1/20

"In this fourth edition of *Messages*, the authors present the essentials of basic communication. From assertiveness and active listening skills to guidelines for digital communication and social media etiquette, every individual, couple, and therapist will benefit from this book. If you wish to deepen your connections to others and to succeed in every social interaction, this book is for you."

—**Michael A. Tompkins, PhD, ABPP**, author of *Anxiety and Avoidance* and codirector of the San Francisco Bay Area Center for Cognitive Therapy

"*Messages* will be warmly and fully welcomed into my clinical practice. This straightforward, easy-to-digest, and wholly useful book on effective communication is completely fit for its purpose. Reading, working through the exercises, and practicing the advised skills could only move those engaged in the process in one direction—toward improved relationships. The plethora of communication process descriptions, exercises, styles, needs, and outcomes provide the reader with a thorough and integrated understanding of what it means to engage in effective communication in the service of connection. An excellent self-help workbook about enhancing how we relate messages to others!"

—**Robyn D. Walser, PhD**, codirector of the Bay Area Trauma Recovery Clinic; assistant professor at University of California, Berkeley; and coauthor of *Learning ACT*, *The Mindful Couple*, and other books

"This is an amazing book. The book will not only help you if you have been struggling to communicate effectively, but also if you just want to hone your skills. Using examples from all walks of life, the book explains the key aspects of effective communication and provides readers with ample opportunities to practice these skills in many different contexts. Although it is based on sound academic research, the book is by no means heavy academic reading. Offering many practical examples and illustrations to bring the content to life, the book is written in a non-technical, clear, concise, and personable style. I recommend this book without any reservations."

—**Georg H. Eifert, PhD**, coauthor of *The Mindfulness and Acceptance Workbook for Anxiety* and *Your Life on Purpose*

"*Messages* is a must-read for any person looking to improve their communication skills; whether the reader needs to augment their relationship's effectiveness with significant others, coworkers, supervisors, or relatives, this book offers 'hands-on' advice about how to effectively relate to others across different settings. All chapters have specific skills and exercises to master interpersonal skills beyond the classic teachings of using 'I statements.' I highly recommend it!"

—**Patricia E. Zurita Ona, PsyD**, East Bay Behavior Therapy Center, coauthor of *Mind and Emotions*, and author of *Parenting a Troubled Teen* and *Escaping the Emotional Rollercoaster*

MESSAGES

FOURTH EDITION

THE COMMUNICATION SKILLS BOOK

MATTHEW McKAY, PhD

MARTHA DAVIS, PhD

PATRICK FANNING

New Harbinger Publications, Inc.

Distributed in Canada by Raincoast Books

Copyright © 2018 by Matthew McKay, Martha Davis, and Patrick Fanning
New Harbinger Publications, Inc.
5674 Shattuck Avenue
Oakland, CA 94609
www.newharbinger.com

Cover design by Amy Shoup

Edited by Brady Kahn

All Rights Reserved

Library of Congress Cataloging-in-Publication Data on file

20   19   18

10   9   8   7   6   5   4   3   2   1   First Printing

Contents

PART III: Conflict Skills

PART IV: **Social Skills**

PART V: **Family Skills**

Part VI: **Public Skills**

Introduction

Communication is a basic life skill, as important as the skills by which you make your way through school or earn a living. Your ability to communicate largely determines your happiness. When you communicate effectively, you make and keep friends. You are valued at work. Your children respect and trust you. You get your sexual needs met.

If you're less effective at communicating, you'll find your life deficient in one or more areas: Work may be all right, but your family shouts at the dinner table. Sex can be found, but friendships never seem to work out. You bounce from job to job and your mate is often cool, but you have a great time with your old school buddies. You get a lot of laughs at parties but go home alone.

Effective communication makes life work. But where can you learn it? Parents are often dismal role models. Schools are busy teaching math and reading. Often there's no one to show you how to communicate your wants, your anger, or your secret fears. No one shows you how to listen actively, how to ask for what you want without blaming others, or how to check out someone's meaning instead of mind reading.

These skills have been known and available for years. They can and should be taught right along with the three Rs. Young adults, for example, should learn parent effectiveness skills in school before having children of their own—not years later when a teenage son is a truant or a daughter runs away. Colleges should provide core courses in the skills of communication in addition to the more traditional courses in communication theory.

This book gathers the most essential communication skills into one volume. They are presented in condensed form, but with sufficient examples and exercises so that you can begin practicing the skills you want to acquire. The book tells you what to do about communicating rather than what to think about it. Pure theory is omitted unless it contributes directly to your understanding of a particular communication skill.

Since its first edition in 1985, this book has become a standard work in its field, used by general readers, students, teachers, therapists, and counselors in a wide variety of settings. Looking over the table of contents of this revised fourth edition, you will see that the emphasis on skills is reflected in the book's organization. The first three chapters cover basic skills. Everybody needs to know how to listen, how to disclose thoughts and feelings, and how to express what's really true.

The section on advanced skills contains five chapters that teach you about using and understanding body language, decoding paralanguage and metamessages, uncovering hidden agendas, applying transactional analysis to your communications, and clarifying your own and others' language.

The next section, on conflict skills, covers skills that are essential in conflict situations: assertiveness, validation, and negotiating. The social skills section that follows contains three chapters on accurate first impressions, making contact with new people, and communicating appropriately and effectively in the digital realm.

The section on family skills teaches you how to communicate with your intimate partner, your children, and your extended family. The final section, on public skills, offers three chapters about skills required for influencing others, when you are called upon to make a speech, and during interviews.

Obviously, you should read the basic and advanced skills chapters first, then go on to the specific chapters appropriate to your relationships and position in life. Not so obviously, you have to do more than read. If you merely read, you will miss the main point of this book—that communication is a skill. The only way to learn a skill is experientially. You have to do it. You actually have to perform the exercises, follow the suggestions, and make these skills your own through practice. For some of the exercises in the book, you'll need a notebook or some blank pieces of paper. You can also download some of the exercises and other useful material at the website for this book: http://www.newharbinger.com/41719. (See the very back of this book for more details.)

Just as you wouldn't expect to become a skilled woodworker after leafing through a back issue of *Woodworking Magazine*, so you can't expect to become a glib, fascinating conversationalist after just perusing the chapter on making contact. Learning by doing applies to communication skills just as much as to woodworking, skiing, or playing a musical instrument. Skill requires knowledge. The knowledge is in this book. But you must put it to work in your everyday life.

PART I

. . . .

Basic Skills

1 Listening

You're at a dinner party. Someone is telling anecdotes; someone is complaining; someone is bragging about his promotion. Everyone there is eager to talk, to tell his or her story. Suddenly you get the feeling that no one is listening. While the talk goes on, you notice that people's eyes wander. They are perhaps rehearsing their own remarks. It's as if they have secretly agreed, "I'll be an audience for you if you'll be an audience for me."

Listening is an essential skill for making and keeping relationships. If you are a good listener, you notice that others are drawn to you. Friends confide in you and your friendships deepen. Success comes a little easier because you hear and understand people; you know what they want and what hurts or irritates them. You get "lucky" breaks because people appreciate you and want you around.

People who don't listen are bores. They don't seem interested in anyone but themselves. They turn off potential friends and lovers by giving the message "What you have to say doesn't matter much to me." As a result, they often feel lonely and isolated. The tragedy is that people who don't listen rarely figure out what's wrong. They change their hairstyle, they get new clothes, they work at being funny, and they talk about "interesting" things. But the underlying problem remains. They aren't fun to talk to because the other person never feels satisfied that he or she has been heard.

It's dangerous not to listen! You miss important information and you don't see problems coming. When you try to understand why people do things, you have to mind-read and guess to fill in the gaps in your listening skills.

Listening is a commitment and a compliment. It's a commitment to understanding how other people feel and how they see their world. It means putting aside your own prejudices and beliefs, your anxieties and self-interest, so that you can look at things from the other person's perspective. Listening is a compliment because it says to the other person, "I care about what's happening to you. Your life and your experience are important." People usually respond to the compliment of listening by liking and appreciating you.

Real vs. Pseudo Listening

Real listening is more than being quiet while someone else talks. It is based on your intention to understand someone, to enjoy someone, to learn something from them, or to give them help. Pseudo listening masquerades as the real thing. The intention is not to listen but to meet some other need, such as:

- Making people think you're interested so they will like you.

- Being alert to see if you are in danger of getting rejected.

- Listening for one specific piece of information and ignoring everything else.

- Buying time to prepare your next comment.

- Half listening so someone will listen to you.

- Listening to find someone's vulnerabilities or to take advantage of him or her.

- Looking for the weak points in an argument, gathering ammunition for a counterattack, so that you can always be right.

- Checking the other's reaction to make sure you produce the desired effect.

- Half listening to be "nice" and avoid hurting or offending someone.

Visit http://www.newharbinger.com/41719 to download this next exercise.

Exercise 1.1

Everyone is a pseudo listener at times. Use the following chart to assess the real versus the pseudo listening you do with significant people in your life. Estimate the percentage of your listening that is *real* for each of the following:

WORK		HOME	
Boss	____ %	Mate	____ %
Coworkers		Children	
_____	____ %	_____	____ %
_____	____ %	_____	____ %
_____	____ %	_____	____ %
Subordinates		Roommate	____ %
_____	____ %	**FRIENDS**	
_____	____ %	Best friend	____ %
_____	____ %	Same-sex friends	
RELATIVES		_____	____ %
Mother	____ %	_____	____ %
Father	____ %	_____	____ %
Siblings		Opposite-sex friends	
_____	____ %	_____	____ %
_____	____ %	_____	____ %
Others		_____	____ %
_____	____ %	_____	____ %
_____	____ %	_____	____ %

To use the information on your chart, ask yourself these questions:

Who are the people you listen to best?

Who are the people with whom you do more pseudo listening?

What is it about these people that makes it easier or harder to listen to them?

Are there any people on the chart with whom you want to do more real listening?

Choose one person you could relate to better. For one day, commit yourself to real listening. After each encounter, check your intention in listening. Were you trying to understand him or her, enjoy him or her, learn something, or give help or solace? Notice if you were doing any pseudo listening and what needs your pseudo listening satisfied. Habits form easily. If you continue this exercise for a week, attention to the quality of your listening will begin to be automatic.

Blocks to Listening

There are twelve blocks to listening. You will find that some are old favorites that you use over and over. Others are held in reserve for certain types of people or situations. Everyone uses listening blocks, so you shouldn't worry if a lot of these blocks are familiar. This is an opportunity for you to become more aware of your blocks at the time you actually use them.

Comparing

Comparing makes it hard to listen because you're always trying to assess who is smarter, more competent, more emotionally healthy—you or the other. Some people focus on who has suffered more, who's a bigger victim. They can't let much in because they're too busy seeing if they measure up. While someone's talking, they have thoughts such as these: "Could I do it that well?" "I've had it harder; he doesn't know what hard is." "I earn more than that." "My kids are so much brighter."

Mind Reading

The mind reader doesn't pay much attention to what people say. In fact, he or she often distrusts it. The mind reader is trying to figure out what the other person is *really* thinking and feeling: "She says she wants to go to the show, but I'll bet she's tired and wants to relax. She might be resentful if I pushed her when she doesn't want to go." If you are a mind reader, you make assumptions about how people react to you, based more on intuition, hunches, and vague misgivings than on what people actually say to you.

Rehearsing

You don't have time to listen when you're rehearsing what to say. Your whole attention is on the preparation and crafting of your next comment. You have to look interested, but your mind is going a mile a minute because you've got a story to tell or a point to make. Some people rehearse whole chains of responses: "I'll say X, then he'll say Y, then I'll say Z," and so on.

Filtering

When you filter, you listen to some things and not to others. You pay only enough attention to see if somebody's angry or unhappy or if you're in emotional danger. Once assured that the communication contains none of those things, you let your mind wander. One woman listened just enough to her son to learn whether he was fighting again at school. Relieved to hear he wasn't, she began thinking about her shopping list.

Another way people filter is simply to avoid hearing certain things, particularly anything threatening, negative, critical, or unpleasant. It's as if the words were never said: you simply have no memory of them.

Judging

Negative labels have enormous power. If you prejudge someone as stupid or nuts or unqualified, you don't pay much attention to what that person says. You've already written the person off. Hastily judging a statement as immoral, hypocritical, fascist, or crazy means you've ceased to listen and have begun a knee-jerk reaction. A basic rule of listening is that judgments should only be made after you have heard and evaluated the content of the message.

Dreaming

You're half listening and something the person says suddenly triggers a chain of private associations. Your neighbor says she's been laid off, and in a flash you're back to the scene where you got fired for playing cards on those long coffee breaks. Hearts is a great game; there were those great card parties years ago when you lived on Sutter Street. And you're gone into dreams of the past, only to return a few minutes later as your neighbor says, "I knew you'd understand, but don't tell my husband."

Identifying

Here you take everything someone tells you and refer it back to your own experience. Someone wants to tell you about a toothache, but that reminds you of the time you had oral surgery for receding gums. You launch into your story before the other person can finish his or hers. Everything you hear reminds you of something that you've felt, done, or suffered. You're so busy with these exciting tales of your life that there's no time to really hear or get to know the other person.

Advising

You are the great problem solver, ready with help and suggestions. You don't have to hear more than a few sentences before you begin searching for the right advice. However, while you are cooking up suggestions and convincing someone to "just try it," you may miss what's most important. You didn't hear the feelings, and you didn't acknowledge the person's pain. He or she still feels basically alone because you couldn't listen and just be there.

Sparring

This listening block has you arguing and debating with people. The other person never feels heard because you're so quick to disagree. In fact, a lot of your focus is on finding things to disagree with. You take strong stands and are very clear about your beliefs and preferences.

One subtype of sparring is the put-down. You use acerbic or sarcastic remarks to dismiss the other person's point of view. For example, Helen starts telling Arthur about her problems in a biology class. Arthur says, "When are you going to have brains enough to drop that class?" The put-down is the standard block to listening in many marriages. It quickly pushes the communication into stereotyped patterns where each person repeats a familiar hostile litany.

Another type of sparring is *discounting*. Discounting is for people who can't stand compliments: "Oh, I didn't do anything." "What do you mean? I was totally lame." "It's nice of you to say, but it's really a very poor attempt." The problem with discounting is that others never feel satisfied that you really heard their appreciation. And they're right—you didn't.

Being Right

Being right means you will go to any lengths to avoid being wrong. You will twist the facts, start shouting, make excuses or accusations, or call up past sins. You can't listen to criticism, you can't be corrected, and you can't take suggestions to change. Your convictions are unshakable. And since you won't acknowledge that your mistakes are mistakes, you just keep making them.

Derailing

This listening block is accomplished by suddenly changing the subject. You derail the train of conversation when you get bored or uncomfortable with a topic. Or you might derail with humor, responding to whatever is said with a joke or quip in order to avoid the discomfort or anxiety of seriously listening to the other person.

Placating

"Right ... Right ... Absolutely ... I know ... Of course you are ... Incredible ... Yes ... Really?" You want to be nice, pleasant, supportive. You want people to like you, so you agree with everything. You want to avoid conflict. You half listen, just enough to get the drift, but you're not really involved. You are placating rather than tuning in and examining what's being said.

Assessing Your Listening Blocks

Now that you've read about the listening blocks, you probably have an idea of which ones apply to you. Make a note of each listening block that seems typical of how you avoid listening. Having identified your blocks, you can begin to explore whom you are blocking out. You can also find out which people or types of people typically elicit certain blocks. For example, you may spar with your mother but derail your best friend, or you may placate and rehearse with your boss but do a lot of advising with your children.

In the following exercises, you will explore the listening blocks you typically use, which blocks you tend to use with which people, and how often and in which situations you resort to listening blocks. After you've assessed your listening patterns, the final exercise will help you make small changes that will enable you to become a better listener in the future. Visit http://www.newharbinger.com/41719 to download exercise 1.2.

Exercise 1.2

For significant people in your life, write down which listening blocks you typically use. Note that for many people, you may use more than one block.

Person	Blocks
WORK	
Boss _____	_____
Coworkers	
_____	_____
_____	_____
_____	_____

Subordinates

_____   _____

_____   _____

_____   _____

RELATIVES

Mother _____   _____

Father _____   _____

Siblings

_____   _____

_____   _____

Others

_____   _____

_____   _____

_____   _____

HOME

Mate _____   _____

Children

_____   _____

_____   _____

_____   _____

Roommate _____   _____

FRIENDS
Best friend _____   _____
Same-sex friends
_____   _____
_____   _____
_____   _____
Opposite-sex friends
_____   _____
_____   _____
_____   _____

Look at your pattern of blocking. Are you blocking more at home or at work, with same-sex or opposite-sex friends? Do certain people or situations trigger blocking? Do you rely mostly on one kind of blocking, or do you use different blocks with different people and situations?

Exercise 1.3

To help systematize your exploration of blocking, reserve a day to take the following five steps. Note that the goal of this exercise isn't to eliminate listening blocks but to increase your awareness of how and when you engage in blocking.

1.   Select your most commonly used block.

2.   Keep a tally sheet: How many times did you use the block in one day?

3.   With whom did you use the block most?

4.   What subjects or situations usually triggered the block?

5. When you started to block, how were you feeling? (Circle every-
    thing that applies.)

    bored   anxious   irritated   hurt   jealous   frustrated   rushed

    down   criticized   excited   preoccupied   attacked   tired

    Other_____

This awareness exercise can be repeated with as many blocks as you
care to explore. Keep track of only one block in any given day.

Exercise 1.4

After gaining more awareness, you may want to change some of your
blocking behavior. Reserve another two days to do the following:

1. Select one significant person you'd like to stop blocking.

2. Keep a tally sheet: How many times did you block the person on
    day one?

3. What blocks did you use?

4. What subjects or situations usually triggered the blocks?

5. On day two, consciously avoid using your blocking gambits with
    the target person. Try paraphrasing instead (see the next section).
    Make a real commitment to listening. Notice and write down how
    you feel and what happens when you resist blocking. (Note: Don't
    expect miracles. If you have a 50 percent reduction in blocking,
    that's success.)

Initially, you may feel anxious, bored, or irritated. You may find yourself avoiding one blocking gambit only to use another. The conversation
may take uncomfortable turns. You may suddenly share and reveal things
you previously kept to yourself. Be a scientist. Objectively observe what
happens. Evaluate it. Does this feel better than the usual way you operate

with the target person? If it doesn't, extend the exercise for a week. Notice how you gradually form the habit of checking how well you are listening.

Four Steps to Effective Listening

There are four steps to effective listening: listening actively, listening with empathy, listening with openness, and listening with awareness.

1. Active Listening

Listening doesn't mean sitting still with your mouth shut. A corpse can do that. Listening is an active process that requires your participation. To fully understand the meaning of a communication, you usually have to ask questions and give feedback. Then, in the give-and-take that follows, you gain a fuller appreciation of what's being said. You have gone beyond passively absorbing information and have become a collaborator in the communication process. Listening actively involves paraphrasing, clarifying, and giving feedback.

Paraphrasing

To paraphrase means to state in your own words what you think someone just said. Paraphrasing is absolutely necessary to good listening. It keeps you busy trying to understand and know what the other person means, rather than blocking. You can paraphrase by using such lead-ins as the following: "What I hear you saying is …" "In other words …" "So basically how you felt was …" "Let me understand; what was going on for you was …" "What happened was …" Do you mean …?" You should paraphrase every time someone says something of any importance to you.

When you paraphrase, people deeply appreciate feeling heard. Paraphrasing stops escalating anger and cools down crisis. It stops miscommunication by clearing up false assumptions, errors, and misinterpretations on the spot. Paraphrasing helps you remember what was said. And finally, paraphrasing is the antidote to most listening blocks—when you paraphrase, you'll find it much harder to compare, judge, rehearse, spar, advise, derail, dream, and so on.

To get practice paraphrasing, do the following exercise. Choose a friend who likes to try new things. Explain that you want to improve your listening skills. The friend's job is to tell you a story of something important that happened in his or her life. Basically, all your friend has to do is talk. Your job, at intervals, is to paraphrase what's just been said. Say in your own way what you've heard so far and find out if you're getting it right. Every time you paraphrase, your friend gets to decide if you've really understood. The friend makes corrections in what you said, and you incorporate those corrections in a new attempt at paraphrasing. You keep at it, paraphrasing and correcting, until your friend is satisfied that he or she has been heard. You may be surprised at how long it can take to clear up confusion and agree on what's been said. Misconceptions occur very easily.

Clarifying

Clarifying often goes along with paraphrasing. It means asking questions until you get more of the picture. Since your intention is to fully understand what's being said, you often have to ask for more details, more background. You have to know the circumstances. Clarifying helps you sharpen your listening focus so that you hear more than vague generalities. You hear events in the context of what someone thought and felt, the relevant history. Clarifying also lets the other person know that you're interested. It gives the message "I'm willing to work at knowing and understanding you."

Giving Feedback

Active listening also depends on feedback. You've paraphrased and clarified what was said and hopefully you understand it. This is the point at which you should share your reactions. In a nonjudgmental way, you can say what you thought, felt, or sensed. This doesn't mean falling back into sparring or identifying as a reaction. It means sharing your perceptions and what happened inside you, without approval or disapproval. Feedback also helps the other person understand the effect of his or her communication. It's another chance to correct errors and misconceptions. It's also a chance for him or her to get a fresh and valuable point of view—yours.

To check perceptions of the other person's feelings, you transform what you saw and heard into a tentative description: "I want to understand your feelings—do you feel more regret or guilt about what happened?" "Listening to what you said, I wonder if maybe you're still angry at him."

Good feedback is immediate, honest, and supportive. *Immediate* means giving feedback as soon as you have paraphrased and clarified what you heard and fully understand it. Putting off your feedback, even for a few hours, makes it much less valuable. *Honest* means giving your real, true reaction—without being brutal about it. You don't have to tear into somebody to give your reaction. In fact, brutality is rarely honest. *Supportive* means that even negative feedback should be gentle, saying what you need to say without causing damage or defensiveness. For example, "I get the feeling that there's something you're not telling me" is more supportive than "You're holding out on me." "I think there's a real possibility that you've made a mistake" is more supportive than "You've been a fool."

2. Listening with Empathy

To listen with empathy, remember that everyone is trying to survive, physically and psychologically, as best they can. You don't have to like everyone or agree with everyone, but recognize that you do share the same struggles. Even the most outrageous, inconsiderate, false, and violent acts are strategies to minimize pain, postpone death, and hold on to life. Some people have better survival strategies than others. And some are plainly incompetent, making a mess of everything they touch. They don't live as long physically, and they die an early psychological death from chronic depression or anxiety. But everyone is doing their best, moment to moment, to survive.

Say to yourself, "This is hard to hear, but it's another human being trying to live." Ask yourself, "How might this belief or this decision, though it may ultimately fail, lower this person's anxiety or get some needs met?" Listening with empathy is especially hard when someone is angry, critical, or self-pitying. When that happens, ask these questions:

What need is the (anger, anxiety, etc.) coming from?

What danger is this person experiencing?

What is he or she asking for?

3. Listening with Openness

It's difficult to listen when your mind is closed, when you're judging and finding fault. All the information gets scrambled coming in, while you build a case to dismiss a person or refute his or her ideas. You listen selectively, filtering out everything that makes sense and pouncing on whatever seems false or silly. You collect and hoard the "stupidities," so you can share them later with a sympathetic audience.

Judgments can be very gratifying, but they cost you a lot: If your opinions are proven false, you are the last to know. You don't grow intellectually, because you only listen to viewpoints you already hold. You dismiss otherwise worthwhile people because you disagree with their ideas. Others lose interest in you because you argue and don't listen. Finally, you miss important information.

Nearly everyone has trouble listening openly. You don't want to hear your sacred cows reduced to hamburger. You don't want to face certain facts about yourself. Nor do you want to believe that an unlikable person has said something worth thinking about. You naturally want to argue, to shout it down. You are afraid of being wrong because your opinions and beliefs are closely tied to your self-esteem. Being wrong can equal being stupid, bad, or worthless.

Listening with openness is a skill you can learn. The following exercise, called a *reversal*, should be tried with someone you trust. Select an old disagreement that isn't too explosive. Each of you states your side of the argument. Now reverse sides and argue for the opposite position. Do it convincingly, really pushing the other person's point of view. Try to win the debate from the other side. Don't stop until you feel immersed in the viewpoint you once opposed. At the end, share with each other what you experienced.

Obviously, you can't practice reversals most of the time. What you can do, as an exercise in openness, is think of yourself as an anthropologist. Imagine that the person you're talking to hails from another country with different customs and ways of thinking, and your job is to find out how the other person's point of view makes sense, to see how it fits with his or her worldview, history, and particular social system. Reserve judgment and strive to hear the whole statement, the entire communication. Refrain from evaluations until you have all the information.

4. Listening with Awareness

There are two components to listening with awareness. One is to compare what's being said to your own knowledge of history, people, and the way things are. You do this without judgment, simply making note of how a communication fits with known facts.

The second way you listen with awareness is to hear and observe congruence. Does the person's tone of voice, emphasis, facial expression, and posture fit with the content of the communication? If someone is telling you that his father has just died, but smiles and leans back comfortably with his hands laced behind his head, the message doesn't make sense. There is no congruence. If body, face, voice, and words don't fit, your job as a listener is to clarify and give feedback about the discrepancy. If you ignore it, you're settling for an incomplete or confusing message.

Total Listening

People want you to listen, so they look for clues to prove that you are listening. Here's how to be a total listener:

Maintain good eye contact.

Lean slightly forward.

Reinforce the speaker by nodding or paraphrasing.

Clarify by asking questions.

Actively move away from distractions.

Be committed to understanding what was said, even if you're angry or upset.

2 Self-Disclosure

Self-disclosure may be as scary to you as skydiving without a parachute. You hold back because you anticipate rejection or disapproval. But you miss a lot. Self-disclosure makes relationships exciting and builds intimacy. It clarifies and enlivens. Without self-disclosure, you are isolated in your private experience.

You can't help disclosing yourself. You do it whenever you're around other people. Even if you ignore them, your silence and posture are disclosing something. The question isn't whether to disclose yourself, but how to do it appropriately and effectively.

For the purposes of this chapter, self-disclosure is simply communicating information about yourself. Contained in that short definition are some important implications, however. First of all, "communicating" implies another human being is on the receiving end of your disclosure. Introspection and writing about yourself in a journal or diary won't pass as self-disclosure. "Communicating" also includes disclosure by nonverbal language such as gestures, posture, and tone of voice.

"Information" in the definition implies that what is disclosed is new knowledge to the other person, not a rehash of old themes and stories. The information can take the form of facts you have observed and are pointing out, feelings you had in the past or are experiencing now, your thoughts about yourself or others, and your desires or needs in the past or present.

The key word in the definition is "yourself." This means your true self. Self-disclosure is not a cloud of lies and distortions or an attractive mask.

To better understand this self that is being disclosed, examine the image below, adapted from the Johari Window (Handy 2000). Imagine that your entire being is represented by a circle, divided into quadrants like this:

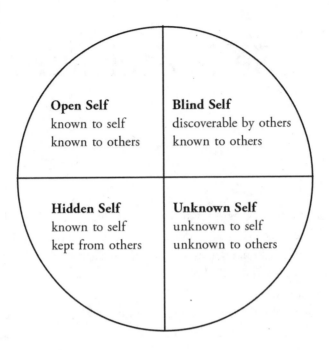

The first quadrant is your Open Self. It contains all your conscious actions and statements. The second is your Blind Self, which is comprised of things others can find out about you that you are unaware of: habits, mannerisms, defense mechanisms, flight strategies. The third quadrant is your Hidden Self. This includes all your secrets—everything you think, feel, and desire that you keep to yourself. The fourth quadrant is your Unknown Self. Since this self is by definition unknown, we can only assume its existence and give it names like the unconscious or subconscious. Dreams and mystical experiences are the strongest evidence for the existence of the Unknown Self.

These are not rigid compartments. Observations, thoughts, feelings, and wants are constantly moving from one area to another as you go about your daily routine. Everything you see and hear and touch in the outside world is taken into the Hidden Self. Some is forgotten, which may mean that it goes down into the Unknown Self. Some experiences contribute to your continuing unconscious habits and thus move into your Blind Self. Some things you remember but never reveal, just leaving them in the

Hidden Self. And some things that you notice you pass on to others, moving them into the Open Self. When you have an insight about how you operate in the world, you move it from the Blind to the Hidden Self. Sharing the insight with someone moves it into the Open Self.

The movement that this chapter studies is the shift of information about your observations, feelings, thoughts, and needs from the Hidden to the Open Self. This is self-disclosure. If you are good at self-disclosure, your Open Self quadrant is large compared to the other quadrants. The larger your Open Self, the more likely you will be to reap the rewards of self-disclosure.

Rewards of Self-Disclosure

Accurately revealing who you are is hard work. Sometimes you think, "Why struggle to explain? Why risk rejection?" And yet the need to be close to others, to be known, keeps reemerging. Several things make self-disclosure worth the trouble.

Increased Self-Knowledge

It's paradoxical but true that you know yourself to the extent that you are known. Your thoughts, feelings, and needs often remain vague and clouded until you put them into words. The process of making someone else understand you demands that you clarify, define, elaborate, and draw conclusions. Expressing your needs, for example, gives them shape and color, adds details, and points up inconsistencies and possible areas of conflict that you need to resolve.

Closer Intimate Relationships

Knowledge of yourself and the other person is basic to an intimate relationship. If you are both willing to disclose your true selves, the relationship deepens. If one or both of you keep large parts withheld, the relationship will be correspondingly shallow and unsatisfying.

Improved Communication

Disclosure breeds disclosure. As you make yourself available to others, they are encouraged to open up in response. The range of topics available for discussion broadens, even with those who are not particularly intimate with you. The depth of communication on a given topic deepens too, so you get more than mere facts and opinions from others. They become willing to share their feelings, their deeply held convictions, and their needs.

Lighter Guilt Feelings

Guilt is a hybrid emotion composed of anger at yourself and fear of retribution for something you have done, failed to do, or thought. Guilt is often unreasonable and always painful. One thing that can relieve the pain a little is disclosure. Disclosing what you have done or thought lightens the guilt feeling in two ways: First, you no longer have to expend energy to keep the transgression hidden. Second, when the thing you feel guilty about is disclosed, you can look at it more objectively. You can get feedback. You can examine whether the guilt is justified, or whether your rules and values are too strict and unforgiving.

Disclosure as first aid for guilt is institutionalized in several forms: Catholics confess, Protestants witness, AA members declare themselves alcoholics, and those in therapy relive traumatic events. But you don't need a priest or a therapist to experience the healing effects of disclosure. A good friend will do.

More Energy

It takes energy to keep important information about yourself hidden. Suppose you quit your job and go home to your family as usual, making no mention of your impending poverty. Here's what happens: You don't notice that your daughter has a new haircut, that your favorite dinner is on the table, or that the living room furniture has been rearranged. You are so concerned with keeping your secret that you can hardly notice anything at all. You are silent, withdrawn, grouchy. Nothing is fun. Life is a burden. All your energy is drained. Until you unburden yourself, you are a walking corpse.

When a conversation seems dead, boring, and hard to keep going, ask yourself if there's something you're withholding. Unexpressed feelings and needs tend to simmer. They build up inside you until you lose spontaneity and your conversation takes on all the liveliness of a funeral oration. That's one way to tell if you should reveal a secret: if withheld feelings or needs are deadening your relationship.

Blocks to Self-Disclosure

Since self-disclosure is so rewarding, why doesn't everybody tell everybody else everything all the time? Because there are powerful blocks to self-disclosure that often keep you huddled in your Hidden Self.

One of these sources of resistance is a societal bias against self-disclosure. It isn't considered nice to talk about yourself too much, or to discuss your feelings or needs outside a narrow family circle.

The biggest block to self-disclosure is fear: fear of rejection, fear of punishment, fear of being talked about behind your back, or fear that someone will take advantage of you. Someone might laugh or say no or leave. If you reveal one negative trait, others will imagine you're all bad. If you reveal something positive, you might be accused of bragging. If you take a stand, you might have to do something about it—vote, contribute, volunteer, or get involved in other people's troubles. Finally, you may be afraid of self-knowledge itself. You instinctively know that by disclosing yourself, you will come to know yourself better. You suspect that there are some unpleasant truths about yourself that you would rather not become aware of.

Optimal Levels of Self-Disclosure

Some people are just more extroverted and forthcoming about themselves than others are. Their Open Selves are relatively larger:

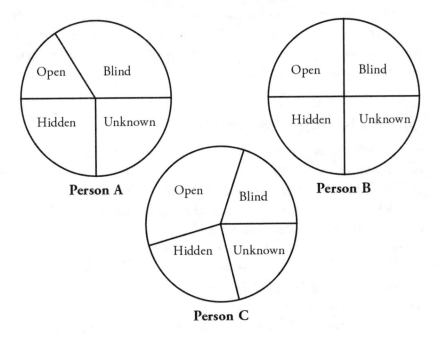

Actually, how much you reveal of yourself is not a fixed quantity. You may have a constant tendency to be more open or reserved than the next person, but within your range of openness, you fluctuate depending on your mood, whom you're talking to, and what you're talking about. The following diagrams represent the same person in different conversations:

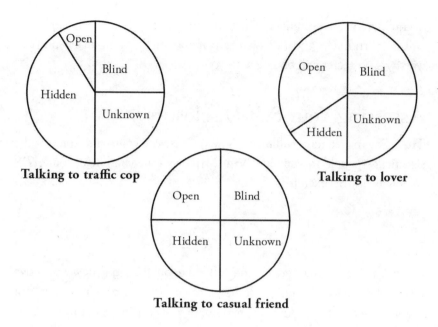

Talking to traffic cop

Talking to lover

Talking to casual friend

Research in self-disclosure confirms what common sense suggests. You tend to be more open with your partner, certain family members, and your close friends. You are more willing to disclose your preferences in clothes and foods than your financial status or sexual preferences. In some moods, you don't want to tell anyone anything. As you age from seventeen to fifty, you'll probably increase your average level of self-disclosure and then become more reserved after fifty.

Healthy self-disclosure is a matter of balance, of learning when to tell what to whom. Generally speaking, the more information you consistently move into the Open Self, the better your communication will be. The more you keep hidden or remain blind to, the less effective your communication will be. Beware of extremes. If your Open Self is too large, you'll be a garrulous, inappropriate blabbermouth; if too small, you'll be closed and secretive. If your Blind Self is too large, you'll be oblivious to how you appear in the world. Unknown to you, you'll get a reputation as a bully, a nerd, a tightwad, and so on. If your Blind Self is too small, you'll be an overanalyzed self-awareness addict. If your Hidden Self is too large, you will be withdrawn and out of reach; if too small, you will be untrustworthy—no secret will be safe with you.

Assessing Your Self-Disclosure

The following exercise will reveal how you disclose yourself to some of the significant people in your life. Visit http://www.newharbinger.com/41719 to download this exercise.

Exercise 2.1

For each topic described on the left, rate on the right how you have talked about it to your mother, father, mate, child, and best friends. If your parents are dead, you have no children, or you can't think of anyone to fill the friends or mate categories, leave those columns blank.

Use this rating scale:

0   You have told the other person *nothing* about this aspect of yourself.

1   You have talked in *general terms* about this. The other person knows some of the facts but not the complete message.

2   You have told the other person about this *completely*, including your observations, thoughts, feelings, and needs.

X   You have *lied* or misrepresented yourself regarding this aspect. The other person has a false picture of you.

	Mother	Father	Mate	Child	Best Female Friend	Best Male Friend
Tastes and Interests						
Your favorite foods and beverages and food dislikes.						
Your likes and dislikes in music.						
Your favorite reading matter.						
The kinds of movies, TV shows, or computer games you like.						
The style of house and the kinds of furnishing you like best.						
The kind of party or social gathering you like best.						
Attitudes and Opinions						
What you think and feel about religion.						
Your views on the issue of racism.						
Your personal views on drinking.						
Your personal views on sexual morality.						
The traits and qualities you regard as desirable in a romantic partner.						

Work (or Studies)						
What you enjoy most.						
What you enjoy least.						
What you feel are your shortcomings and handicaps.						
What you feel are your special strong points.						
How you feel that others appreciate your work.						
Your ambitions and goals in your work.						
Money						
How much money you make at your job.						
Whether or not you owe money; if so, how much and to whom.						
Whether or not you have savings and the amount.						
Whether or not others owe you money, the amount, and who owes it to you.						
Whether or not you gamble and how much.						
All of your present sources of income.						
Personality						
The aspects of your personality that you dislike.						
The feelings you have trouble expressing or controlling.						

	Mother	Father	Mate	Child	Best Female Friend	Best Male Friend
The facts of your present sex life—how you get sexual gratification; any problems; with whom you have relations.						
Whether or not you feel you are attractive sexually.						
Things in the past or present that you feel ashamed and guilty about.						
What you fear most.						
Body						
Your feelings about the appearance of your face.						
How you wish you looked.						
Your feelings about different parts of your body—legs, hips, waist, weight, chest or bust, and so on.						
Whether or not you now have any health problems.						
Your past record of illness and treatment.						
Whether or not you now make a special effort to keep fit, healthy, and attractive.						

Notice which topics seem easier to talk about. Notice what you consistently remain quiet or lie about. How much energy are you devoting to keep that stuff hidden?

Notice to whom you talk and from whom you are hiding. Are there any obvious patterns along family lines? Along gender lines?

Make a note of the topics or people you want to concentrate on, and keep them in mind for the next exercise.

Practice in Self-Disclosure

The following exercise will give you practice in self-disclosure. It proceeds in three stages, from telling someone else a few facts about yourself to revealing your current thoughts, feelings, and needs.

Information

Here you deal with facts only. Choose an acquaintance and tell him or her about your job, your last vacation, or some interesting experience you've had. Stick to the facts of when, where, what, who, and so on. Don't include any of your feelings or opinions. When you are comfortable with disclosing the facts, go on to the next step.

Thoughts, Feelings, and Needs About the Past or Future

Facts are only part of the story. The next step in practicing self-disclosure is to include your thoughts, feelings, and needs. Refer to exercise 2.1 to find topics for this step. You can talk about your tastes in music, your religious convictions, your ambitions at work, your finances, what you're especially proud of, your health, and so on. Tell someone you trust about your chosen topic. Besides just the facts, say what you think about the matter, how you feel about it, and what needs or wants you have regarding it.

Don't try to talk with this person about what you are feeling or thinking right now. Practice only on topics that relate to the past or future.

When you are comfortable with this step, you can practice here-and-now communications.

Here-and-Now Communications

This is the most difficult type of self-disclosure because you have to take the risk of sharing with someone else what you think, feel, and need right now.

For example, you can talk about how you're feeling attracted to the other person, how his or her responses are affecting you, how you're holding something back, how you're slanting your story to make yourself look good, how you want the conversation to come out, what you need right now, how relaxed or nervous you're feeling, and so on. This is the most complete and satisfying mode of self-disclosure and is explored more fully in chapter 3.

To get into here-and-now communications gradually, select one thing to concentrate on for a week. For example, you might practice giving feedback to others on how conversations are affecting you. Go slowly. Scare yourself a little bit, but not so much that you give up talking about the here and now.

3 Expressing

This chapter is about expressing your thoughts and feelings to the people who matter to you, when something important is at stake, or when you need to make a clear and complete statement about your inner experience. There are four types of expression: observations, thoughts, feelings, and needs. Each type has its own style and vocabulary.

Observations

This is the language of the scientist, the detective, the appliance repairperson. It means reporting what your senses tell you. There are no speculations, inferences, or conclusions. Everything is simple fact. Here are some examples of observations:

"I heard on the news that an ice age is due to start within five hundred years."

"My old address was 1996 Fell Street."

"She plans to wear a red strapless evening gown."

"I broke the toaster this morning."

All of these statements adhere strictly to what the person has heard, read, or personally experienced.

Thoughts

Your thoughts are conclusions, or inferences drawn from what you have heard, read, and observed. They are attempts to synthesize your observations so you can see what's really going on and understand why and how events occur. They may also incorporate value judgments in which you decide that something is good or bad, wrong or right. Beliefs, opinions, and theories are all varieties of conclusions. Here are some examples:

"Selflessness is essential for a successful marriage." (*belief*)

"I think the universe will keep exploding and collapsing, exploding and collapsing, forever." (*opinion*)

"He must be afraid of his wife; he always seems nervous around her." (*theory*)

"Real maple syrup is the only syrup worth buying." (*value judgment*)

Feelings

Talking about your feelings is the most difficult type of expression. It's scary because people might reject you or judge you harshly. Some people don't want to hear anything about what you feel. Some are bored or upset when feelings come up. Others are selectively receptive—open to hearing about your sadness but afraid of your anger.

So you may keep many feelings to yourself. And yet how you feel is a large part of what makes you unique and special. Shared feelings are the building blocks of intimacy. When you allow others to know what angers, frightens, and pleases you, they have greater empathy and understanding. They are more likely to meet your needs.

Here are some examples of feeling statements:

"I missed Al and felt a real loss when he left for Europe."

"I feel like I let you down, and it really gnaws at me."

"I sit alone in the house, feel this tingling going up and down my spine, and get this wave of anxiety."

"I light up with joy when I see you. I feel this incredible rush of affection."

Note that feeling statements are not observations, value judgments, or opinions. For example, the statement "Sometimes I feel that you are very rigid" has nothing to do with feelings. It's just a slightly softened judgment.

Needs

No one except you knows what you need. You are the expert, the highest authority on yourself. However, you may have a heavy injunction against asking for what you want. You hope friends and family will be sensitive or clairvoyant enough to know what you want. "If you loved me, you'd know what's wrong" is a common assumption. Since you feel it's bad to ask for anything, you can express your needs only when spurred by anger or resentment. The anger says, "I'm wrong to ask, and you're wrong to make me have to."

Relationships change, accommodate, and grow when both people can clearly and supportively express what they need. Trying to have a close relationship in which you don't express your needs is like driving a car without a steering wheel. You can go fast, but you can't change directions or steer around potholes.

Needs are simple statements about what would help or please you. They are not judgmental. They don't blame or find fault. Here are some typical expressions of need:

"Can you be home before seven? I'd love to go to a movie."

"I'm exhausted. Will you do the dishes and see that the kids are in bed?"

"I need a day to myself this weekend. Can we get together Sunday night instead?"

"I need to reserve time with you so we can sit down and work this out."

Whole Messages

Whole messages include all four kinds of expression: what you see, think, feel, and need. Intimate relationships thrive on whole messages. Your closest friends, your mate, and your family can't know the real you unless you share all of your experiences. That means being willing and able to share your feelings, even uncomfortable emotions like anger. It means revealing your needs, even when they might seem selfish or petty. It means giving accurate feedback about what you observe, clearly stating your inferences and conclusions, making straightforward requests or suggestions.

Not every relationship or situation requires whole messages. Effective communication with your garage mechanic probably won't involve a lot of deep feeling or discussion of your emotional needs. Even with intimates, the majority of messages are just informational.

However, when you leave something important out, it's called a *partial message*. Partial messages create confusion and distrust. People sense something is missing, but they don't know what. They're turned off when they hear judgments that are not tempered by your feelings and hopes. They resist hearing anger that doesn't include the story of your frustration or hurt. They are suspicious of conclusions without supporting observations. They are uncomfortable with demands growing from unexpressed feelings and assumptions.

You can test whether you are giving whole or partial messages by asking yourself the following questions:

> "Have I expressed what I actually know to be fact? Is it based on what I've observed, read, or heard?"

> "Have I expressed and clearly labeled my inferences and conclusions?"

> "Have I expressed my feelings without blame or judgment?"

> "Have I shared my needs without blame or judgment?"

Contaminated Messages

Contamination takes place when your messages are mixed or mislabeled. For example, you might be contaminating feelings, thoughts, and observations if you said to your daughter, "I see you're wearing that old dress again." What you needed to say were four very distinct things:

> "That dress is a little frayed and still has the ink spot we were never able to get out." (*observation*)

> "I don't think it's nice enough for a Sunday visit to Grandpa's." (*thought*)

"I feel anxious that your grandfather will think I'm not a very good parent if I let you wear a dress like that." (*feeling*)

"I would prefer that you wear something more presentable." (*need*)

Contaminated messages are at best confusing and at worst deeply alienating. The message "I see your wife gave you two juicy oranges for lunch" is confusing because the observation is contaminated by need. The need is only hinted at, and the listener has to decide if what he heard was really a covert appeal. The message "While you were feeding your dog, my dinner got cold" is alienating because what appears to be a simple observation contains undercurrents of anger and judgment ("You care more about your dog than me").

Contaminated messages differ from partial messages in that the problem is not merely one of omission. You haven't left the anger, the conclusion, or the need out of the message. It's there all right, but in a disguised and covert form. The following are some examples of contaminated messages:

"Why don't you act a little human for a change?" In this message, need is contaminated with a value judgment (*thought*). A whole message might have been "You say very little, and when you do, it's in a soft, flat voice [*observation*]. It makes me think that you don't care, that you have no emotions [*thought*]. I feel hurt [*emotion*], but what I really want is for you to talk to me [*need*]."

"Every year you come home to visit with a different man. I don't know how you move from one to another like that." Said in an acid tone, this would be an observation contaminated with a value judgment (*thought*). The whole message might be "Each year you come home with someone else [*observation*]. I wonder if it creates a sort of callousness, a shallow affection [*thought*]. I worry, and also feel disappointed when I start liking your friend and never see him again [*feeling*]. I hope you'll make a commitment to a life partner [*need*]."

"I need to go home ... my head is killing me." Said in an angry voice at a party, this is an example of feelings contaminated with need. What the person really wants to say is this: "I've been standing all by myself [*observation*]. You don't seem to notice me or draw me into the conversation [*thought*]. I start feeling hurt and angry [*feeling*]. I want you to involve me in things, or I don't want to be here [*need*]."

"You eat your breakfast without a word, you get your laptop, you leave, you get home, you mix a drink, you read the paper, you talk about golf and your secretary's legs at dinner, you fall asleep in front of the TV, and that's the way it is." In this case, observation is contaminated with feelings. It seems like a straightforward recital of events, but the speaker really wants to say, "I'm lonely and angry. Please pay attention to me."

A common way to contaminate your messages is to make the content simple and straightforward but to say it in a tone of voice that betrays your feelings. "I want to stop interviewing people; we have enough already" can be said in a matter-of-fact or very annoyed voice. In the first case, it's a clear statement of need. In the second, need is contaminated with unacknowledged anger.

Preparing Your Message

When you have something important to say, there are three types of awareness that can help you deliver whole messages:

Self-awareness. The only way you can be sure to give whole messages is to examine your own inner experience. What are you observing, thinking, feeling, and wanting? What is the purpose of this communication? Is the stated purpose the same as your real purpose? What are you afraid of saying? Self-awareness may require some mental rehearsal, particularly when you are getting used to delivering whole messages. Run things over in your mind until each part of the message is clear and distinct. Separate what you observe and know from what you surmise and believe. Contact your feelings and find a way to say them. Arrive at a nonthreatening way to express your need.

Awareness of the other person. A certain amount of audience analysis should precede any important message. If your friend just lost a job, he or she may not be receptive to a rant about your low rate of pay. What kind of shape is the other person in? Rushed, in pain, angry, or able to listen? Awareness also means keeping track of the listener's response while you're talking: paying attention to facial expressions, eye contact, and body language. Is the other person asking questions, giving feedback, or sitting like a lump in the chair?

Place awareness. Important messages are usually delivered when two people are alone, in a nondistracting environment. Talking where you can be overheard discourages whole messages. Partial and contaminated messages increase as you feel the need to compress and sanitize your comments for public consumption. So find a private place where you won't be interrupted, a place that's quiet, comfortable, and with few distractions.

Practicing Whole Messages

You can practice communicating whole messages by taking partial or contaminated messages and adding the missing observations, thoughts, feelings, or needs.

Exercise 3.1

Make a whole message out of each of the following statements. Write it using first-person sentences ("I noticed that you've been very quiet ...").

1. "I see you're getting uptight again." (This is said in an annoyed voice, covering a certain amount of anxiety and hurt. The speaker's wife has been silent for thirty minutes following his late arrival home.)

   Observations: _____

   _____

   Thoughts: _____

   _____

Feelings: _____

_____

Needs: _____

_____

2. "Should we be talking like this?" (Between new lovers who've sud-
    denly launched into fantasies of kids and marriage. The speaker
    is anxious that her partner may feel pressured and may withdraw.)

    Observations: _____

    _____

    Thoughts: _____

    _____

    Feelings: _____

    _____

    Needs: _____

    _____

3. "A person runs out of time. Something just changes in them." (A
    man trying to explain why he quit his job. Passed over for pro-
    motion, he was depressed and fearful of getting older without
    finding satisfying work. He's trying to get his fourteen-year-old
    daughter to understand.)

    Observations: _____

    _____

    Thoughts: _____

    _____

Feelings: _____

_____

Needs: _____

_____

4. "I'm here, aren't I?" (Said to the boss after being asked how he felt having to work overtime. He's missing his ten-year-old's performance in a school play and wants to be home in time to help with the cast party.)

Observations: _____

_____

Thoughts: _____

_____

Feelings: _____

_____

Needs: _____

_____

5. "I know, I know. You don't have to tell me." (After being reminded of upcoming finals for the fourth time, a sixteen-year-old is feeling overcontrolled by her parents.)

Observations: _____

_____

Thoughts: _____

_____

Feelings: _____

_____

Needs: _____

_____

Here are examples of whole messages for the above statements. See how yours compare.

1. "You haven't said anything since I got home, and I assume you're angry. When you withdraw like that I get angry too. I'd rather talk about it instead of just getting mad."

2. "We're fantasizing about a lifetime together after knowing each other two weeks. I'm worried that one of us may get scared and withdraw. Does it feel okay to you to talk about this?"

3. "I'd been passed over for a long time and didn't really like what I was doing anyway. I don't think it's healthy to grow old someplace doing work you don't like. I was getting depressed and wanted to take a chance on finding something that really felt good. It's hard, and I need your support."

4. "I'm missing my ten-year-old's performance in her school play. I should be there. It's frustrating. I do want to be home by nine to help with the cast party."

5. "You've reminded me four times, and I get the impression you think I'm stupid or irresponsible. I feel watched and it makes me angry. Let me handle this myself, and we can talk about it if I mess up."

The ability to make whole rather than partial or contaminated messages is a skill. It is acquired with practice.

Exercise 3.2

Try this exercise to practice communicating in whole messages:

1. Select a friend or family member whom you trust.

2. Explain the concept of whole messages.

3. Arrange a time to practice.

4. Select something you want to talk about, something that was important enough to affect you emotionally. It can be something in the past or something going on right now, something involving others, or something directly related to the person you are practicing with.

5. Talk about your chosen subject using the four components of a whole message: what happened, what you observed, what you thought, how you felt, and what you need in the situation.

6. When you finish, have your partner repeat back in his or her own words each part of the message.

7. Correct anything that he or she didn't get quite right.

8. Reverse the whole process, and let your partner describe an experience using whole messages.

Then make an agreement with your friend or family member that every significant communication between you will involve whole messages. Commit yourself to practicing whole messages for two weeks. Always be sure to give each other feedback about what was heard and what was left out of the message. At the end of two weeks, evaluate your experience.

The goal is for whole messages to become automatic. Eventually you can expand your exercise program to include other significant people. The exercises will sharpen your awareness, so you can rapidly look inside yourself for the information necessary to make whole messages.

Rules for Effective Expression

To communicate effectively, you need to make sure that your messages are direct, immediate, clear, straight, and supportive. The following sections discuss these five characteristics in more depth.

Messages Should Be Direct

Indirectness can be emotionally costly. One man whose wife divorced him after fifteen years complained, "She knew I loved her. I didn't have to say it in so many words. A thing like that is obvious." But it wasn't obvious. His wife withered emotionally without the direct expression of his affection. A woman who had been distressed by her child's performance in school stopped nagging when his grades went up. She was surprised to learn that her son felt unappreciated and wanted some direct approval. A man who had developed a chronic back problem was afraid to ask for help with gardening and household maintenance. He suffered through these tasks in pain and experienced a growing irritation and resentment toward his family. A fifteen-year-old retreated to her room when her divorced mother became interested in a new man. She complained of headaches and excused herself whenever the boyfriend arrived. Her mother, who once told the children they would always come first, assumed that her daughter was just embarrassed and would soon get over it.

These are all examples of people who had something important to communicate, but didn't know it. They assumed others would realize how they felt. Communicating directly means you don't make any assumptions. In fact, you should assume that people are poor mind readers and haven't the faintest idea what goes on inside you.

Sometimes people know they need to say something but are afraid to. So they try hinting or telling third parties in hopes that the target person will eventually hear. This indirectness is risky. Hints are often misinterpreted or ignored. One woman kept turning the sound down on the TV during commercials. She hoped her husband would take the hint and converse a little at the breaks. Instead he used the time to check his messages and sports scores on his phone, until she finally blew up at him. Third-party communications are extremely dangerous because of the likelihood that your message will be distorted. Even if the message is accurately delivered, no one wants to hear about your anger, your disappointment, or even your love secondhand.

Messages Should Be Immediate

If you're hurt or angry or needing to change something, delaying communication will often exacerbate your feelings. Your anger may smolder, your frustrated need become a chronic irritant. What you couldn't express at the moment will be communicated later in subtle or passive-aggressive ways. One woman was quite hurt at the thought of not being invited to Thanksgiving at her sister's house. She said nothing, but she broke a date they had to go to the planetarium and "forgot" her sister's birthday. Sometimes unexpressed feeling is stockpiled to the point where a small transgression triggers a major dumping of the accumulated rage and hurt. These dumping episodes alienate family and friends.

There are two main advantages to immediate communication. First, immediate feedback increases the likelihood that people will learn what you need and adjust their behavior accordingly. This is because with immediate communication you establish a clear relationship between what they do (for example, driving too fast) and the consequences (your expressed anxiety). Second, immediate communication increases intimacy because it's more exciting and interesting when you share your responses now instead of waiting three weeks for things to get stale.

Messages Should Be Clear

A clear message is a whole message, a complete and accurate reflection of your observations, thoughts, feelings, and needs. You don't leave things out or obscure them with vague, abstract language. Even when you are nervous about saying what must be said, you don't resort to jargon, pseudo psychological interpretations, or explaining everything by the "vibes." One woman who was afraid to tell her boyfriend that she was turned off by public displays of affection said that she felt "a little strange" that day and thought that her parents' upcoming visit was "repressing her sexuality." This ambiguous message allowed her boyfriend to interpret her discomfort as a temporary condition. He never learned her true needs.

Here are some tips for staying clear:

Don't Ask Questions When You Need to Make a Statement

Husband to wife: "Why do you have to go back to school? You have plenty of things to keep you busy." The statement hidden in the question is "I'm afraid that if you go back to school, I won't see you enough. I'll feel lonely. As you grow in independence, I'll feel less control over the direction of our lives."

Wife to husband: "Do you think we need to make an appearance at your boss's barbecue today?" Embedded in the question is an unexpressed need to relax and putter in the garden. As the woman fails to plead her case clearly, her husband can either miss or safely ignore her needs.

Father to son: "How much did that paint job cost?" This man really wants to talk about the fact that his son lives above his means and then borrows from Mom without any intention of paying her back. He's worried about his son's relationship to money and angry because he feels circumvented.

Keep Your Messages Congruent

Congruence promotes clarity and understanding. Your content, your tone of voice, and your body language should all fit together. If you congratulate someone on getting a fellowship, the response is congruent if voice, facial gestures, and spoken messages all reflect pleasure. Incongruence is apparent if the person thanks you with a frown, suggesting that he or she doesn't really want the compliment.

Incongruence confuses communication. A man who spent the day in his delivery truck arrived home to a request that he make a run to the supermarket. He responded, "Sure, whatever you want." But his tone was sarcastic and his body slumped. His wife got the message and went herself. But she was irritated by the sarcastic tone and later started a fight about the dishes. A college student asked soothingly to hear about her roommate's boyfriend trouble. But while the story unfolded, her eyes flitted always to the mirror, and she sat on the edge of her chair. Her voice said, "I care," but her body said, "I'm bored. Hurry up."

Avoid Double Messages

Double messages are like kicking a dog and petting it at the same time. They occur when you say two contradictory things at once. Husband to wife: "I want to take you, I do. I'll be lonely without you. But I don't think the convention will be much fun for you. Really, you'd be bored to death." This is a double message, because on the surface the husband seems to want his wife's company. But when you read between the lines, it's evident that he's trying to discourage her from coming.

Father to son: "Go ahead to the party, have a good time. I guess we can talk about your grades tomorrow. If ever." One message undercuts the other, and the son is left unclear about his father's real position. The most malignant double messages are the "come close, go away" and "I love you, I hate you" messages. These communications are found in parent-child and lover relationships and inflict heavy psychological damage.

Be Specific About Your Wants and Feelings

Hinting around about your feelings and needs may seem safer than stating them clearly. But you confuse your listener. Friend to friend: "Why don't you quit volunteering at that crazy free clinic?" The clear message would be "I'm afraid for you, struggling in that conflict-ridden place. I think you are exhausting yourself, and I miss the days when we had time to spend an afternoon together. I want you to protect your health and have more time for me."

Husband to wife: "I see the professors and their wives at the faculty party, and I shudder at some of the grotesque relationships." The real message that wasn't said was this: "When I see that terrible unhappiness, I realize what a fine life we have and how much I love you."

Mother to daughter: "I hope you visit Grandma this week." On the surface this statement seems straightforward, but underneath lurks the guilt and anxiety the mother feels about Grandma's loneliness. She worries about the old woman's health and, without explaining any of this, badgers her daughter to make frequent visits.

Two lovers: "I waited while you were on the phone, and now our dinners are cold." The underlying statement is "I wonder how much you care about me when you take a phone call in the middle of dinner. I'm feeling hurt and angry."

Distinguish Between Observations and Thoughts

You have to separate what you see and hear from your judgments, theories, beliefs, and opinions. "I see you've been fishing with Joe again" could be a straightforward observation. But in the context of a long-standing conflict about Joe, it becomes a barbed judgment. Review the section on contaminated messages for more discussion of this issue.

Focus on One Thing at a Time

This means that you don't start complaining about your daughter's Spanish grades in the middle of a discussion about her girlfriend's marijuana use. Stick with the topic at hand until both of you have made clear, whole messages. If you get unfocused, try using one of the following statements to clarify the message: "I'm feeling lost … What are we really talking about?" or "What do you hear me saying? I sense we've gotten off track."

Messages Should Be Straight

A straight message is one in which the stated purpose is identical with the real purpose of the communication. Disguised intentions and hidden agendas destroy intimacy because they put you in a position of manipulating rather than relating to people. You can check if your messages are straight by asking yourself these two questions: "Why am I saying this to this person?" and "Do I want him or her to hear it or something else?"

Hidden agendas are dealt with at length in chapter 6. They are usually necessitated by feelings of inadequacy and poor self-worth. You have to protect yourself, and that means creating a certain image. Some people take the "I'm good" position. Most of their communications are subtle opportunities to boast. Others play the "I'm good, but you aren't" game. They are very busy putting everyone down and presenting themselves, by implication, as smarter, stronger, or more successful. Hidden agendas such as "I'm helpless," "I'm fragile," "I'm tough," or "I know it all" are defensive maneuvers to keep you from getting hurt. But the stated purpose of your communication is always different from your real purpose. For example, while you are ostensibly discoursing on intricate Middle East politics, the real purpose is to show how knowledgeable you are. We all succumb to little vanities, but when your communications are dominated by one such agenda, you aren't being straight.

Being straight also means that you tell the truth. You state your real needs and feelings. You don't say you're tired and want to go home if you're really angry and want more attention. You don't angle for compliments or reassurance by putting yourself down. You don't say you're anxious about going to a couples therapist when actually you feel angry about being pushed to go. You don't describe your feelings as depression because your mate prefers that to irritation. You don't say you enjoy visiting your girlfriend's brother when the experience is one step below fingernails scraping on the chalkboard. Lies cut you off from others. Lies keep others from knowing what you need or feel. You lie to be nice or you lie to protect yourself, but you end up feeling alone with your closest friends.

Messages Should Be Supportive

Being supportive means you want the other person to be able to hear you without getting upset or defensive. Ask yourself, "Do I want my message to be heard defensively or accurately? Is my purpose to hurt someone, to aggrandize myself, or to communicate?" Steer clear of the following unfair tactics if you want to avoid hurting your listener:

Global labels. "Stupid," "ugly," "selfish," "evil," "asinine," "mean," "disgusting," "worthless," and "lazy" are a few of a huge list of hurtful words. Such labels are most damaging when used in a "You're a fool, a coward, a drunk ..." format. Making your point this way creates a total indictment of the person instead of just a commentary on some specific behavior.

Sarcasm. This form of humor clearly tells the listener that you have contempt for him or her. It's often a cover for feelings of anger and hurt. The effect on the listener is to push him or her away or make him or her angry.

Dragging up the past. This destroys any chance of clarifying how each of you feels about the present situation. You reopen old wounds and betrayals instead of examining your current dilemma.

Negative comparisons. "Why aren't you generous like your brother?" "Why don't you come home at six like other people?" "Sarah's getting As, and you can't even get a B in music appreciation." Comparisons are deadly because they not only contain "you're bad" messages but also make people feel inferior.

Judgmental you-messages. Known as *you-messages* or *you-statements*, these attacks take an accusatory form: "You don't love me anymore." "You're never here when I need you." "You never help around the house."

Threats. Threatening to move out, to quit, or to harm another is sure to bring meaningful communication to a halt. People use threats as violent topic changers, avoiding uncomfortable issues by talking about the hostile things they plan to do.

Communicating supportively means that you avoid win/lose and right/wrong games. Real communication produces understanding and closeness, while win/lose games produce warfare and distance. Your intention in communication will guide you toward a predictable result. Ask yourself, "Do I want to win, or do I want to communicate? Do I want to be right, or do I want mutual understanding?" If you find yourself feeling defensive and wanting to criticize the other person, that's a clue that you're playing win/lose.

PART II

· · · · · · · · · · · · · ·

Advanced Skills

 # 4 Body Language

You can't not communicate with others. Without making a sound, you reveal your feelings and attitudes. Your smile says, "I'm happy," your frown and crossed arms say, "I'm mad," and your drumming fingers and explosive sighs say, "I'm impatient—get moving." Even when you try to show nothing, your closed-off stance and refusal to speak say, "I don't want to talk about it. Leave me alone."

There are two ways you communicate without making a sound: with body movements such as facial expressions, gestures, and posture, and with spatial relationships, by how much distance you put between yourself and the other person. Understanding body language is essential because over 50 percent of a message's impact comes from body movements (Mehrabian 2007).

Body language not only conveys more information than words but is often more believable than verbal communication. For example, you ask your mother, "What's wrong?" She shrugs her shoulders, frowns, turns away from you, and mutters, "Oh … nothing, I guess. I'm just fine." You don't believe her words. You believe her dejected body language, and you press on to find out what's bothering her.

The key to interpreting body language is congruence. First, do a person's gestures and movements all match each other, adding up to a congruent message? Second, do those gestures and movements match the verbal portion of the message? Your mother's shrug, frown, and turning away are congruent among themselves. They could all mean "I'm depressed" or "I'm worried." However, her body language is not congruent with her words. They don't match. As an astute listener, you recognize this incongruence as a signal to ask again and dig deeper.

In another situation, you may find a lack of congruence among the nonverbal cues themselves. Body language cues usually occur in clusters of gestures and movements that go together. But sometimes not: A salesperson may be standing close to you, shaking your hand with a warm, firm grip and smiling. However, at the same time, the salesperson refuses to meet your eyes. These conflicting nonverbal cues are often a sign of conflicting feelings or incomplete communications. Perhaps while talking to you, the salesperson is hoping that you won't ask about the guarantee. Or maybe she is aware of her boss, who's standing nearby.

Awareness of incongruence in your own body language messages can make you a much more effective communicator. For example, you might have a good idea for improving morale at work, but you hang back at meetings, slouch in your chair, fold your arms protectively, and keep your eyes downcast. Verbally, you might be saying, "I've got a great idea," but your body says, "Please ignore me."

As you become aware of your own nonverbal cues, you will discover that your body language provides a wealth of information about your unconscious feelings and attitudes. For instance, in an awkward social situation, you might notice that your arms are folded and your fingers are wrapped tightly around your biceps. You realize that you are nervous and defensive. With this increased awareness of your internal state, you can move to reduce your tension rather than just continue tensing up.

You'll also discover that a particular gesture or expression may have different meanings in different contexts. Covering your mouth as you watch a truck smash into the back of your parked car communicates your horror. But you may use the same gesture during a tedious lecture to express your boredom. Or you could use this gesture with a policeman as you say, "Oh no, officer, I was only going the legal speed limit," reflecting your uncertainty or perhaps your untruthfulness. Sometimes the context is difficult for others to ascertain. As you walk from your house to the car, you cover your mouth and then hurry back to your house. Only you know the full context of this situation: you forgot your keys or left the oven turned on.

Body Movements

Social kinesics, or body communication, is largely learned. Gestures are passed from one generation to the next without any special training. A boy learns to walk bowlegged like his rancher father, and a girl learns to laugh and flutter her hands like her mother. Many gestures are restricted to a specific peer group, others are typical of a particular region or culture, and some body movements are universal.

While there are more similarities in body language between cultures than there are in verbal language, the differences are sufficient to create considerable confusion. For example, maintaining steady eye contact while answering the question of someone in authority is a sign of sincerity in the American Midwest. For a Puerto Rican to maintain eye contact under similar circumstances would be a sign of disrespect. Hence a respectful Puerto Rican might be judged untrustworthy by someone from Wisconsin.

Within a culture there is room for much individual variation. For instance, you may indicate annoyance by using quick, jerky movements, while your partner may express annoyance by frowning and standing rigidly at attention, arms folded. Tuning into each other's unique ways of expressing feelings and attitudes helps communication.

Body movements serve several communication purposes. Besides indicating attitudes and conveying feelings, body movements can serve as illustrators and regulators. *Illustrators* are nonverbal movements that accompany and illustrate verbal communication. You say to the butcher, "I want that one," and point to the T-bone steak. You nod your head up and down to indicate yes and shake it from side to side to indicate no. You use your hands to draw a picture in the air of something you are discussing. You imitate the movement you are verbally describing or move in a way that underscores the significance of a particular word or phrase.

Regulators are nonverbal cues that monitor or control the speaking of the other person. As you listen, you nod your head, indicating to the speaker that you understand and want him or her to keep talking. You lean or look away to communicate that you want the speaker to stop talking. You raise your eyebrows in disbelief, suggesting that the speaker needs to defend a position. The sensitive speaker modifies his or her conversation in response to the listener's regulators.

Facial Expression

The face is the most expressive part of the body. The next time you're reading a magazine or looking at Facebook, look at some photos of people in action. Use your hands to cover up everything but their faces. What kind of information do you get from the face alone? What kind of information do you lose?

You'll probably find that, although you can't tell what the people are doing, you can still identify feelings and attitudes. Try covering up everything but the eyes and see if you can still sense feelings and attitudes. Try it with everything but the mouth area covered. You'll see that some emotions can be interpreted reliably by looking only at the eyes and mouth. But the more of the face you cover, the harder it is to identify emotions and attitudes.

When observing facial expressions, you will also want to note if the person's eyebrows are raised or lowered, forehead is wrinkled or smooth, and chin is set or flaccid. How flushed or pale a person's face is can also provide useful information.

As an experiment, try using different facial expressions in your daily interactions with people. But for normal situations, try smiling and looking directly at people whom you normally would not give the time of day. Stare vacantly into space as you address your best friend. Tell an amusing story with a straight face. Tell the same story again with animated facial expressions. Deliver a very serious message with a broad smile. Deliver it again with a serious facial expression. In each case, note how you feel and the reaction you get from other people. What differences do you notice between when you are being congruent and when you are being incongruent?

Gestures

Other parts of the body besides the face can communicate a great deal about what you are thinking or feeling.

Arms and Hands

You have probably known people who talk with their hands. Even when on the phone, they may unconsciously use regulating and illustrating gestures that are lost on their listener. People scratch their heads in puzzlement, touch their noses in doubt, rub their necks in anger or frustration, tug on their ears when they want to interrupt, wring their hands in grief, and rub their hands in anticipation. They will put their hands on their knees to indicate readiness or on their lips to indicate impatience; lock their hands behind their back as a signal of self-control or behind their head as a statement of superiority; stick their hands into their pockets to hide their meaning; and clench their fists as a sign of anger or tension. They will extend their arms out in front of them with palms up to indicate sincerity, and then shrug their shoulders in this position, as if to say, "How should I know?" or "I just couldn't help it." They'll cross their arms in front of their chest when feeling defensive or unwilling to communicate openly. They'll use their arms and hands to create non-verbal emblems that translate directly into words or phrases such as "Peace" or "Up yours."

Legs and Feet

When you sit with your legs uncrossed and slightly apart, you communicate openness. When you straddle a chair, you are indicating dominance. When you put one leg over the arm of a chair, you are suggesting indifference. Sitting with one ankle over the other knee or sitting with ankles crossed can be a sign of resistance. Sitting with one leg crossed over the other and swinging or kicking it back and forth is often a sign of boredom, anger, or frustration. Agreement is most likely when all limbs are uncrossed. The direction in which the legs and feet are pointed is often the direction in which the individual feels most interest.

To experience how much you rely on body movements to communicate, try telling a story without using gestures. You may have to plant your feet firmly on the floor and hold your hands behind your back. After talking for a few minutes, allow yourself to use body movements, and notice the difference it makes. Note how you felt when you couldn't illustrate your points with your hands. How do you imagine your communication was affected? Ask your listener what differences he or she noticed.

You can practice another exercise to experiment with regulators when you are having a casual conversation. As your friend is talking, use different gestures to indicate nonverbally that you want your friend to do the following: go on talking, speed up, slow down, get to the point, expand on a point, defend a point, stop and let you talk, stop and end the conversation.

Posture and Breathing

Slumped posture can be a sign of feeling "low," fatigue, a sense of inferiority, or not wanting to be noticed. Keep in mind, however, some sensitive tall people will slump so as not to tower over and intimidate shorter people. Erect posture is generally associated with higher spirits, greater confidence, and more openness than slumped posture. Leaning forward tends to suggest openness and interest. Leaning away suggests lack of interest or defensiveness. A tense, rigid posture tends to be a sign of defensiveness, while a relaxed posture indicates openness.

Breathing is another important indicator of feelings and attitudes. Rapid breathing can be associated with excitement, fear, irritability, extreme joy, or anxiety. A pattern of holding your breath, alternating with short gasps for air, is a sign of anxiety or built-up tension. Shallow breathing in the upper chest often indicates thinking that is cut off from feelings. Deep breathing into the stomach is more likely to be associated with strong feelings and action.

You can find out a lot about people by watching and imitating their breathing for a few moments. It is probably easiest to follow a person's pattern of breathing by focusing on his or her collar as it rises and falls. Notice the speed and depth of breathing, then imitate it with your own breathing for a few minutes. As you do so, notice what changes occur in your own body. What feelings come up for you? Often people find that in the process of imitating, they take on the feelings of the other person.

In the course of everyday events, you can pause at times to notice how you are breathing and feeling. Experiment with varying your breathing pattern. For instance, if your breathing is shallow and you are feeling tired or depressed, try breathing more rapidly and deeply for a few minutes and observe what happens. If your breathing is very rapid and you feel anxious or annoyed, try slow deep breaths for a few minutes. Changing how you breathe will often change how you feel.

Exercise 4.1

Observe on TV or in your everyday life how people use body movements to convey meaning. At first, concentrate on facial expressions. Then look at their arm and hand gestures. Notice what they're doing with their feet, balance, and posture. Watch their breathing for a while.

Notice how much meaning can be understood from each movement considered by itself. Then take into account the context in which the movement occurs. What is going on in the interaction that defines the meaning of a body movement?

Notice how body movements tend to occur in clusters. Are these groups of movements congruent? Do they mean the same thing? Or is one part of the body sending a different message from the rest?

Finally, is the nonverbal message conveyed by the body the same as the verbal message? Are there any jarring incongruities that would indicate anxiety, anger, withheld communication, or outright lying? What feelings and attitudes are missing from the verbal message but conveyed by the nonverbal part?

Spatial Relationships

Proxemics is the study of what you communicate by the way you use space. How far you stand from a person you're talking to, how you arrange the furniture in your home, and how you respond to others invading your territory are important nonverbal statements.

The father of proxemics was Edward T. Hall (1990), an anthropologist who described four distinct zones that people unconsciously use as they interact with others: intimate distance, personal distance, social distance, and public distance. Imagine that each person is surrounded by four concentric bubbles of personally defined space. The bubbles are largest in front of people and smallest at their sides and back. Each zone also has a *close* and a *far* subphase. Generally speaking, the greater the distance between two people interacting, the less intimate their relation.

Intimate distance has a close subphase of actually touching and a far subphase of 6 to 18 inches from the body. The intimate zone is appropriate for lovers, close friends, and children holding on to their parents or each other. Nonintimates usually feel embarrassed or threatened if circumstances force them to share this space without nonverbal barriers to protect themselves. Observe on a crowded bus or elevator how people avoid eye contact and draw away or tense up if touch is unavoidable. If eye contact is made, it is brief and often combined with a polite, nonintrusive smile.

Personal distance has a close subphase of 1½ to 2½ feet, which is a comfortable zone for talking at a party. You can still easily touch your partner, whereas in the far subphase of 2½ to 4 feet, you can discuss something relatively privately without risking touch. In the far subphase, you are literally keeping your partner at arm's length.

Social distance has a close subphase of 4 to 7 feet, in which you are most likely to transact such interpersonal business as talking to a client or service person. This subphase is often used manipulatively to indicate dominance. A supervisor will stand over a seated employee at this distance as an indication of his or her higher status. The far subphase of 7 to 12 feet is most frequently used for formal business or social interactions. The president of the company will often sit behind a desk at about this much distance from his or her employees, for doing so conveys a superior status even when looking at an employee from a seated position. This distance is also useful in an open office setting, where it allows employees to continue working without feeling rude for not interacting with coworkers nearby. At home, a husband and wife could sit at this distance from one another as they read, watch TV, and occasionally chat.

Public distance has a close subphase of 12 to 20 feet, which is usually used for relatively informal gatherings, such as a teacher working with a classroom of students or a boss talking with a group of employees. The far subphase of 20 feet or greater is reserved for politicians and celebrities.

These four zones vary greatly from culture to culture, and people from different cultures often misinterpret one another for lack of an understanding of their differently defined zones. For instance, the personal zone of people from Latin American countries is generally much closer than that of Anglo Americans. A conversation between acquaintances from these two distinct cultures can start at one end of a room and end at the other, as the Latin American tries to move closer to the personal zone where he or she feels most comfortable, and the Anglo American draws away, feeling uncomfortable in this intimate zone. The Latin American goes away thinking that Anglos are standoffish, and the Anglo leaves with the perception that Latin Americans are pushy.

Individual variations in the size of these zones for members of the same culture can also lead to discomfort when the wrong people slip into the wrong zone. Hall's model of four zones should be used only as a general guide.

The old double standard between the sexes may still apply to how they interact spatially. A woman can usually move into a man's space more easily than a man can move into a woman's space. Both woman and man may read the gesture as flirtation, but the woman is more likely to read the intrusion as a sign of disrespect.

Spatial zones are routinely ignored when people are treated as objects. Patients often become nonpersons while doctors and nurses discuss their cases in front of them as though they were not there. Similarly, parents might discuss plans for their thirteen-year-old daughter in front of her without asking her opinion on the matter, or two men might tell a lewd sexual joke in front of their female colleague. In these cases, the other person's humanness is not respected. Treating others as nonpersons can also be achieved by staring at them as though they were an object or by not talking to them when they would ordinarily be part of the conversation.

Territory is similar to personal space. It is a place you have staked out as your own and where you feel safe. In your territory you can relax and not have to worry about constant intrusion. Your territory may be your home, your office, your favorite chair, or, for a few hours, the spot on the beach where you lay out your towel to sunbathe. The instinct to take and defend territory is well known among animals, and humans are no exception. From street gangs to entire nations, people react strongly in defense of their territory when they feel it is being threatened.

As an exercise, stand in the middle of an empty space and have someone walk slowly toward you. Tell the person to stop as soon as you begin to feel uncomfortable. Instruct him or her to move backward until you are at a comfortable distance. The space between you and the other person is your body's buffer zone. Does this zone change when you have different people walk toward you and stand at the point at which you feel comfortable? Can you explain any differences?

You can also experiment with invading someone else's buffer zone. For instance, stand "too close" in a waiting line, elevator, or bus. Observe how the person standing next to you responds. (Do this exercise with caution, preferably with members of your own gender.)

A few times during each day, take note of the distance between yourself and the people with whom you are speaking. Are the zones you are in consistent with your relationships with the other people? If not, can you explain why?

5 | Paralanguage and Metamessages

In chapter 4 you learned that body language accounts for over 50 percent of the impact of a typical communication (Mehrabian 2007). The rest of the impact comes from verbal content and vocal but nonverbal content. Here is the complete breakdown from that research:

7 percent verbal (words)

38 percent vocal (volume, pitch, rhythm, etc.)

55 percent body movements (mostly facial expressions)

That 38 percent of vocal but nonverbal content is the subject of this chapter. The vocal component of speech, considered apart from the verbal content, is called *paralanguage*. It includes pitch, resonance, articulation, tempo, volume, and rhythm. Through paralanguage, you unintentionally betray your moods and attitudes. No matter what you say, the sound of how you say it will reveal a great deal about who you are and what you feel.

When you intentionally alter your rhythm or pitch for emphasis or include special verbal modifiers, you are sending *metamessages*. Metamessages add another level of meaning to a sentence, often a contradictory or disapproving meaning. The statement "*We* like you, of course" is very different from "We like you." By emphasizing "we" and adding "of course," the meaning has been subtly changed to imply that others don't feel the same way and that your personal charm may be somewhat doubtful. A few innocuous words and a change in rhythm are all it takes to make a metamessage.

The Elements of Paralanguage

The six elements of paralanguage are pitch, resonance, articulation, tempo, volume, and rhythm.

Pitch

As you tighten your vocal cords, you raise the pitch of your voice. Intense feelings of joy, fear, or anger make your voice go higher in pitch. When you are depressed, tired, or calm, the muscles of your vocal cords relax and the pitch of your voice goes down. Though your pitch varies in normal conversations, it will move toward the extremes when you're expressing intense feelings.

Resonance

Resonance refers to the richness or thinness of your voice. The shape of your vocal cords and chest determines resonance. A man with heavy vocal cords and a large chest is likely to have a deep, full voice. A woman with tight, thin vocal cords is apt to have a thin, high voice. With some practice, you can control both pitch and resonance—as singers and public speakers regularly do. Deep chest tones communicate firmness, self-assurance, and strength. Thin, high-pitched voices suggest insecurity, weakness, and indecisiveness.

Articulation

How carefully do you enunciate your words? Do you speak in so relaxed a manner that many of your sounds are slurred together, or do you pronounce each syllable precisely? Different levels of articulation are appropriate in different situations. A slight slur or drawl may add to an atmosphere of comfort or intimacy. But slurred words would be inappropriate in a board meeting, where clear, decisive speech is expected.

Tempo

The tempo or speed at which words are spoken reflects emotions and attitudes. Fast talkers convey excitement and can be expressive and persuasive. Speaking too fast, however, can make the listener nervous. Rapid speech can also signal insecurity. A slow, hesitant speaker may give an impression of laziness or indifference. To another listener, the slow speaker may sound sincere, thoughtful, and interested.

The speed at which you speak often reflects the region of the country where you grew up. People from New York City speak more rapidly than those from Atlanta, and people raised in large cities generally tend to speak faster than those from the country. Fast talkers and slow talkers often feel frustrated when they converse with one another. The fast talker feels uncomfortable with long pauses and often will attempt to finish the sentences of slow talkers for them. The slow talkers have difficulty keeping up and may eventually give up trying to communicate.

Volume

On the positive side, loud volume is usually associated with enthusiasm and confidence. On the negative side, it may be associated with aggressiveness, an overinflated ego, or an exaggerated belief in the importance of a message. A person of higher status may raise the volume of his or her voice over that of a subordinate. A loud voice in this case says, "I'm in command. You do what I tell you to do." A soft voice may convey, "Don't attack me. I know my place. I know I'm helpless."

In everyday settings, a soft voice is often heard as a sign of trustworthiness, caring, and understanding. It can also indicate a lack of confidence, a feeling of inferiority, or a sense that the message is unimportant. At the same time, an extreme version of the soft voice, a whisper, accentuates communication. A whisper can imply special intimacy, meaning "This is just between the two of us." It can also convey sadness, fear, or awe.

Rhythm

Rhythm determines which words will be emphasized in a sentence. In the question "What time is it?" the emphasis is normally on the word "time." If you were to place the emphasis on the word "what," you would upset the rhythm. Notice the change in meaning as you vary the rhythm in the following sentence:

"Am I happy!"

"Am I happy?"

The sentence changes from an exuberant statement of fact to a message of doubt and uncertainty.

Just as every song has its particular rhythm, so does every language. As a baby, you imitated the language rhythms of the adults around you before you could speak words. Later, as you began using words, you would simply fit them into the familiar rhythms. By now, rhythm patterns are so natural for you that you rarely pay any attention to them. But despite its invisibility, rhythm is extremely important. The words you choose to emphasize in a sentence ("Am I happy?" versus "Am I happy!") make a vital difference in the meaning of what's being said.

Changing Your Paralanguage

If you did not vary your pitch, resonance, volume, tempo, or rhythm as you spoke, you would sound like a robot. Others would experience your speaking style as monotonous and tune you out. They would assume that you were bored with what you were saying. To assess your own paralanguage and learn what it says about you, record your voice as you carry on a normal conversation. Wait at least twenty-four hours before listening to the replay, so you can be more objective. Also, if you haven't heard your recorded voice frequently, you should listen to it for a while until the novelty wears off and it sounds relatively natural to you. As you listen to the recording, consider the following:

Does your voice reflect what you want to say?

Is your voice congruent with the words you speak?

Is there something about your voice that you dislike?

If you discover something about your paralanguage that you want to change, practice again with a recorder. Speak or read into the recorder, varying your voice and always keeping in mind how you want to sound. Play the original recording of your voice for a friend to get some feedback on your voice quality. Experiment with any changes he or she suggests.

Cindy, a cocktail waitress, found that her customers were often a little light on tips. When she listened to a recording of her own voice, she found that it had a monotonous, high-pitched, flat, nasal-sounding tone. She also noticed that she spoke so fast and slurred so many words that she was hard to understand. Her voice reminded her of her aunt, who was thirty years older than Cindy and incredibly boring. Cindy began practicing the three exercises that follow and she read into the recorder for five minutes each day for a month. While she was reading, she focused on deep, slow breathing and relaxing her vocal cords. Over time she noticed an improvement in her resonance and greater variations in pitch, speed, and rhythm. Cindy's tips improved a little and her dating life got better.

The following vocal exercises were provided by John Argue, dramatic voice teacher.

The body-vocal stretch. Your body is the instrument you use to produce your voice. To increase your range of pitch, resonance, and volume, you need to loosen up your body. If you speak too softly, if your resonance is too thin, or if your pitch is unpleasantly high, low, or monotonous, this exercise will help you gain greater range. It will open up your throat and upper chest as well as exercise your vocal cords.

Begin by yawning—widely and loudly. Open your mouth as wide as you can and empty your lungs of air. Then inhale deeply. As you yawn, let your voice travel up and down the tonal scale. After a few minutes, try speaking while yawning.

Volume modulation. How loud is loud enough? If you speak too loudly or too softly, this exercise will help you modulate your volume. It allows you to connect your visual sense with your vocal sense so that you can choose an appropriate volume for each situation.

Focus your attention on an object near you and say the word "touch" slowly and precisely. Imagine your voice going out and touching that object. Then look at a more distant object and say the word "touch" louder.

Again imagine your voice actually touching that object. Let your eyes find other items in the room to "touch." Find out how far away you can touch an object with your voice. With practice, you will be able to sense when the volume of your voice is falling short of or overshooting another person.

Articulation and tempo. If people have difficulty understanding you because you speak too rapidly, mumble, or otherwise distort your words, this exercise in articulation is for you. It will help you slow down and enunciate your words in normal, everyday conversations.

Recite something you know by heart, such as a favorite saying, poem, or nursery rhyme, or even your phone number and address. Say it over and over again, out loud. Speak s-l-o-w-l-y. Draw out all the vowel sounds to three or four times their normal duration. Exaggerate all the words so that hard consonants such as *b*, *p*, *k*, and *t* explode from your lips.

Metamessages

Many statements have two levels of meaning. One level is the basic information being communicated by a series of words. The second level, or metamessage, communicates the speaker's attitudes and feelings. The metamessage is largely communicated by rhythm, pitch, and verbal modifiers.

Consider the sentence "You're late tonight." If the word "late" is emphasized with a slightly rising inflection, the sentence communicates surprise. It may also imply a question about the cause of the delay. If the word "you're" is emphasized, the metamessage is irritation.

Metamessages are a source of much interpersonal conflict. On the surface, a statement may seem reasonable and straightforward, but underneath, the metamessage communicates blame and hostility. Consider the statement "I'm trying to help." If the verbal modifier "only" is inserted and given the emphasis of a rising inflection, the metamessage becomes very different. "I'm *only* trying to help" communicates hurt feelings and defensiveness. The message is now an attack.

It's hard to defend against the anger and disapproval expressed in negative metamessages. The attack is often so subtle that you aren't aware of exactly how you've been hurt. For example, John has just moved out of a college dormitory into his own apartment. When his mother visits, she remarks, "Of course, it *is* your first apartment." By adding the modifier "of course" and emphasizing the verb "is," the metamessage becomes "This place isn't very nice, but what can you expect from a novice homemaker?" John feels irritated for the rest of her visit but has no idea of how he has been put down.

You can learn to recognize your own metamessages and deal with the negative metamessages of others. The trick is to be aware of how a metamessage is constructed. Step one is to listen for rhythm and pitch.

Rhythm and Pitch in a Metamessage

A sentence in which each word gets equal emphasis is unlikely to contain a metamessage. But by accentuating one or more of the words, a speaker may communicate a great deal about his or her emotional state. For example, examine the phrase "just a minute." When every word has equal emphasis, the phrase is a simple request. When the words "just" or "minute" are emphasized, the message is annoyance or impatience.

Now consider the sentence "I'm not going home with you." Depending on which word receives rhythmic emphasis, the sentence will have a very different metamessage. "*I'm* not going home with you" has the metamessage of "Somebody else might, but not me." When "home" is emphasized, the message is "I might go somewhere with you, but not home." If the word "you" is emphasized, the metamessage is "I might go home with someone but certainly not with you." The same words have very different meanings depending on your emphasis.

Many compliments have hidden metamessage barbs in them. The simple sentence "You're sweet" changes considerably, depending on rhythm and pitch. When "you're" is emphasized with a rising inflection, the metamessage is surprise, perhaps distrust. The statement reads as "You're being sweet, but that's an unusual occurrence." When "sweet" is emphasized, the message is clearly appreciation or affection. A sarcastic, cutting metamessage is achieved by giving both words a strong emphasis and "sweet" a falling inflection.

Some metamessages function as warnings. Consider the phrase "in my opinion." If the word "opinion" is emphasized, you get the message that it's okay to disagree. When "my" is strongly emphasized, the message is "Listen, but don't contradict me."

Pitch and rhythm are an important component of sexual metamessages. At a party, a man sees a woman wearing an attractive, tight-fitting sweater. He remarks, "That's quite a nice … *sweater* you have on." The words are the same, but the metamessage is a covert sexual invitation.

Verbal Modifiers

Verbal modifiers are special words that add nuances of meaning to a sentence. The following is a list of words often used to modify verbs: "certainly," "only," "merely," "naturally," "now," "later," "sure," "just," "still," "again," "slightly," "supposedly."

Some phrases like "of course," "come on," "I'm sure," or "I guess" show up frequently in metamessages. In general, any word that denotes quantity (either a lot or a little) can be crafted into a sarcastic metamessage: "You're a *little* bit on the messy side" or "I got *slightly* wet waiting for you."

In the column on the left are a series of sentences that include verbal modifiers. The column on the right contains the metamessage implied by each modifier.

Statement	Metamessage
"It's *only* a game."	There's something wrong with you. You're taking this too seriously.
"You *sure* have been tired lately."	There's something wrong with you, or you're up to no good.
"I was *just* being frank."	There's something wrong with you if you can't take honesty.
"*Naturally*, you'll want to come."	There's something wrong with you if you don't want to come.

"Are you *still* here?"	You shouldn't be here.
"I was *merely* making a point."	There's something wrong with you if you can't be reasonable.
"You *certainly* are quiet."	You're too quiet and it bugs me.
"*Come on*, let's relax."	There's something wrong with you, and you're annoying me.
"You tried your best, I'm *sure*."	I'm not so sure you tried your best.
"*Now* what do you want?"	You ask for too much. You're trying my patience.

The verbal modifiers in these sentences create an undertone of irritation and disapproval. Go back and read the lines in the left-hand column without the modifiers. Notice that they turn back into simple statements of fact. Gone are the covert barbs and the implied rejection.

Coping with Metamessages

The basic function of metamessages is to say something covertly that you're afraid to say directly. Since a metamessage attack is covert, there is little chance of overt retaliation. Here are two simple steps for coping with an attacking metamessage:

1. Repeat the message over in your own mind, listening to rhythm and pitch, noticing any verbal modifiers.

2. Say out loud what you think the metamessage is, and ask if that's what the person really thinks or feels.

The second step is absolutely necessary. If you don't check out your interpretation, you're stuck in a position of guessing the other person's intent. You'll act as if the assumed metamessage were true, without ever knowing for sure. Checking it out is also a good way of teaching metamessagers to talk straight. When you call them on their covert attack, they are more likely to be direct with you. The thoughts and feelings hidden in the metamessage can then be looked at openly and honestly.

Harry, who often worked late, knew how to deal with metamessagers. When a coworker remarked, "I guess *you're* staying late *again* tonight," Harry ran the statement over in his mind. He noticed the emphasis and rising inflection on the word "you're." He also noticed the verbal modifier "again." Harry still couldn't decide whether the statement was critical ("Your diligence makes us all look bad") or sympathetic ("Please take care of yourself"). He decided to repeat back the negative metamessage to check out his perceptions. "I wonder if it irritates people that I work late, like I'm showing them up or something?" To his relief, Harry found that the comment had been made out of genuine concern.

Sometimes it requires real tenacity to get the speaker to acknowledge a metamessage. Lisa's father was famous for his subtle sarcasm. When he asked, "Are you *still* interested in that ... *young* man?" Lisa heard the message for what it was: a disapproving put-down. She ran the message over in her mind to verify what she'd heard. She recalled the emphasized verbal modifier "still." She recalled the pause, and the heavy emphasis on "young."

Lisa: Dad, is there something about him you don't like?

Dad: I suppose he's the usual sort of man one sees these days.

Lisa: Dad, I have the feeling from what you said that you don't like him very much. You think I'm foolish to go out with him.

Dad: He's all right, I guess.

Lisa heard how the "I guess" modified the sentence to give the impression that there was a great deal of doubt about her boyfriend's worth. She decided to specify exactly what she had heard.

Lisa: Dad, when you asked me if I was still going out with him, you gave a lot of emphasis to the word "still." The way you referred to him as "that … young man" also gave me the feeling that you felt that there was something foolish about him and our relationship.

Dad: I don't know him, but I guess he does bother me.

Lisa is finally talking with her dad about what's important. In a few moments, they will be talking openly about his negative feelings. If she can remain undefensive, Lisa will really have the opportunity to hear and directly respond to her dad's point of view. The need for metamessage attacks will be over.

6 Hidden Agendas

On the bus you overhear, "Every night he's got his nose to the TV while I'm still cleaning up. I could break a leg and he'd just sit there. He says he works all day. He doesn't know what work is. I've got the shopping, the constant care of kids, three meals, the cleaning up. When I complain, he says, 'Take time to relax.' But when I do a job, I have to do it right. I guess I'm too good."

You invite a couple to dinner. The man sits upright at the table like he's at a podium. He begins by holding forth on politics. The subject changes to the economy, and he argues for the flat tax. The subject is sports, and he proves that baseball is dying. The subject is child rearing, and he describes the seven developmental stages. The subject is ecology, and he pronounces on climate change. Your dinner is one long lecture.

You've known people like this. Their stories and remarks all have the same theme, the same hidden agenda. The point is to prove that they are good, smart, blameless, successful, and so on.

Hidden agendas are common defensive maneuvers if you don't feel very good about yourself. They protect you from rejection by creating a desired impression. Over and over, they help you make a case for your essential value as a person.

Hidden agendas hinder intimacy. Nobody gets to see the real you. You show others only carefully crafted stories and calculated remarks. They hear how brave, helpless, or fragile you are. You can usually tell if you are using hidden agendas by listening to yourself. Do your anecdotes all make the same point? Are you always trying to prove something?

The Eight Agendas

There are eight major hidden agendas. As you read about them in the descriptions that follow, notice which ones may apply to you.

"I'm Good"

You are the hero of all your stories. Each anecdote highlights the attributes you value most. If you want people to know about your wealth or power, your stories tell them. If you want the word out about your strength or generosity, your stories do that for you. A frequently encountered "I'm good" agenda is the caring and sensitive person. This role is played as if you were on the stage—you create an undeniably fine character, but not your authentic self. You have to prove your caring constantly by a gesture, a recollection, a sensitive remark.

Here are some typical "I'm good" messages: "I'm honest ... successful ... hardworking ... powerful ... courageous ... strong ... loyal ... wealthy ... generous ... self-sacrificing ... ambitious ... adventurous."

Everyone is a little phony, but the "I'm good" agenda is more than that. It's a life's work. It's a way of distorting yourself so that only very selected parts get seen. It means you don't trust anyone with the parts of yourself that are less than wonderful.

There are two big disadvantages to the "I'm good" agenda. It's hard to get close to people, because they only know you through your "I'm good" stories. And people get bored. They get tired of seeing the same mask, hearing the same theme over and over. They listen for a while, then tune out or go away.

"I'm Good (But You're Not)"

In this agenda, you prove that you're all right by showing how bad everyone else is: "Everyone's stupid, incompetent, selfish, unreasonable, lazy, frightened, or insensitive but me." Every story is a variation on this theme. You're always the one who does it right, who reasons clearly, who really cares. One nurse often complained, "I'm always willing to stop and answer a light even if it's not my patient. I'll help another nurse lift someone who's heavy, but do you think I can get anyone to help me? Not on your life."

There are several versions of "I'm good (but you're not)." One is the implied criticism. You point out how hard you've worked or how much you've compromised—with the implication that the other person is lazy or rigid. Another version of this agenda is a game that Eric Berne (1996), the father of transactional analysis, calls *Courtroom*. This involves spouses who are each trying to prove how awful the other is. The courtroom judge is usually played by a next-door neighbor, a therapist, or one of the children. Berne (1996) has also identified *If It Weren't for You*, a game for spouses who blame each other for restricted, joyless lives.

"I'm good (but you're not)" can give a boost to your self-esteem, but you pay a price. Your family and friends feel threatened and put down by you, and they soon begin defensive maneuvers of their own.

"You're Good (But I'm Not)"

The simplest version of this agenda is flattery. More complex forms involve a kind of worship of smart, beautiful, or strong people. The worship often means putting yourself down by comparison: "You do that so well; I'm all thumbs." "I wish I had your gumption and guts; I'm too afraid of blowing it." "I've never had a head for business; I look at what you've done and think how clever you are." This one-down position is sometimes used to extract favors or strokes. "You're good (but I'm not)" can be a token to buy inferior relationships. Sometimes it's a strategy to ward off anger and rejection. After all, how can you really get angry at someone who's already down on themselves? The agenda is also useful to block uncomfortable demands and expectations. Nobody's going to expect much of an incompetent.

"You're good (but I'm not)" can be the agenda of the depressed person. The basic statement is "I'm wrong, bad, damaged, stupid, boring, or unlovable. Take pity on me." The alcoholic, the chronic gambler, and the philandering spouse may also emphasize an "I'm no good" position as a way to head off rejection and also as an excuse not to change.

"I'm Helpless, I Suffer"

This is the agenda of the victim. The stories focus on misfortune, injustice, or abuse. The stories are about someone who's stuck, who tries but can't escape, who endures without hope of remedy. The person implicitly says, "Don't ask me to do anything about all this pain; I'm not responsible."

Berne (1996) describes several games that depend on the "I'm helpless" agenda. *Ain't It Awful* is played by people who want to complain about their spouses; the injustices they suffer always seem beyond solution. *Why Don't You … Yes But* is a game for two that maintains helplessness. One person makes a series of suggestions that the helpless second person shoots down, one after another. The helpless person is vindicated in the end by proving nothing will work, that the suffering is beyond his or her ability to control.

A classic "I'm helpless, I suffer" game is *Why Does This Always Happen to Me?* One man who'd gotten a little break from his ulcer symptoms complained of a reoccurrence after he got stuck in traffic without his antacids: "This always happens. I feel a little better, and then some crazy thing comes up to set me back. Somebody puts pepper on my salad, or sales take a plunge at work. It never fails." The "I'm helpless, I suffer" agenda is often employed to avoid scary new solutions or put off the need for a major life decision. "I'm ugly," "I'm ill," or "I'm too nervous" will often help put off change indefinitely.

A past-tense version of this agenda can dominate the early phase of courtship. Horror stories are traded back and forth about the previous spouse or lover. A bond of sympathy is built on the old hurts, the former years of immobility and pain.

"I'm Blameless"

This is the agenda of choice when things go wrong. You've heard people with a thousand excuses for their failures. You've watched them cast about for something or someone to blame. The basic position is "I didn't do it." Painful marriages often breed "I'm blameless" agendas. Each spouse looks for proof that the fault lies elsewhere: "She didn't give enough." "He never was home." "The children took all our time." "If we hadn't moved to Long Island." "It was different after she quit her job."

One of the games played from the "I'm blameless" position is *See What You Made Me Do.* You ask for suggestions or advice, follow the advice, and then blame your advisor for everything that went wrong. It's like taking out a kind of psychological insurance that you'll never have to be responsible for anything.

"I'm Fragile"

The basic statement from the "I'm fragile" position is "Don't hurt me." The statement is made by telling stories about how you have been betrayed and wounded in the past. You make it clear that you need protection, that you cannot hear the whole truth. You speak in a soft voice, and your vulnerability is often quite attractive: "How did you do at school today? Oh. You know, it really upsets me when I hear about you playing alone without any friends." "Everything that goes on with you is important to me, dear. But why do you have to tell me things that upset me?" "Please don't cry. I'm getting another one of my headaches." "My parents always fought about money. Let's not get into that."

"I'm Tough"

You muscle your way through life, both psychologically and physically. You are a student who carries forty units during freshman year and holds down a full-time job. You are a superwoman who works forty hours a week, raises four kids, bakes bread, does all the cleaning and cooking, and heads up the Community Chest campaign in the neighborhood. You are the workaholic man who has a high-paying, stressful job and spends twelve-hour days on the weekend replacing all the plumbing by himself.

With this agenda, a typical communication is often a harried listing of things you have done or are in the process of doing. You recite your schedule and overwhelm the other person with news of where you've been, details of your current labors, and a litany of all the places you have to rush off to as soon as the conversation is done. Your underlying message is that you are stronger and work harder, faster, and longer than anyone else. The payoff is admiration and assurance that you won't be criticized. People won't ask you for much because you are so busy. You are in control, in charge, and, most importantly, above reproach. With this agenda, you don't slow down; you collapse.

"I'm tough" is also the position of the hard, the dangerous, and the sometimes violent. In this posture, gesture and speech combine to create a studied invulnerability. "Don't attack me, or I'll cut you up" is the message. For some people, "I'm tough" is an ideal. But the sole purpose of the agenda is to ward off hurt and protect a fragile self-esteem. The only thing that is really hidden is the vulnerability of those who use it. Inside the wall of defenses is a person who's afraid of rejection and unsure of his or her worth.

"I Know It All"

This is the agenda of the endlessly lecturing dinner guest described at the beginning of the chapter. The purpose of the communication is not to inform or entertain but to prove how much you know. "I know it all" can take the form of moralizing or teaching. You are the perpetual instructor, comfortable only behind the imaginary lectern. People don't get too close. This agenda works best with younger people who may be impressed or intimidated. But peers soon learn that they can't be heard or appreciated, except as an audience. The real function of "I know it all" is to prevent you from reencountering early experiences of shame at not knowing and not feeling adequate.

Purpose of the Agendas

The agendas serve two functions. The first is to build up and preserve an existential position, a basic stance in the world. The agenda becomes your individual strategy for coping with core feelings of inadequacy. You deal with those feelings by asserting your worth in the "I'm good" agenda or by borrowing some worth by denigrating others with "I'm good (but you're not)." You protect your vulnerability with "I'm tough," "I'm fragile," or "I know it all."

The second function of your agendas is to promote ulterior motives and needs. If you need a friend but don't know how to get one, you might flatter someone with "You're good (but I'm not)." You can solicit comfort and assistance from the "I'm helpless, I suffer" position. You can excuse your failures with "I'm blameless." Consider the accusation "I'm trying to save our marriage, and you're not." It communicates the existential position of blamelessness and simultaneously promotes the ulterior motives of producing guilt and forcing change.

There is no doubt that the agendas are adaptive and serve a purpose, but ultimately your maneuvers isolate you. In the end, they wall you off from the relief of being known and accepted for who you are. The following exercise will help you see which agendas you use most often and with whom.

Exercise 6.1

For one day, count the number of times you use your agendas. Keep track of your stories, reminiscences, and remarks. Carry a file card with a list of the eight agendas and make a note each time you use one.

Now make an assessment. If the agendas are a major influence on your interactions, try keeping track a second day. This time, write down the names of everyone you talk to. Next to each name, write a percentage— how much of what you said was influenced by agendas. One woman who did this exercise found that 80 percent of her communication with her boss was a mixture of "I'm good" and "I'm blameless" agendas. Conversations with coworkers were about 30 percent "I'm good." At home, there were no agendas with her children, but 20 percent of her contact with her husband was "I'm good (but you're not)."

If you did the counting exercise, you're beginning to notice your agendas. Should an important relationship be dominated by agendas, you may want to take additional action. Here are four suggestions:

1. Let the person in question know about your agenda: "I know I'm always telling you stories of my heroics, but I'm trying to take a break from that." "I notice I'm always telling you how I'm down on someone. I'm going to try looking on the bright side." "I always seem to make myself out as helpless, but I don't think it's really me."

2. Keep track of your agendas with the target person ("There I go again").

3. Reward yourself with something nice when you block an impulse to use the old agendas.

4. If you are stuck on one agenda, mentally rehearse a new position. The following list gives some examples of new positions to take.

Agenda	Your New Position
"I'm good."	"I'm a mixture of strengths and weaknesses. I can shape both sides of myself."
"I'm good (but you're not)."	"I don't have to tear you down to make me good. I'm no longer in the business of comparing."
"You're good (but I'm not)."	"I can get attention with my strengths and abilities. I don't need to make excuses."
"I'm helpless, I suffer."	"My life is a balance of pleasure and pain, hope and sadness. I can share each side of myself."
"I'm blameless."	"Nobody's perfect. Decisions I make sometimes affect things that go wrong."
"I'm fragile."	"It scares me a little when someone is upset, but I can listen to it."
"I'm tough."	"I can take care of myself. I can relax and people will still like me. I can be safe without scaring people."
"I know it all."	"I can listen, can be interested, can ask questions. There are interesting things to learn and discover."

Notice that these new positions are in the form of simple self-instructions. They are like mantras that you can say over and over to yourself in situations that traditionally elicit your agendas. You can even turn them into personal mottos, taping them to your bathroom mirror or to the inside of your briefcase.

7 | Transactional Analysis

Transactional analysis was introduced by Eric Berne in the early 1960s as a way of examining communication. Berne (1996) suggested that every human being has three ego states: a parent, an adult, and a child. In any given day, you will probably spend some time in each ego state, and each will affect how you behave and how you communicate.

Parent, Child, and Adult Messages

Your communication style will vary markedly depending on whether you are functioning from the parent, adult, or child position.

The Parent

Your internal parent is a huge collection of rules, moral dictums, and how-to-do-it instructions that your parents gave you. These rules and instructions are recorded inside you, probably during your first five years, and they continue to play throughout your entire life. The parent rules include everything you ever heard your parents say, every pronouncement, every favorite adage: "Don't be lazy." "Don't brag." "Never let anyone make a fool of you." "A marriage lasts forever." "Always finish everything on your plate." "Never trust wealthy people." "All politicians are crooks." "Avoid risks." "Strangers are dangerous." "Don't walk under ladders." These rules were important to you as a child because you had no way of predicting danger and no knowledge of the ways of the world. As a child you didn't know what "hot" meant or what a burn did to the skin, so there were strong rules to govern your behavior with the stove.

Parental rules also provided how-to information. They gave you instructions on how to shake hands, how to eat at the table, how to fill a glass, how to make conversation, and how to navigate in your neighborhood. The rules helped you cope with your first social encounters and gave you confidence as you stepped tentatively into the world.

In many ways, the parent rules are good and helpful. They provide a structure for your life. Some have a supportive, caring quality. Like a good teacher, they remind you of the right way to do something, but without coercion or attack. If your parents were strict and rigid, however, then the parent inside you may be equally strict and unforgiving. Your internal parent may have a punitive, rejecting voice that leaves you feeling hemmed in and controlled by absolute rules.

You can usually tell when you are talking from your parent position because you use words like "always," "never," "stop," and "don't." Your communications are full of commands and value judgments. The punitive parent, in particular, will use judgmental words like "disgusting," "stupid," "ridiculous," and "idiotic." The supportive parent may describe things as "perfect," "wonderful," or "excellent." Functioning from your parent, you tend to discuss problems in terms of what "ought to" and "should" be done. Using these words is a tip-off that you're in your parent state.

The Child

Just as your parents are still inside you, so also is the child that you once were. Your child consists of all your urges to know, to feel, to touch, and to experience a new world. Your child is hungry for discovery and sensation. But your child is also a product of all the disapproval, punishment, and negative feelings brought on by confrontations with parental mandates. A child concludes very early, "I'm not okay." The child decides this because inexplicable frightening episodes of disapproval continually mar his or her existence.

Your child is the part of you where your emotions reside: your attractions, your love, your delight, and also your fear, your anger, and your feelings of not being okay left over from the turmoil of growing up. Your child is full of healthy appetites and, at the same time, raw and wounded from the inevitable parental rejections.

When you are communicating from a child position, there is usually a great deal of energy: tears, pouting, temper tantrums, and whining. Your child is also the source of exuberance, giggling, and sexual excitement. Your child uses phrases like "I hate," "I wish," and "Why do I have to?" It can't stand being told it isn't okay and retreats into hurt and anger when it senses rejection.

The Adult

There is a part of you that has to juggle the intense feelings and needs of the child and the rules and mandates of the parent. This is your adult. Your adult is like a computer, a data processing center that sorts through and keeps you aware of what's going on inside and outside of you. The adult has to make decisions. To do so, it examines the conditions of the outside world and makes predictions about likely outcomes. On the inside, the adult listens to the advice of the parent and hears out the needs and reactions of the child.

The focus of transactional analysis is to strengthen the adult. Sometimes the adult is overwhelmed or contaminated by the child or the parent. You can tell when your adult has succumbed to your child because you tend to act on intense feelings and impulses without examining them. Your feelings overwhelm you. You may express them by whining, complaining, or having crying jags or tantrums. Spending sprees and ill-advised sexual adventures are also indications that your impulsive child has gotten the upper hand. When your adult is contaminated by your parent, the result is usually a large supply of unquestioned prejudices. You have strict, unexamined beliefs. You are straitjacketed in rules that you have no permission to evaluate. Often you communicate with an attacking, blaming style.

The healthy adult knows the needs of the child and is aware of the rules of the parent. But it can function independently. It communicates and makes decisions without blocking out or giving up control to either of them.

Communications that come from your adult position are direct and straight. Your adult describes, it asks questions, it assesses probabilities; it evaluates the known and the unknown, the true and the false. It has opinions rather than judgments or beliefs. It is aware, but the awareness has no emotional charge.

Analyzing Your Communications

The skill of transactional analysis is learning to identify whether you are talking from your parent, adult, or child. If you are talking from a hurt, angry place while a customer is railing about the poor service, it probably means that your child is involved. If you're making stern threats and warnings, it probably means that your parent has gotten activated. In his book *I'm OK, You're OK*, Thomas Harris (2004) suggested these rules for analyzing your communications:

> Learn to recognize your child, its vulnerabilities, its fears, and its primary ways of expressing these feelings.

> Learn to recognize your parent, its rules, its injunctions, its fixed ideas, and its primary ways of expressing these commands.

Harris's rules mean that you have to develop an ear for the language characteristically used by your parent and child. Once you are sensitive to the child and the parent in yourself, you can more easily recognize these ego states in other people. They will use language similar to yours when expressing their punitive parent. Their child will be angry, frightened, and impulsive, just as yours is.

The following exercises are designed to help you get practice in identifying parent, adult, and child statements. For the purpose of these exercises, the focus will be on the punitive rather than the supportive parent and the not-okay rather than the healthy child.

Exercise 7.1

Identify the following statements as those of parent, child, or adult:

1. "I won't go, forget it. That's it, that's final, no way."

2. "You're just lazy. There's no other word for it."

3. "Get a move on, we're late."

4. "You've been here three hours and haven't accomplished a thing."

5. "I'll need some help with the packing when you're free."

6. "Why do I always have to go to the store?"

7. "Don't mope around. Straighten up and get on with life."

8. "Please, let's eat out tonight."

9. "You call that makeup? You look like a dead carp."

10. "One of us can get more dip for the party."

Answer key: 1. child 2. parent 3. parent 4. parent 5. adult 6. child 7. parent 8. child 9. parent 10. adult

Exercise 7.2

Write the following statements from the parent, adult, and child positions.

1. John wants to tell Susan that he'd like her to call if she's going to be late. How would he express his need from the three ego states?

   Parent: _____

   Adult: _____

   Child: _____

2. Sylvia wants to tell Ramone that she's lonely when he goes to political meetings at night. How can Sylvia express her feeling from each of the three ego states?

   Parent: _____

   Adult: _____

   Child: _____

3. David wants to ask his boss for a raise.

    Parent: _____

    Adult: _____

    Child: _____

4. How would Sam tell the butcher that the meat was tough?

    Parent: _____

    Adult: _____

    Child: _____

5. Ron wants to tell Enid that it frightens him when she expresses her anger through coldness.

    Parent: _____

    Adult: _____

    Child: _____

Possible answers: Compare your parent, adult, and child statements with these examples.

1. Parent: "If you can't be punctual, at least have the courtesy to call." Adult: "When you're going to be late, Susan, I'd appreciate it if you'd call." Child: "Why do I have to wait for you all the time? At least you could call."

2. Parent: "It's thoughtless and uncaring to go to all those late meetings while I'm left alone." Adult: "I'm lonely in the evenings when you're out at meetings." Child: "Can't you see how lonely I am at night?"

3. Parent: "You're paying a ridiculously low wage. I want a raise." Adult: "I'm asking for a raise. The figure I have in mind is ..." Child: "I wish I could get a bit more money. Do you think I could?"

4. Parent: "It's outrageous to sell meat like that. It's a rip-off." Adult: "The last meat I bought here was pretty tough." Child: "I hate it when I get tough meat. My meal was ruined."

5. Parent: "Your coldness is a stupid, ugly way to act." Adult: "Enid, you seem to get cold when you're angry. The coldness frightens me." Child: "Why do you have to get cold like that? Why do you do it to me?"

Exercise 7.3

Change the following child statements to adult statements.

1. "I wish you'd leave me alone."

_____

2. "Do you think we could be home by ten?"

_____

3. "I hate cooking!"

_____

4. "Why do I have to do everything?"

_____

5. "Why do you get to read the front page first?"

_____

Possible answers: Compare your statements with these examples. 1. "I'd like to be alone now." 2. "I need to be home by ten." 3. "I prefer not to cook." 4. "I'm overworked and tired." 5. "I'd like to read the front page first today."

Exercise 7.4

Change the following parent statements to adult statements.

1. "That's a sloppy way to make a bed."

_____

2. "What's the matter with you, buying that ridiculous tea set?"

_____

3. "Get back to work!"

_____

4. "You're sure tight with money."

_____

5. "Don't sit on the coffee table!"

_____

Possible answers: Compare your statements with these examples. 1. "I'd prefer it if the bed was tucked in neatly." 2. "What prompted you to buy that tea set?" 3. "It's time to return to work." 4. "I'd prefer it if we had a different policy about money." 5. "The coffee table won't support your weight."

You'll notice from the exercises that the punitive parent commands, accuses, and attacks. This ego state is easily recognizable by its critical, evaluative language. The not-okay child complains, pouts, and functions as a victim. The adult makes clear statements without blaming and without whining complaints.

Kinds of Transactions

There are three common ways your ego states interact with the ego states of others during conversations. Note that by paying attention to your own ego state and the ego state of your conversation partner, you can actually deescalate existing conflict or avoid provoking new conflict.

Complementary Transactions

One type of *complementary transaction* can be defined as messages that are sent or received by the same ego state for each of the participants. Person A's messages are sent by the same ego state that person B is addressing. And B's messages are sent by the same ego state that A is addressing. Figure 1 shows the same ego states communicating with each other: adult communicates with adult, parent with parent, and child with child.

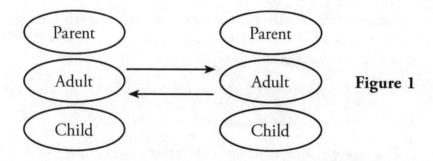

Figure 1

In another type of complementary transaction, each person is in a different ego state, but each addresses messages to the other's current state (figure 2).

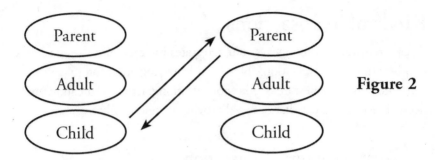

Figure 2

A typical example is the child addressing the parent and the parent therefore responding to the child.

A: Let's buy the couch anyway.

B: Now you know we can't afford it; we can barely make the rent.

Complementary transactions can usually go on indefinitely because they don't create conflict. For example, when people address each other's parent, they are usually in agreement.

A: Workmen all do shoddy work nowadays.

B: It's disgusting; they certainly do.

When people are addressing each other's child, there is also agreement.

A: I hate it when we have to go right home from work on Friday nights.

B: It's awful; we miss out on all the fun.

Crossed Transactions

Crossed transactions occur when you address an ego state that the other person isn't in. Some crossed transactions cause conflict, and others solve conflict. Figure 3 shows how crossed transactions can precipitate conflict.

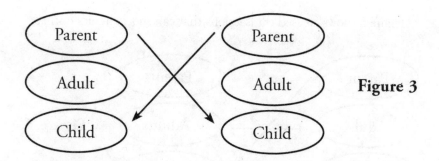

Figure 3

In figure 3, parent A punitively addresses child B, while parent B attacks child A. Here's how it might sound:

A: Why don't you stop bringing food into the bedroom?

B: Why don't you cook a dinner worth eating once in a while, so I don't have to snack all night?

Both A and B are using their punitive parent voices to attack the vulnerable child in the other. The result is that the child in each of them is wounded while they escalate the hostilities.

Figure 4 shows child A complaining to parent B, while child B complains to parent A.

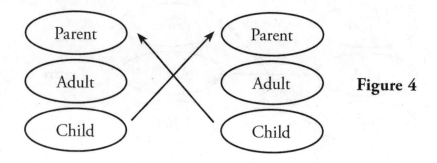

Figure 4

Here's how it could sound.

A: I hate French movies. Why do we have to go to French movies all the time?

B: If you don't like them, then I see no point in going to the movies with you anymore.

Figure 5 shows crossed transactions that can short-circuit conflict.

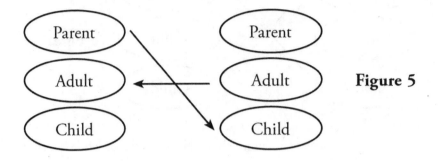

Figure 5

In figure 5, parent A is punitively addressing child B. However, adult B responds to adult A to cut off the conflict. Here's how it might sound:

A: Why don't you stop wasting time with those endless TV sitcoms and read a good book?

B: I prefer to look at the TV tonight.

Figure 6 shows child A whining to parent B. B, however, refuses to engage in conflict, and uses an adult-adult communication.

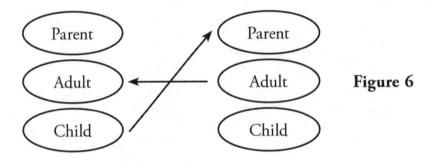

Figure 6

Here's how it might sound:

A: Why do I have to take out the garbage all the time? Why don't you do it? I hate taking out the garbage.

B: Each of us has a job. I'd like you to take out the garbage as soon as possible.

Exercise 7.5

When someone addresses your child with a punitive parent or addresses your parent with a complaining child, the only way to stop the conflict is to function in the adult position. Here is an exercise to help you get some practice.

1. Punitive parent to your child: "You're always in a lousy mood after work." Your adult-adult response:

    _____

2. Child to your parent: "Why can't we ever go dancing like other couples?" Your adult-adult response:

    _____

3. Punitive parent to your child: "Your desk is a complete mess. No wonder you can't find anything." Your adult-adult response:

    _____

4. Child to your parent: "I hate it when you don't pay attention to me." Your adult-adult response:

    _____

5. Punitive parent to your child: "You're talking a lot of nonsense." Your adult-adult response:

    _____

Possible answers: Compare your statements with these examples. 1. "I do feel tired after work. I didn't know I was upsetting you." 2. "I'm not much of a dancer, but there are other things we might go out to do." 3. "I'm comfortable with my desk the way it is." 4. "I wasn't aware that you needed my attention right now." 5. "They may be nonsense to you, but they are my opinions."

Ulterior Transactions

A third class of transactions is ulterior transactions, the basis of what Eric Berne called games. In ulterior transactions there are more than two ego states involved at the same time. For example, when communication is ostensibly adult-adult, there might be ulterior and sometimes nonverbal messages between an adult and a child (see figure 7).

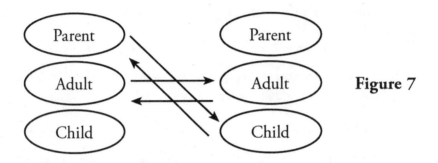

Figure 7

Salesperson A says, "This is better, but you can't afford it." Car-buyer B says, "That's the one I'll take, then." The transaction operates at the adult level, but the salesperson has provided a hook for the buyer's child. He is covertly addressing the child with the challenge, "You can't afford it." The child responds, "Oh yes I can."

You can keep track of ulterior transactions by asking yourself, "What am I trying to get this person to do? What covert feeling am I trying to express?" The game *Now I've Got You, You Son of a Bitch* is an example of how a hidden need to express hostility becomes an opportunity for an ulterior transaction. During an argument over an agreement that adult B has not honored, adult A says, "You've done wrong." Adult B says, "I guess you're right." But an ulterior communication is also going on between parent and child. The parent of person A says, "I've been hoping you'd make a slip." Child B says, "I guess I'm gonna get it now." Parent A responds, "Yes, and I'm really going to blast you." The ulterior transaction progresses while the adult communication is apparently focused on solving the disagreement.

Keeping Your Communications Clean

The following are basic transactional analysis rules for effective communication:

Know the ego state from which you are communicating.

Know the ego state to which you are sending your message.

Be sensitive to the child in others, protect that child, and recognize the not-okay burden that it must carry.

Protect your own child. Keep it safely tucked away when others are angry and attacking.

Don't use your punitive parent to communicate. No one wants to hear it, and people are likely to react by trying to hook your child with not-okay attacks. When appropriate, use your supportive parent, or rely on your adult.

Solve problems and conflicts with your adult only. Listen to your parent and listen to your child, but communicate through your adult when resolving issues.

Give your adult time to process data. Count to ten if necessary in order to analyze the communication. Your own parent or child may be clamoring inside you to get on stage and make a statement. It's important to sort out what really needs to be said from the impulsive statements your parent and child may demand that you make.

8 Clarifying Language

You don't experience the world directly. You experience your subjective representation of it. What you see, hear, and feel is converted into a thought or an interpretation, a *model* of the world that becomes your reality.

Everyone has his or her own particular model of the way things are. If you were raised in a low-income farming community, your model of the world would be likely to contrast sharply with the model held by someone raised in Beverly Hills. Depending on whether you were born nearsighted or with 20/20 vision, whether you're an orphan or a rabbi's son, whether A's came easy or you had to labor for a C+, you form a model of the world that fits your experience.

A model of the world helps you make sense of what happens. It tells you what's really important, what should be noticed or ignored, why people do things, and what choices are best for you. It says who you are in relationship to other people. For example, the person who has to study to get C's might place enormous importance on intelligence and tend to see others as brighter and more confident. The same person might also value hard work and see most people as lazy, just coasting on natural talent.

It is therefore your model of the world, and not the world itself, that determines what choices you see as open and what limitations you think constrain you. You use your model to guide you in making the best choices you can. No matter how odd it may seem to others, each person's behavior makes sense when considered within the context of the choices generated by his or her model.

You limit your choices when your model is full of very strict rules about what you can and cannot do, or when your model is full of absolutes: "I'm always going to have trouble with math." "My mother-in-law will never like me." "Everybody enjoys a party." You might limit your choices by simply mind-reading rejection: "She thinks I'm stupid." "He thinks I'm too quiet." "They know I work too slow." A limited model that restricts or distorts reality results in a limited life.

Your model of the world also determines how well you listen and communicate. Consider the following dialogue:

Sarah: I can't wait until we're married, so we can really start building a home together.

Jim: Yes, and we'll have the security to do things we haven't been able to do.

Sarah: No more apartments, a real house, a place you can move around in.

Jim: One of us could go back to school or make a career change, and the other one would provide support.

Sarah: A real living room where people can sit quietly and talk. I want to feel like a couple. I want to have couples over.

Jim: There are so many possibilities. We can go anywhere together, do anything.

Sarah: Yes, but I still want a house that has enough room for children.

Jim: Yes, sure. We'll have kids when we're ready, but there's so much we can do now.

Jim and Sarah have a very different model of marriage. Sarah sees marriage as settling down, building a home, making a social network with other couples, and preparing for children. Jim sees marriage as an opportunity to take risks that wouldn't otherwise be possible. Because they aren't able to listen to each other's different personal model of the world, Sarah and Jim are in for some big surprises.

Many relationships are made up of Jim-and-Sarah dialogues. People use the same words, but the words mean something different. "Marriage," "family," "love," "selfishness," "duty," "fairness," and "loneliness" are words that can have particular, idiosyncratic meanings to each person. Someone says, "I feel exhausted." You say to yourself, "I know what exhausted means; it's a feeling of being very tired, worn down from too much work." The speaker, however, may have a completely different model of what exhaustion is. The word might stand for pent-up rage, confusion, or a sense of powerlessness.

A way of clarifying language so that each person's model of the world can be communicated has been developed by Richard Bandler and John Grinder (2005). In their book *The Structure of Magic*, Bandler and Grinder adapted many of the concepts of transformational grammar into a set of linguistic information-gathering tools that you can use to explore and expand personal models. They describe certain universal language patterns that do one of three things:

1. Keep people from understanding your model.

2. Keep your model of the world limited.

3. Keep your model of the world distorted.

Understanding a Model

Most people talk in ways that make it very difficult for others to fully understand their experience. Because someone else's model of the world remains hidden, it's tempting and easy for you to assume that you both see things the same way. But different people draw on very different experiences, and words very rarely mean exactly the same thing to others that they mean to you. Four important language patterns that prevent people from really understanding each other are deletion, vague pronouns, vague verbs, and nominalizations.

Deletion

Deletion refers to material that has been completely left out of a sentence. You don't know exactly what the speaker means, but you fill in the blanks with your own set of assumptions. A better way to deal with deletions is to ask for the information that is missing. For example, when the speaker says, "I'm happy," you can ask, "About what?" or "About whom?" The following are statements that contain deletions and examples of questions you can use to clarify them.

Statements	Questions
"I'm confused."	"About what? About whom?"
"I'm ready."	"What are you ready to do?"
"My mood is better."	"About what? Better than what?"
"I want help."	"What kind of help do you want?"

Exercise 8.1

To get practice with clarifying deletions, write down your own questions that challenge the deletions in the following statements.

Statements	Questions
"I'm sad."	
"The empire was destroyed."	
"James is too good."	
"I just don't know what to do."	

Vague Pronouns

Confusion and misinterpretation are the usual results when a speaker relies on vague pronouns. Here are some examples of vague pronouns and clarifying questions.

Statements	Questions
"It's unbelievable."	"What is unbelievable?"
"It's unfair."	"What is unfair?"
"They say artificial sweeteners cause cancer."	"Whose research shows that artificial sweeteners cause cancer?"
"It's going wrong."	"What is going wrong?"

Exercise 8.2

Write down questions that uncover the missing pronoun references in the following statements.

Statements	Questions
"They aren't listening to me."	
"This is easy!"	
"It was sensational."	
"This can't go on this way."	

Vague Verbs

Some verbs, such as "tickle," "yawn," and "blink," are much more specific than others, such as "move," "touch," and "see." If someone said to you, "I grew a lot last year," you might wonder to yourself, "Well, how did you grow? Are you two inches taller? Did you put on weight? Overcome your hang-ups?" By challenging a speaker with the question "How did you grow last year?" you get clarification of the other person's experience and model of the world. The following are statements containing vague verbs, with questions that challenge them.

Statements	Questions
"She makes me so mad!"	"In what way does she make you mad?"
"My parents pushed me to become a doctor."	"What did your parents do to push you toward medicine?"
"He just faded away."	"How did he leave? Where did he go?"
"We just had to keep moving."	"What forced you to keep moving?"

Exercise 8.3

Write questions challenging the statements with vague verbs.

Statements	Questions
"You frustrate me!"	
"They liked your work."	

"She seemed to miss us."	
"I feel like I'm running down."	

Nominalizations

Nominalizations are abstract nouns that give the false impression of being concrete things or events. "The problem," "our relationship," "this discussion," and "your guilt" are examples of nominalizations.

There are two ways to create a nominalization. One way is to use extremely vague nouns that don't clearly denote anything that people can agree on. If other people talk about "your guilt," they may have a very good idea of what they mean. But you may have a very different model of how guilt operates in your life.

The second way to create nominalizations is to turn verbs into nouns. "Let's make a decision" is an example of this sort of nominalization. A more dynamic, understandable sentence would read, "Let's decide on how many shade trees to plant." By turning the noun "decision" into the verb "decide," you make a sentence that requires more specific information. The indefinite "decision" to be made is replaced by the specific thing to be decided.

Nominalizations are easy to distinguish from other nouns. Visualize a green wheelbarrow. Now imagine putting a young tree, a little girl, or a couple of sacks of cement in the wheelbarrow. These are all nouns. Now try putting guilt, problems, or relationships in the wheelbarrow. As you can see, nominalizations are not persons, places, or things; they are too abstract to visualize. When speakers use a static nominalization, you can get them to turn it into a dynamic process word by doing one of two things: demand a specific definition of the nominalization, or ask a question using the nominalization as a verb. For example, if someone says that he or she wants more attention, you could demand a definition of attention by asking, "Specifically, what kind of attention do you need?" If someone tells you, "I'm feeling a lot of disapproval," you can turn the nominalization into a verb by asking, "How am I disapproving of you?" The following are statements with nominalizations and questions that challenge them.

Statements	Questions
"Our relationship seems strained."	"How are we relating that you're feeling strained?"
"Work is nothing but problems."	"Exactly what kinds of problems have been bothering you?"
"The day was full of rejection."	"How were you rejected during the day?"
"The excitement is gone."	"What excited you that isn't happening now?"

Exercise 8.4

Write down questions that clarify the nominalizations.

Statements	Questions
"He's a success."	
"I want guidance."	
"It is all a misunderstanding."	
"I felt a lot of anger."	

Challenging the Limits of a Model

There are three important language patterns that artificially restrict your experience: absolutes, imposed limits, and imposed values.

Absolutes

Absolutes are overgeneralizations typified by words such as "always," "never," "all," "none," "everyone," and "no one." You can challenge a speaker's absolutes by exaggerating them with your tone of voice and by adding even more absolutes. When a speaker says, "My mother's always late," you can reply, "She's *always* and *forever* late?" Another way to challenge statements containing an absolute is to ask the person if he or she has ever had an experience that contradicts the generalization: "Can you think of even one time when your mother was punctual?" The following are statements containing absolutes and questions to challenge them.

Statements	Questions
"I'm always in pain."	"You're absolutely always in pain?"
"Nobody cares about me."	"There's not a single person on earth who cares about you? Not even one?"
"I never win."	"There has never been an instance when you won?"
"She's always brusque with me."	"She's always brusque with you? Do you ever recall her being cordial?"

Exercise 8.5

Write down questions challenging the following statements containing absolutes.

Statements	Questions
"I can never get a date."	
"I'm always the last one to be served."	
"Everybody says he's right."	
"All the good ones are married."	

Imposed Limits

Imposed limits are words or phrases that suggest you have no choice. Examples of such words are "can't," "must," "have to," "should," "ought," "it's necessary," and "it's impossible."

Imposed limits fall into two categories. The "I can't" and "it's impossible" category defines reality in such a way that certain options are absolutely excluded. The "must," "should," and "have to" category often carries the weight of a moral imperative. Such *should-statements* are extremely limiting because they imply that you're a bad person if you break the rules that the statements impose.

Many people hem themselves in with unquestioned limits. You might overhear a man say, "I can't speak in front of any kind of crowd." His model of the world says that such experiences are out of the question, completely beyond his capability. You can challenge his imposed limits by asking either of these questions: "What would happen if you did speak to a large crowd?" or "What stops you from speaking to a large crowd?" The first question propels the speaker into the future to imagine the possible consequences of his actions, and the second forces the speaker into the past to discover the experience on which his fear is based.

"Shoulds" and moral imperatives can be challenged in the same way. A friend remarks, "I have to finish my work before I can relax." You might challenge that imposed limit: "What would happen if you didn't finish your work before relaxing?" The following are statements containing imposed limits and questions that challenge them.

Statements	Questions
"I'd like to go, but I can't."	"What stops you from going?"
"You must not say things like that."	"What will happen if I say things like that to you?"
"I have to do what my boss says."	"What would happen if you didn't do what your boss says?"
"I can't cook."	"What about cooking is too difficult for you?"

Exercise 8.6

Write down questions that challenge the following imposed limits.

Statements	Questions
"I can't get very far with my homework."	
"I can't wait for her any longer."	
"You have to get a more mature attitude."	
"You must think of their feelings."	

Imposed Values

When people state a generalization about the world, they make a judgment based on their personal model. Essentially, they are taking values that they find appropriate to themselves and applying them to other people. You can tell that you are encountering imposed values when you hear people using global labels: "stupid," "money hungry," "corrupt," "gutless," "ugly." People who rely on this language pattern are typically unaware that there is any legitimate alternative viewpoint. Challenging such statements forces the speaker to examine his or her personal opinions and, at the same time, acknowledge that the rest of the world has its own values and opinions. When someone says, "All modern art is a waste of paint," you can ask, "For whom is all modern art a waste of paint?" The following are statements containing imposed values and questions that challenge them.

Statements	Questions
"That's a worthless piece of junk."	"For whom is it worthless?"
"Communism is evil."	"To whom does communism seem evil?"
"Walking out was the wrong thing to do."	"For whom was walking out wrong?"
"Sex therapy is stupid."	"For whom is sex therapy foolish or ineffective?"

Exercise 8.7

Write down questions challenging the following statements containing imposed values.

Statement	Questions
"Modern popular music is just noise."	
"Jogging is the best form of exercise."	
"Fanaticism is dangerous."	
"Anger is an unnecessary emotion."	

Challenging Distortions in a Model

When your personal model of the world is distorted, it cuts you off from considering other alternatives and your experience becomes severely impoverished. Three language patterns that distort reality are cause-and-effect errors, mind reading, and presuppositions.

Cause-and-Effect Errors

Cause-and-effect errors result from the belief that one person can cause another to experience some emotion or inner state and that the second person has no choice about how he or she will respond. When you challenge this belief, you are asking whether this causal connection does indeed exist and whether the second person does have any alternative ways of responding. For example, if your mother says, "I'm anxious because you're leaving," you can ask, "How does my leaving make you anxious?" The point is to gently remind her that she is responsible for her own feelings and that she generates her own responses to events. The following are statements that contain cause-and-effect errors and questions that challenge them.

Statements	Questions
"You make me sad."	"How did I make you sad? What did I do that you got sad about?"
"Your baby gives me a headache."	"Gives you a headache? Did my baby actually make your head hurt?"
"Your silence makes me angry."	"How does my silence anger you? What is it about my silence that irritates you?"
"The work bored me."	"What was it about the work that you found boring?"

Exercise 8.8

Write down questions challenging the statements containing cause-and-effect errors.

Statements	Questions
"I'm tense whenever you're near me."	
"He infuriates me."	
"Your procrastination frustrates me."	
"Your judgmental attitude ties me in knots."	

Mind Reading

Mind reading is the belief that you can know what another person is thinking or feeling without direct communication with that person. Mind reading distorts your model of the world because it invariably leads you to form beliefs that are simply untrue. Mind reading depends on a process called projection—the expectation that people feel and react in the same way as the mind reader. The mind reader doesn't watch or listen closely enough to notice that others are actually experiencing the world differently. To challenge the language pattern involving mind reading, you ask, "How do you know such-and-such?" Speakers then have the opportunity to become aware of and question assumptions that they previously took for granted. The following statements contain mind-reading errors and questions to challenge them.

Statements	Questions
"My coworkers think I'm lazy."	"How do you know that your coworkers think you're lazy?"
"My husband knows what I want."	"How do you know that your husband is aware of what you want?"
"He only married her for her money."	"What makes you feel that he only married her for her money?"
"Please don't be mad at me."	"What gives you the impression that I'm mad at you?"

Exercise 8.9

Write down questions challenging the following statements containing mind-reading errors.

Statements	Questions
"Tony doesn't like me."	
"You think that I don't care about the kids."	
"I think that you're pretty anxious."	
"You're expecting too much of me."	

Presuppositions

Presuppositions are parts of a statement that must be true in order for the whole statement to be valid: "Since you got so jealous the last time we went dancing, let's not go again." The conclusion of this statement, "let's not go again," can only be valid if the assumption that "you got jealous" is true. To challenge this statement, you could ask, "In what way did I seem to you to be jealous?" The following are statements that contain presuppositions and the questions that challenge them.

Statements	Questions
"If Tom would only listen to me, I would tell him how I really feel."	"How does Tom seem not to listen to you?"
"If you really loved me, you'd spend more time with me."	"In what ways do I seem not to really love you?"
"I'm in serious trouble, so I need an immediate appointment."	"In what way is the trouble serious?"
"Your dog menaces my children. Either lock it up or put it to sleep."	"How does my dog seem to menace your children?"

Exercise 8.10

The following statements contain presuppositions. Write down opposite each statement a question that would challenge the assumption it makes.

Statements	Questions
"If you're going to be greedy, let's stop playing cards."	
"Since he's so cheap, I won't ask him for a loan."	
"I wouldn't work overtime if they didn't really need me."	
"If Stella weren't so lazy, she would have gotten better grades."	

The list of language patterns presented in this chapter was adapted from Bandler and Grinder's meta-model, discussed in *The Structure of Magic* (2005). Some of the terms were changed to promote simplicity and ease in memorization. Additional challenges were also included.

Some Final Clarifications

The clarifying techniques you've learned in this chapter shouldn't be used excessively. Constantly demanding clarification of the casual remarks others make would be obnoxious. But the techniques should be used when someone's statement doesn't make sense, is vague, or misses some vital piece of information. Consistent use of absolutes, mind reading, and other language patterns indicates that the speaker's model is limited or distorted, and you should judiciously use clarifying techniques. Be gentle. Explore or challenge with an attitude of interest rather than hostility.

PART III

· · · · · · · · · · · · · · ·

Conflict Skills

9 Assertiveness Training

Assertiveness training teaches you to express your feelings, thoughts, and wishes, and to stand up for your legitimate rights without violating the rights of others. Assertiveness is a skill you can acquire, not a personality trait that some people are born with and others are not. Like aggression and passivity, assertiveness is a social behavior that can be learned.

Nobody is consistently assertive. You may be assertive with your children in one instance, aggressive with them in another, and passive in still another. You might have no trouble being assertive with your family yet find it almost impossible to be assertive with strangers. Assertiveness training can expand the number of social situations in which you can respond assertively rather than passively or aggressively.

Learning to be assertive doesn't mean that you must always behave assertively. When your life, well-being, or property is being threatened, it's entirely appropriate to be aggressive. When a judge is lecturing you, it's certainly appropriate to be passive. Learning to be assertive helps you match your style to the situation.

Your Legitimate Rights

You learned a set of beliefs early in your life to help guide your social conduct. These beliefs are essentially a set of rules about "good" and "bad" behavior passed on to you by your parents and later role models. While these rules helped you get along with the people you grew up with, they are not cast in bronze and lightning won't strike you down if you decide to act differently.

Read the following list of traditional assumptions, adapted from *The Relaxation and Stress Reduction Workbook* (Davis, Eshelman, and McKay 2008). Do any of them remind you of rules you learned as a child? Do you still believe that they apply to you as an adult? Listed beside each traditional assumption is a statement of your legitimate right as an adult. These rights are a reminder that you have a choice about what you believe and that you are no longer an unquestioning child, but rather an adult with alternatives.

Mistaken Traditional Assumptions	Your Legitimate Rights
It is selfish to put your needs before others' needs.	You have a right to put yourself first sometimes.
It is shameful to make mistakes. You should have an appropriate response for every occasion.	You have a right to make mistakes.
If you can't convince others that your feelings are reasonable, then your feelings must be wrong.	You have a right to be the final judge of your feelings and accept them as legitimate.
You should respect the views of others, especially if they are in a position of authority. Keep your differences of opinion to yourself. Listen and learn.	You have a right to have your own opinions and convictions.
You should always try to be logical and consistent.	You have a right to change your mind or decide on a different course of action.
You should be flexible and adjust. Others have good reasons for their actions, and it's not polite to question them.	You have a right to protest any treatment or criticism that feels bad to you.
You should never interrupt people. Asking questions reveals your stupidity to others.	You have a right to interrupt in order to ask for clarification.

Things could get even worse. Don't rock the boat.	You have a right to negotiate for change.
You shouldn't take up others' valuable time with your problems.	You have a right to ask for help or emotional support.
People don't want to hear that you feel bad, so keep it to yourself.	You have a right to feel and express pain.
When someone takes the time to give you advice, you should take it very seriously. They are often right.	You have a right to ignore the advice of others.
Knowing that you did something well is its own reward. People don't like show-offs. Successful people are secretly disliked and envied. Be modest when complimented.	You have a right to receive recognition for your work and achievements.
You should always try to accommodate others. If you don't, they won't be there when you need them.	You have a right to say no.
Don't be antisocial. People are going to think you don't like them if you say you'd rather be alone instead of with them.	You have a right to be alone, even if others would prefer your company.

Three Communication Styles

The first step in assertiveness training is learning to distinguish between passive, aggressive, and assertive behaviors.

Passive Style

When you are communicating passively, you don't directly express your feelings, thoughts, and wishes. You may try to communicate them indirectly by frowning, crying, or whispering something under your breath. Or you may withhold your feelings and wishes entirely.

In the passive style, you tend to smile a lot and subordinate your needs to those of others. You also probably do more than your share of listening. If you do speak up directly, you make disclaimers such as "I'm no expert ... ," "I'm really not sure ... ," or "I really shouldn't be saying this, but ..." You find it difficult to make requests. When someone asks you to do something that you don't want to do, you're inclined to do it or make an excuse rather than say no.

A passive speaking style includes a soft, weak, even wavering voice. Pauses and hesitations are common. You are likely to be at a loss for words. You may ramble, be vague, and use the phrases "I mean" and "you know" often. You frequently rely on others to guess what you want to say. Your posture is likely to be slouched, and perhaps you will lean against something for support. Your hands are apt to be cold, sweaty, and fidgety. Eye contact is difficult for you; you tend to look down or away. Because you are often not saying what you mean, you don't look like you mean what you say.

Aggressive Style

In the aggressive style, you are quite capable of stating how you feel, what you think, and what you want, but often at the expense of others' rights and feelings. You tend to humiliate others by using sarcasm or humorous put-downs. You are likely to go on the attack when you don't get your way, and you stir up guilt and resentment in others by pointing a finger of blame. Your sentences often begin with "You ..." followed by an attack or a negative label. You use absolute terms such as "always" and "never" and describe things in a way that implies that you're always right and superior.

When you are behaving aggressively, you tend to move with an air of superiority and strength. Your style may run the gamut from cold and deadly quiet to flippant and sarcastic to loud and shrill. Your eyes are narrowed and expressionless. Your posture is that of a solid rock: feet planted apart, hands on hips, jaw clenched and jutting out, and gestures rigid, abrupt, and intimidating. Sometimes you point your finger or make a fist, raise your voice, or bang the table to emphasize your words. You are so intent on being right that you don't really hear what others are saying, even when you ask them a direct question.

Assertive Style

When you communicate assertively, you make direct statements regarding your feelings, thoughts, and wishes. You stand up for your rights and take into account the rights and feelings of others. You listen attentively and let other people know that you have heard them. You are open to negotiation and compromise, but not at the expense of your own rights and dignity. You can make direct requests and direct refusals. You can give and receive compliments. You can start and stop a conversation. You can deal effectively with criticism without becoming hostile or defensive.

When you are behaving assertively, you convey an air of assured strength and empathy. Your voice is relaxed, well modulated, and firm. While you are comfortable with direct eye contact, you don't stare. Your eyes communicate openness and honesty. Your posture is balanced and erect.

Exercise 9.1

A good way to become familiar with the passive and aggressive styles is to role-play them. But unless you're reading this book as part of a class or sharing it with friends, role-playing will be difficult. You can either act out or imagine yourself acting the following parts.

1. Passive Style

Pretend to be a very dependent spouse. Move one of your feet back and put your weight on it. Extend your arms, palms up. Bend over a bit, so you don't get enough air to have a full, rich voice, and so you are slightly off balance. Your voice will be soft as you look up and say, "Whatever you say is all right with me. I'm just here to make you happy." "I don't have any power of my own. I depend on you to make the decisions and take care of me." "I'd be too vulnerable without you, so whatever you say goes." "I'm sorry if I have inconvenienced you in some way." "I'd offer an opinion, but it isn't worth much."

Continue to repeat statements like these in this voice and posture for three minutes. Notice what your voice sounds like. How do you feel? How are you breathing? How are your muscles?

Most people find it exhausting to play this role. They report feeling off balance, tense, sad, vulnerable, resentful, dependent, dishonest, upset, worthless, and childish.

The major advantage of being passive is that you don't have to take responsibility for your feelings and needs. There is someone else around to make decisions and to protect you. The disadvantages are your loss of independence, your stifled needs, and your stifled feelings. It's hard sometimes to like yourself because you can't seem to change anything or express how you really feel.

People often behave passively in order to avoid conflict. The irony is that passivity creates conflict. The needs and feelings that you hide make you frustrated and angry. You have to manipulate others to get what you want. When others sense your dissatisfaction, they feel attacked or pressured by it. They often resent your covert manipulations.

2. Aggressive Style

Now pretend you're an aggressive supervisor bawling out an employee. Stand up and lean forward slightly on one foot. Put one hand on your hip and point the index finger of the other at the imaginary employee. In a loud, accusatory voice, say such things as the following: "You never do anything right. You're always late." "You're always doing some stupid thing." "What's wrong with you? You're just a lazy SOB. We could rent you out as a doorstop. I'm the only one around here who does anything." "I get sick and tired of having to make all the decisions." "You never take any initiative."

Continue for three minutes in this vein, using plenty of you-messages, negative labels, and sarcasm. What the other person thinks is irrelevant. Never ask a question as though you really expect an answer. Your only interest is in being right and on top. Notice how you feel. How are you breathing? How are your muscles? What do you sound like?

If you are like most people, you enjoy this role more than the passive one. You feel strong and solid. Nothing can touch you. All of your energy is directed outward. You notice that your muscles are tense, especially in the throat, neck, and shoulders. Your voice tends to become shrill and your breath comes in little gasps as your throat tightens.

The primary objective of being aggressive is to win, to establish your primacy over others. You often achieve your short-term goals, but in the end people resist and resent you. You end up feeling frustrated and alone. You're able to vent your anger, but you always have to stay on guard. You can't express your softer feelings or your uncertainty.

Your Assertiveness Goals

Learning assertiveness skills is one thing. Using them is another. Before you go to the effort of learning assertiveness skills, ask yourself if it is really worth it to you to change. Ask yourself:

What do you get out of being passive?

What would you have to give up if you behaved assertively instead of passively?

What do you get from being aggressive?

What would you have to give up if you behaved assertively instead of aggressively?

What would you gain from being assertive?

Visit http://www.newharbinger.com/41719 to download the next exercise.

Exercise 9.2

List at least five goals in terms of social situations in which you would like to be more assertive. Write down specifically how you would like to behave differently, not how you would like to feel or be. For example, you might write the following: "I want to present my ideas on a new product in a business meeting with my boss and colleagues."

_____

_____

_____

_____

_____

Assertive Expression

If you're like most people, you tend to be fairly indirect about expressing your feelings and needs. Perhaps you were told as a child that it was self-centered to talk a lot about yourself or to overuse the pronoun "I." Or maybe you're afraid of how people will react if you are more direct.

When you share your thoughts indirectly, you often call on the invisible expert: "They say the economy is getting worse. Of course, some say it's getting better. But you never know who you can trust." When you state your feelings indirectly, you are apt to sound something like this: "They just laid our whole department off. Makes me feel kind of ... you know. You work all those years, and then it's all gone in a moment. It's frustrating, but what can you do? You just go home and wait." When you can't express your wants directly, you have to hint: "It looks like a nice day for an outing ... What do you think?"

An assertive statement has three parts: what you think, what you feel, and what you want. These are known as *I-statements* or *I-messages*:

I think. This is your perspective of the situation, described objectively, without blaming the other person or making negative judgments.

I feel. In an assertive statement, any feelings—positive or negative—belong to the speaker. This is where you can include the emotions you feel in the situation, but again without blaming or harsh judgments. Use I-statements such as "I feel lonely" or "I'm very nervous about my new job." Avoid you-statements like "I feel that you are too self-centered." That's a you-statement masquerading as an I-statement.

I want. Express your needs in the situation as clearly and directly as you can. The more specific you are, the better. The more you hedge, the easier it will be for the other person to ignore or misunderstand your message.

Here are some examples using the three components of an assertive statement:

"When I think about giving a speech, I get nervous. I've been feeling butterflies in my stomach since yesterday when I told you I would talk at the next general board meeting. I realize that I don't want to give that talk. Please find someone else."

"I think we have a lot in common. Spending the evening with you has been a lot of fun. I want to get to know you better, and I'd like to go out with you again next Friday night."

"We spend a lot of time talking about your situation at work. I feel irritated and a bit bored when you come home and only discuss office politics. I'd like to have time to tell you about my day, and also to talk about us, how we're feeling about being together."

Visit http://www.newharbinger.com/41719 to download the next exercise.

Exercise 9.3

For each of the situations described in your assertiveness goals, write three assertive I-messages:

1. "I think _____."

   "I feel _____."

   "I want _____."

2. "I think_____."

   "I feel _____."

   "I want _____."

3. "I think_____."

   "I feel _____."

   "I want _____."

4. "I think_____."

    "I feel _____."

    "I want _____."

5. "I think_____."

    "I feel _____."

    "I want _____."

Assertive Listening

When you listen assertively, you concentrate your attention exclusively on the other person, without interrupting, so that you accurately hear feelings, opinions, and wishes. There are three steps in assertive listening: preparing, listening, and acknowledging.

Preparing. Tune in to your own feelings and needs to find out if you are ready to listen. Check to be sure that the other person is also ready to speak.

Listening. Put your full attention on the other person. Try to hear feelings and what is wanted. If you are uncertain about the other person's feelings or wishes, ask him or her for more information. For example, "I'm not really sure how you feel about that ... Can you tell me more? What is it that you want?"

Acknowledging. Let the other person know that you heard his or her feelings and wants. For example, "I hear that you are exhausted from a hard day and want to spend an hour before dinner taking a nap." You may want to acknowledge the other person's feelings by sharing your feelings about what has been said. For example, "I'm angry to hear that you had to do so much extra work today."

Combining Assertive Expression and Listening

When you're in conflict with someone and you both have strong feelings, the two of you can take turns using assertive listening and expression.

Simply stating clearly what you each think, feel, and want can solve many problems. Misunderstandings are often cleared up, or solutions to problems quickly appear. Here's an example:

Paul: This house is a mess! It's maddening to come home to chaos after a long day at work.

Mary: I don't understand. What's upsetting you?

Paul: I get really pissed off when I come home to a cluttered, noisy house. I want some peace and quiet when I first get in. I want to be able to walk into my study without tripping over toys, and I want to spend some time alone.

Mary: I hear that you're angry because the house is noisy and chaotic when you first get home, and that you need to have some quiet time alone, and that you wish that the place could be picked up.

Paul: Yes, that's right.

Mary: Well, I have my own perspective on the problem. Ever since I took that part-time job, I haven't had time to keep this place spotless. I get exhausted and frustrated trying to work, take care of the kids, keep house, and do all my errands. I want you to help me more with the housework and the errands.

Paul: I wasn't aware you were feeling overworked to the point of exhaustion. What exactly do you want me to do?

Paul and Mary make a deal: he'll do the vacuuming and fold the clothes if she'll have the living room picked up and give him an hour to decompress when he gets home.

As an exercise, with a friend or family member, practice combining the assertive listening and expression skills. Begin practicing on a small issue such as what to do next weekend. When you feel comfortable with the skills, try using them with more emotionally laden problems.

Responding to Criticism

One of the major reasons people have difficulty being assertive is that they experience criticism as rejection. This is often a leftover from childhood, when you faced criticism from a one-down position. Each time you erred, your critical parents or teachers would pass judgment on you. You were wrong, and therefore you were bad. In time, you learned to feel bad each time you were criticized. You may even have learned to use self-criticism as a club to beat yourself until you felt guilty and wrong.

Because criticism can be so painful, you may have developed special strategies to minimize the hurts. You may respond to criticism aggressively by verbally blowing up. Or you may respond in kind, bringing up old sins to fault your critic. Couples are particularly good at this: "You say I'm a spendthrift? Why, you bought yourself a whole new wardrobe last year and then put on thirty pounds so you couldn't wear a stitch of it!" Some partners respond to criticism with sarcasm: "Look at Mr. Perfect who knows so much!"

If you respond to criticism passively, you may become silent, turn red, cry, or try to escape your critic as soon as possible. You might either pretend you didn't hear what was said or, in order to avoid conflict, quickly agree with everything the critic says. When you respond passively, you hold in your anger and hurt. Sitting on your feelings is a very good way to get depressed or develop physical symptoms such as headaches and stomachaches.

Storing resentments and hurts can propel you into the "getting even" syndrome. Either consciously or unconsciously, you start "forgetting" important dates, procrastinating, arriving late, going too slow or too fast, being silent, or talking nonstop in an annoying whine—whatever will most irritate your critic. The advantage of this tactic is that you don't have to take responsibility for how you feel and what you do. When challenged, you can respond innocently: "Who me? You've got to be kidding. You're too sensitive." Or, you might say, "I'm sorry, I didn't mean it." The major disadvantage of this tactic is that your feelings and wants often get lost in the process of rationalizing and defending. Your little revenges also tend to alienate your critic and bring on more criticism.

The best response to criticism is an assertive response, based on the assumption that you are the most qualified person to decide what's best for you. As the final judge regarding your feelings, thoughts, wants, and behavior, you are also responsible for their consequences. Since you have a unique genetic heritage and life history, you have your own expectations, likes, dislikes, and values. Your set of rules is likely to differ from those of other people, so it's understandable that you will not always agree with them.

When criticized, you can choose from several good assertive responses described next.

Acknowledgment

When you receive criticism with which you agree, whether it is constructive criticism or just an unnecessary reminder, acknowledge that the critic is right: "You're right, boss, I should always spell-check my work." "Yes, I don't have the report in that was due last week." "Yes, I was half an hour late for work today."

Don't fall into the trap of making excuses or apologizing for your behavior. This is an automatic response left over from childhood, when you accidentally spilled milk, soiled your clothes, or came home fifteen minutes late and your parents asked, "Why did you do that?" They expected a reasonable answer, and you learned to supply an excuse. As an adult, you might choose to give an explanation for your actions, but you don't have to. Stop and ask yourself if you really want to, or if you are just reacting out of an old habit. For example, you might say, "Yes, Jack, I haven't submitted that report that was due last week," and decide not to give Jack any explanation, since he's your peer and not in charge of when you get your work done.

On the other hand, when responding to your boss, you wouldn't merely acknowledge that you were "half an hour late this morning." Since you value your job, you would hasten to explain, "My car battery was dead, and I had to ask a neighbor to jump it."

Exercise 9.4

Write an acknowledgement to this criticism:

"If you drive like a madman, we're going to have an accident. You're in too much of a hurry."

Clouding

Clouding is a useful technique for dealing with nonconstructive, manipulative criticism with which you disagree. It provides a quick way to dispense with statements that have a grain of truth in them but are intended mostly as put-downs. When you use clouding, you find something in the critical comment to agree with while inwardly sticking to your own point of view. This calms critics down and gets them out of the win/lose game so that you can either communicate about more important things or end the conversation. There are three ways that you can agree with your critic:

Agreeing in Part

You find some part of what the critic is saying that you agree with and acknowledge that they are right about that part. You ignore the rest of the criticism. You modify any words the critic uses that are sheer exaggeration, such as "always" and "never." You rephrase the sentences that you almost agree with, but you do not distort the essence of the critic's original meaning.

Critic: You're always working. You think the world would fall apart if you took a day off.

You: Yes, I do work a lot.

Critic: You never have time for your friends anymore. You've become driven and obsessed by work.

You: You're right, I don't have much time for my friends right now.

Agreeing in Probability

You agree in probability when there's some chance that your critic is right. Even if the odds are one in a thousand, you can make such replies as "It may be ..." or "You could be right." Using the last example, you could respond to the critic with the following: "It may be that I work too much." Or you might say, "It could be that I don't have time for my friends anymore."

Agreeing in Principle

Sometimes you can agree with the logic of your critic without agreeing with his or her premise. You can agree that "if X, then Y" and still not admit that X is true.

Critic: If you don't study more than you do, you're going to fail your classes.

You: You're right. If I don't study, I will fail my classes.

Exercise 9.5

Write a clouding response to this criticism:

"You spend a lot of time with your bonsai trees, but very little else gets your attention around here."

Probing

Assertive probing is useful when you can't tell if the criticism is constructive or manipulative, when you don't understand the criticism, or when you think you're not getting the whole story. Criticism is often a way of avoiding important feelings or wishes, so if you're confused by a critical comment, probe for what's underneath it.

To use probing, pick out the part of the criticism that you think the critic feels most strongly about. Generally this will be something that affects his or her self-interest. Ask, "What is it that bothers you about …? and add the part of the criticism you think is most important to the critic. If necessary, ask the critic to provide a specific example. Listen to the critic's response carefully to determine what he or she feels, thinks, and wants. Continue to probe: "What is it that bothers you about … ?" until you are satisfied that you understand the critic's intent. Don't use phrases like "So what's the matter this time?" or "What's wrong with what I did?" or "What's bothering you?" They will make you sound defensive and will deter the critic from expressing authentic feelings and wants.

Here's an example of effective probing:

Critic: You're just not pulling your weight around here. Your work is half-assed.

You: What is it about my work that bothers you?

Critic: Well, everybody else is working like a dog—doing overtime. You waltz out of here every night at five o'clock.

You: What is it that bothers you about me leaving the office on time when other people work overtime?

Critic: I hate working overtime myself. But the work has to be done. I'm responsible to see that it is, and I get angry when I see you just working by the clock.

You: What is it that bothers you when I work by the clock?

Critic: When you leave, somebody else has to finish your work. I want you to stick around until it's done.

You: I see. I appreciate your explaining the situation to me.

In this case, probing got you to a clear understanding of the critic's gripe and to a clear request for you to do something about it. If your critic had continued to criticize you in vague terms, you could have turned to clouding.

Exercise 9.6

Write a probing response to this criticism:

"You never really get involved. You bail out of a relationship at the first sign of trouble. One harsh word and you're gone."

Special Assertive Strategies

Here are some strategies you can use to set limits or assert your own needs in a situation.

Broken Record

The broken record is a useful technique to use when you want to say no or otherwise set limits with someone who is having difficulty getting your message. You can use it to say no to your five-year-old, to tell a phone solicitor that you're not interested in contributing to his charity, or to inform your enthusiastic hostess that you really don't want a drink. The broken record is most handy in situations where an explanation would provide the other person with an opportunity to drag out a pointless argument. It has five steps:

1. Clarify in your own mind exactly what you want or don't want. Be aware of your feelings, your thoughts about the situation, and your rights.

2. Formulate a short, specific, easy-to-understand statement about what you want. Keep it to one sentence if you can. Offer no excuses, no explanations. Avoid saying, "I can't." This is an excuse of the worst kind. The other person will probably return with "Of course you can," and then proceed to tell you how. It's much simpler, more direct, and more honest to say, "I don't want to." Review your statement in your mind. Try to get rid of any loopholes that the other person could use to further his or her own argument.

3. Use body language to support your statement. Stand or sit erect, look the other person in the eye, and keep your hands quietly at your sides.

4. Calmly and firmly repeat your statement as many times as necessary for the person to get your message and to realize that you won't change your mind. The other person will probably come up with several reasons for not going along with your wishes. But most people run out of nos and excuses eventually. Don't change your broken record unless the other person finds a serious loophole in it.

5. You may choose to briefly acknowledge the other person's ideas, feelings, or wishes before returning to your broken record: "I understand you're upset, but I don't want to work any more overtime." "I hear what you want, but I don't want to do any more overtime." Don't allow yourself to become sidetracked by the other person's statements.

Here's a dialogue that exemplifies the broken record:

Customer: I bought this blouse here a couple of weeks ago, and I want to return it and get my money back.

Salesperson: Do you have a receipt?

Customer: Yes. (Shows it to the salesperson.)

Salesperson: It says you bought the blouse over a month ago. That's too long. How can you expect us to take back something you bought so long ago?

Customer: I understand I bought it a month ago, and I want to return it and get my money back.

Salesperson: This is highly irregular. Our store policy is that all returns must be made within one week.

Customer: I understand that, and I want to return this blouse and get my money back.

Salesperson:	Given the policy, I would feel uncomfortable authorizing your return.
Customer:	I can appreciate your feeling uncomfortable about accepting it, but I want to return this blouse and get my money back.
Salesperson:	I could lose my job for doing such a thing.
Customer:	I hear your worry about losing your job, and I still want to return this blouse and get my money back.
Salesperson:	Look, I don't want to take any chances. Why don't you return it tomorrow when the manager is here?
Customer:	I hear you would rather have me come back tomorrow, but I want to return this blouse and get my money back now.
Salesperson:	You sound like a broken record. You're unreal.
Customer:	I know I sound that way, but I want to return this blouse and get my money back now.
Salesperson:	Okay, okay, okay. Gimme the blouse.

A good rule of thumb is to try the broken record at least four times. You will feel awkward practicing this technique at first, especially if people respond by telling you that you sound like a broken record. But the results you get from this simple but powerful skill will convince you that it's worth the initial discomfort.

Content-to-Process Shift

When you think that the focus of a conversation is drifting away from the topic you want to talk about, use the content-to-process shift. You simply shift from the actual subject being discussed (the content) to what is going on between you and the other person (the process). For instance, you could say, "We've drifted away from what we agreed to discuss into talking about old history" or "I realize that I'm doing all the talking on this subject, and you're being very quiet."

A content-to-process shift often involves some self-disclosure about how you are feeling or thinking in the interaction at that very moment. You may try to quash an interaction: "I'm afraid to go on talking about this. You're turning red and grinding your teeth." "I'm feeling uncomfortable discussing this issue in a public place, and I notice that we're both whispering." Alternatively, you can use a content-to-process shift to provide positive feedback: "I feel great about getting this problem resolved. We're really communicating! I feel very positive about you right now."

Content-to-process shifts are especially helpful when voices are being raised and both people are angry: "I see we're both getting upset. It's a touchy issue." "We're talking a lot louder and seem squared off for combat." The trick is to comment on what's going on between you in a neutral, dispassionate way so that your statement won't be experienced as an attack.

Momentary Delay

You may feel compelled to respond immediately to any situation. If asked a question, you feel you have to answer right away. As a result, you may often end up doing or saying things you regret. If you don't take time to check in with your own feelings and needs, you may be letting others make your decisions for you.

Momentary delays let you do four things: make sure that you understand the other person; analyze what has been said; go inside and become aware of what you feel, think, and want in this situation; and consciously influence the situation so that you are more likely to get the outcome you want. Momentary delay is very helpful when you are just learning to use the other assertive techniques presented in this chapter. It gives you time to think and prepare.

Here are some examples:

"Slow down! This is too important to race through."

"That's interesting. Let me think about that for a moment."

"I don't quite understand that. Would you please say it in a different way?"

"This seems important. Would you repeat it?"

"Did I get what you were saying?" (You repeat what you think you heard while you take time to digest it and reflect.)

"I must be getting tired. Let's go over this again, only more slowly."

"Wait a minute. I want to give you my honest answer."

"There may be something to what you are saying ... Let me think about it for a little bit."

Time-Out

When you know that what you're discussing is important but the discussion is at an impasse, delay the conversation until another time. A time-out is valuable when the interaction is too passive or too aggressive. One of you may be silent, tearful, or frozen into agreeing with everything the other says. Or one of you may be acting hurtful, name-calling, and dragging up old complaints.

A time-out can also be used when you just want some room to think. For example, you're having difficulty deciding which car to buy and the car salesperson is pressuring you. Or your girlfriend has just told you that she loves you and wants to know how you feel about her. Or you've just been invited to spend the weekend at your in-laws' beach house.

These are typical examples of time-out situations:

In response to an inflexible, blaming coworker, you say, "I think what we're talking about is important, and I'd like to discuss it with you tomorrow."

You're about to dissolve into tears or rage, or you're feeling very anxious. Further discussion would be fruitless or just too painful. So you say, "Time-out. I'm upset right now. I know that I will be able to deal with this issue much more effectively tomorrow."

You are feeling pressured to do something that you're not sure you want to do. You say, "I want to sleep on it," "I'll get back to you next week," "I want to talk to my spouse [attorney, accountant, friend] about this before I make a decision," or "This is important; when's a good time next week for you to discuss it?"

Don't abuse time-out by using it repeatedly to avoid a difficult problem. Set up a specific time in the near future to continue your discussion.

Assertiveness Skills Practice

Using the skills in this chapter will feel awkward at first. Ideally, you will practice them with a sympathetic friend before you apply them in your daily life. If you are learning these skills on your own, you will find the following empty chair technique helpful in rehearsing them:

1. Imagine that the person with whom you want to be assertive is sitting in a chair facing you. See the person's face in your mind's eye. How is he or she sitting and dressed? Try to see as clear a picture as you can.

2. Now make your assertive statement as though the person were really in the chair listening.

3. When you are finished, move to the empty chair. Pretend you are the other person and respond as you think that person would respond.

4. Return to your own chair and notice how you feel and what you think of the other person's response. Make an appropriate assertive statement.

5. Continue this process, moving back and forth between the two chairs until you have finished the interaction.

If you feel too self-conscious using this technique, try going through its steps in your imagination. Or write out a script with your statements and the responses of the other person. Many people find it helpful to rehearse their assertive lines in front of a mirror in order to make sure that their body language is consistent with what they're saying. Recording an imaginary conversation can also be useful. All of these techniques give you an opportunity to slowly integrate assertiveness skills into your everyday life.

10 Validation Strategies

Validation is a powerful tool that can be used in any situation where there is real or potential conflict. Most conflicts erupt because people feel attacked, misunderstood, or not acknowledged. In many cases, our first instinct during a conflict—and sometimes this is what ignites the fight in the first place—is to tell the other person how he or she *should* be acting, feeling, or thinking and to invalidate the other person's position so that we can feel in the right. Validation works by stopping this cycle of overwhelming emotions, defensiveness, attack, and counterattack before it even starts. When you validate another person, the situation is immediately defused, and the conversation can be about solutions rather than anger and defensiveness. The validation strategies in this chapter were developed by Marsha Linehan (1993).

What Is Validation?

Validation is communicating to the person with whom you're in conflict that you understand his or her experience in that moment. It doesn't mean you have to agree with the person, but it means that you recognize how that person sees things and why he or she feels this way.

Validation can be as simple as looking someone in the eye as he or she talks, nodding, and saying "uh-huh" or "okay" to show that you're listening and that you understand. Or it can be a more complex exploration of that person's issues through questions, clarifications, and statements that encourage dialogue rather than defensiveness.

Even if you don't immediately understand someone else's experience, it is possible to act in a validating way by gently asking clarifying questions and checking out your assumptions. Question such as "How did you feel after that happened?" or "What is it about what I just said that bothered you?" can help the other person open up and share his or her feelings and experiences.

How Does Validation Work?

When people are in conflict, all of the conflicting parties are on the defensive. They feel under attack and are busy putting up walls and readying verbal weaponry to throw back at their opponent. Validation works by stopping the fight before it begins. When someone feels heard and understood, there's no need for a battle. By taking defensiveness out of the equation, validation disarms the other person. It opens a door to understanding that is all too often held shut by arguing, convincing, advising, or problem solving.

For example, John wanted a raise at work and prepared himself for a fight with his boss. He researched salaries in competing companies and made a comprehensive list of the successful projects he'd completed for his company. He even asked his wife to listen to a speech where he threatened to quit if he didn't get the raise. The morning of the confrontation, John felt anxious as he drove to work, and by the time he got into the office, he was a wreck. His boss saw him coming and noticed how tense he looked. When John sat down across from her, she said in a caring voice, "You look stressed-out, John. Is anything the matter?" John could tell from her voice, body language, and eye contact that she genuinely wanted to know. Instead of delivering his speech, he was honest with her about his need for more money and his belief that he'd earned a raise. Together, he and his boss worked out a plan that would give him a small raise but, more importantly, put him on a track to get more frequent promotions. John's boss used validation to open up a dialogue and to defuse a potentially tense situation.

Validation Opens the Way for Communication

Validation lets the parties in conflict truly communicate about the root of the problem rather than resort to attacks or defensiveness.

Helen and Dan always fought around the holidays about a present for Dan's mother. He would buy his mom a book or a gift certificate, which Helen considered too cheap and impersonal. She would take it upon herself to buy his mother a nice, expensive, and tasteful gift, and every year she felt resentful about Dan's nonparticipation. One Christmas, after taking a work seminar on communication skills, Dan decided to use validation when Helen started in about his mother's gift. Instead of acting with defensiveness, Dan said, "Helen, I can see that buying a present for my mother is really important to you. You seem to feel very close to her, and I can see that it upsets you when I don't participate as much as you'd like. I'm curious: What exactly bothers you?" Rather than telling her she was wrong to have her feelings, Helen felt like Dan was open to understanding her experience. Eventually, as they talked, it came out that Helen felt she hadn't given her own mother enough attention before she died, which is why it seemed so important for Dan to acknowledge his mother with a special gift. Dan, on the other hand, could finally communicate how he felt belittled and childlike when Helen got after him to do what was important to her but not necessarily to him. He explained that he and his mother saw each other often during the rest of the year and that his mother had let him know that she was more interested in his company than in receiving more gifts to cram into her small apartment. After this conversation, Helen and Dan felt closer than they had in years.

Validation Soothes Arousal and Builds Trust

Often when people are on the defensive, they are in a *negative arousal state*. In this state you feel flushed and anxious, your heart beats fast, and your breathing is rapid. You are physically preparing to either fight or flee, the fight-or-flight response that evolved to help us escape danger. When two people are in this state, it's more difficult for them to concentrate on what is being said, and they may say things or do things they regret afterward. Validation strategies can soothe negative arousal, calming you so you can fully participate in the conversation. This dynamic can be seen in the previous example of John, who wanted to ask for a raise. By the time he got into the office, he was in a full fight-or-flight state. He expected the conversation with his boss to go badly, and he was preparing for a conflict.

When his boss validated him, his arousal diminished and he was able to think straight and fully engage in the conversation.

Validation also builds trust. When you validate others, you are letting them know that you really see and understand them. You are letting go of your own agenda for the moment and being attentive to your conversation partner's experience and needs. You help the other person feel that his or her experience is understandable, not bad, wrong, or crazy. When you make validation strategies a part of your daily communication repertoire, the people around you start to trust that you want to make things work for all involved. When conflicts or tensions arise, this trust allows others to come to you with problems or issues that may be getting in the way of your relationship.

Validation Builds Self-Esteem

Validation is good for the validator as well as the person being validated. In any conflict situation, negative emotional arousal goes up for both parties. Both people may say or do things they regret, and things said in anger can often do incredible and permanent damage to relationships. When you become practiced at the validation strategies outlined later in this chapter, you'll be less likely to say or do things that cause damage to your relationships. This can ultimately enhance all the relationships in your life, as well as increase your own self-esteem and sense of being in control of your reactions and emotions.

Validation does not mean agreeing with someone just to keep the peace, and it's not the same thing as throwing your own beliefs or opinions out the window. Validation also does not mean repeating mindless phrases back at the other person, trying to convince the person that you understand. Nodding and saying "Oh, I see," when you actually don't see, serves neither of you. The problematic misunderstanding will continue, leading to more conflict down the road.

Components of Validation

The key components of validation are listening, acknowledgment, acceptance of what is, and validating the legitimacy of another's experience.

Listening

The first rule of validation is to show the other person that you are listening. Stop anything else you may be doing and turn toward the other person. Lean slightly toward him or her and make good eye contact. If you're talking on the phone, turn off the television or music and step away from the computer or any other task that may distract you. Even if the person you're talking to can't see you, he or she will know if you're distracted. Chapter 1 discussed listening skills. To refresh your memory, good listening skills include the following.

Active listening. By paraphrasing what the other person has just said, you can clarify your understanding of his or her experience and can get feedback to make sure you understand the message the other person is trying to get across.

Empathy. Understanding that those you are talking to are trying their best and are simply trying to get their needs met, even if their methods aren't ones you feel are effective, can move you a long way toward feeling empathy for them.

Openness. We all judge other people, but as you are listening, notice your judgments and let them drop away. If you need to, take deep, even breaths as you listen, especially if you feel your emotions are getting aroused. Remember that your conversation partner is trying to be understood.

Awareness. People communicate with more than just words, and one part of listening is being aware of the nonverbal messages you are getting in addition to the verbal ones. Paying attention to your conversation partner's body language, facial expression, and tone of voice will help you understand his or her message.

Acknowledgment

Validation is all about expressing your understanding and acceptance of another person's experience. Acknowledgment can go far in showing others that you are listening and engaged, and are not about to attack them or tell them they are wrong for feeling the way they do about a given situation.

When Terri heard that her boyfriend, Darrin, had accepted an invitation for lunch with Jenny, an ex-coworker with whom he'd once had a sexual fling, she felt terribly jealous. In the back of her mind, Terri wondered if something was still going on between them. At first, she pretended that Darrin's lunch plans didn't bother her, but Darrin could tell something was wrong. She wouldn't look him in the eyes when they talked, and she seemed distant and distracted. Finally, Darrin asked her outright what was wrong. Terri broke down and tearfully admitted that she was jealous and afraid that he and Jenny would rekindle their old relationship. As he listened, Darrin's first reaction was to be hurt and angry. He noticed these angry feelings and that he had an impulse to interrupt her to defend his innocence and to bring up her history of jealousy. But instead of going into a defensive mode, he noticed how afraid she seemed, with her tear-stained face, her arms crossed in front of her, head down, and body slightly slumped as she leaned against the kitchen counter. He looked Terri in the eyes and gently said, "I can see this is really hurting you. I understand how you might be jealous and scared considering what happened between Jenny and me before. And I understand how my not inviting you might make you feel even more afraid that I want to start up something with her again." This simple acknowledgment of her experience allowed both of them to calm down and discuss the situation in a thoughtful, constructive, and compassionate way.

Acceptance of What Is

We generally expect that other people experience things the same way that we do (Ross, Greene, and House 1977). It's very difficult for most of us to truly accept that our experience isn't universal. But the truth is that other people have different reactions, experiences, and feelings from ours. Genetics, brain chemistry, history, personality, and culture all affect how differently people experience the world.

Accepting another person's experience is the cornerstone of validation. If your coworker lets you know that a joke you made at a staff meeting upset her, you would not be accepting her experience by saying, "Well, I didn't mean it that way, so I don't see why you'd be hurt." A more validating response would be to say, "I'm sorry you were hurt by what I said. I certainly didn't mean to be offensive, but I can see that you were upset by my comment." In this way, you're acknowledging her experience and accepting that she was offended, while also owning your own experience, which is that you did not mean to be hurtful.

Validating the Legitimacy of Experience

Most of us are influenced by past experience when reacting to current situations, whether we realize it or not. One important aspect of validation is realizing that even if someone else is reacting in a way that may seem out of proportion, unhealthy, inappropriate, or harmful, chances are that the reaction is based on a past experience. You can validate this without actually supporting the other person's behavior. Dan found this out when he opened a discussion with Helen about buying gifts for his mother. Her past experience with her own mother was at the root of her anxiety about making Dan's mother feel valued. With this piece of information, Dan felt his resentment fade. He was then able to let Helen know that her behavior had been troubling him and how he experienced her actions.

As you can see, validation strategies can be powerful tools for defusing potential conflicts, by letting others know that you're open to hearing their experience and working out the problem, and giving yourself a chance to state your own experience without invalidating anyone else's. Using these strategies will serve to deepen your relationships with the people close to you, enabling you to enjoy more satisfying, fruitful inter-actions with family members, friends, business partners, coworkers, and romantic partners.

11 Negotiation

Everybody negotiates—not just union officials, diplomats, and contractors. You negotiate when you ask for a raise, apply for a job, dispute a grade with a teacher, buy a car or a house, sue somebody, or ask your landlord to paint your apartment. Any time you want something from someone who may have conflicting interests, you are potentially in a negotiating situation.

Negotiation is a skill that helps you get what you want from others without alienating them. It's for people with whom you are not intimate, with whom you cannot count on a give-and-take of clear self-expression and respectful listening. Negotiation is a process whereby people with different or even opposing needs can arrive at a fair agreement. Though both sides want to win, their best interests are served by generating a mutually acceptable option.

Four Stages of Negotiation

Even the most complicated negotiations can be broken down into four stages: preparation, discussion, proposal-counterproposal, and agreement/disagreement.

1. *Preparation.* Before you actually meet the opposing side, you need to figure out what outcome you want most, what would be less satisfactory but still acceptable, and what constitutes the worst deal you'd accept. During time-outs from negotiation, you'll do more preparation by looking up information, planning your strategy, and brainstorming to create optional proposals.

2. *Discussion.* You and your opponent describe the facts of the situation, how you feel about it, and what you think about it. You

explain to your opponent how the situation looks to you in terms of both of your interests and needs. Discussion is the major means of resolving deadlocks: you ask for more information about the other side's interests, and you elaborate your own point of view.

3. *Proposal-counterproposal.* You make an offer or a request. Your opponent makes a counteroffer. This cycle is repeated several times, perhaps interspersed with more discussion or with time-outs to think things over. As new proposals and counterproposals evolve, their terms move ever closer together in the classic ballet of compromise.

4. *Agreement/disagreement.* Disagreement returns the negotiation to the discussion stage, or if a time-out has been called, to the preparation stage. Disagreement is a natural step in negotiation. It's a signal to try again, not a brick wall. Eventually you'll come to agree on a mutually acceptable option.

Here's how the four stages of negotiation work when Terry approaches Alfred about buying Alfred's car:

1. *Preparation.* Terry wants to buy a dependable car that's comfortable, gets reasonably good gas mileage, and won't cost him more than $7,000. He researches the want ads, talks to a mechanic, and consults a knowledgeable friend. He decides to look for a five- to ten-year-old midsize sedan that has had good care. He'll accept an older car if it's in exceptional shape and has low mileage. He wants a radio, but isn't interested in paying extra for a fancy stereo or other exotic accessories.

2. *Discussion.* Terry calls up Alfred, who has advertised an eight-year-old Ford for $7,500. Terry tells him that he is looking for a dependable car in good shape. He gathers information: Mileage? 79,000 miles. Engine? Recent valve job. Tires? Fair. Body? One small dent in right fender. Paint? Faded. Based on this discussion, Terry sets up an appointment to test-drive the car. He does not mention money at this stage, since he doesn't really have enough information to make a definite offer. Although the car is priced over his limit, he suspects that Alfred will probably come down.

3. *Proposal-counterproposal.* Terry drives the car and finds it satisfactory. At the end of the test-drive, he says to Alfred, "Well, you're right, it's a nice car. I like everything about it, but the price is just a little more than I want to pay. How about $6,500?" Terry arrived at this amount by figuring that if the car was priced at $500 more than he wanted to pay, he'd better offer about $500 less than he wanted to pay, so he'd have some room to negotiate.

4. *Disagreement.* Alfred isn't pleased with the offer and declines. He says that he has to get at least $7,200 for the car. Terry knows that Alfred's disagreement is actually an invitation to return to discussion.

5. *Discussion.* Terry asks for more information: $7,200 seems like quite a bit for an eight-year-old car. "Is there something special that sets it apart?" he asks. Alfred points out the car's new stereo and mag wheels. He shows the receipt for a rebuilt transmission. He says that the car has always had regular maintenance and has had only two owners.

6. *Proposal-counterproposal.* Terry agrees that these considerations are important, although he isn't interested in extras like a fancy stereo and mag wheels. He offers $6,900. Alfred comes down to $7,100 and says it's as low as he can go. Terry says, "Look, it seems like we're stuck because you want an extra $200 for a stereo system that I don't even care about. How about taking the stereo out? You can keep it."

7. *Agreement.* Alfred laughs. "Forget it," he says, "it's too much trouble. Let's split the difference. You can have it for $7,000." Terry drives home in his new car, stereo blasting.

Dealing with Conflict

Your attitude toward conflict will determine your success at negotiation. Conflict is inevitable, no matter how you try to avoid it. The smart way to think about conflict is to see it as a positive opportunity for change. With skillful negotiating, you can make the change a favorable one for you.

Dealing with conflict often seems to boil down to a no-win decision: should you be softhearted and make friends, or should you be hardheaded and make enemies? In the softhearted approach, the goal is agreement at all costs. You make concessions, you trust everybody, you yield to pressure, you disclose your bottom line early in the game, and you end up paying too much for a car you don't really like.

In the hardheaded approach, the goal is winning at all costs. You demand concessions, you distrust everybody, you apply pressure, and you lie about your bottom line. You end up with either a cheap car and an enemy for life or no car and an enemy for life.

You can steer between these two extremes by taking the principled approach. In the principled approach, the goal is a fair, mutually agreeable outcome. Personalities and trust don't enter into it, so you can stay friends or stay strangers and still benefit from the outcome. You avoid talking in terms of a firm bottom line or digging into a position. You reason with your opponents and are open to reason. You yield to principle but never to pressure. Proposals and counterproposals are judged according to objective criteria rather than seen as contests of will. You end up paying a fair price for the car you want.

Rules of Principled Negotiation

Once you have begun negotiations, there are four important principles to remember: separate the people from the problem, understand your opponent's needs, state the problem in terms of interests, and list the options.

Separate the People from the Problem

Conflict doesn't have to mean hostility. Conflict becomes hostile when both sides choose positions. You settle on your position in the matter and dig into it. You identify with that position so strongly that an attack on your position becomes an attack on your self-worth.

The way out of this trap is to keep the people separate from the problem at hand. Don't enter negotiations with a single rock-solid position. Instead, enter with the attitude that many options are open to you. You and your opponent are decent, reasonable people who want to reach a fair solution to a problem in which you both have some legitimate interests.

For example, suppose you and three other tenants are meeting with the owner of your apartment building to discuss maintenance of common areas. You want the halls cleaned more often, you want burnt-out bulbs on landings replaced promptly, and you want the back fence repaired. The wrong way to approach this meeting is to show up with a typed list of non-negotiable demands, throw it in your landlord's face, and say, "You've got one week to shape up, slumlord, or it's rent strike time."

This approach will get you nothing but a crash course in local eviction law. The right approach is to quietly say, "We've come to discuss how we might improve the common areas of the building. When you hear our requests, we think you'll agree that they're reasonable, and probably you'll want to make some suggestions of your own."

Understand the People

Empathy, active listening, and honest self-expression are as important in negotiation as in everyday communication with intimates. Put yourself in your opponent's shoes. Imagine what he or she feels and thinks about the situation and needs to get out of it. But don't project your own fears on to his or her intentions. Just because you're afraid the boss has picked someone else for a promotion, don't automatically assume that your boss has.

Use your active listening skills to elicit your opponent's feelings, thoughts, and needs: "The way I understand it, you're afraid a younger person in that job might not be effective. You think experience is important in the department. You need a capable, hardworking employee who can start making changes right away." Feeding back information makes an opponent feel that he or she has been heard and shows that you take the opposing side seriously. You sound intelligent, considerate, and fair.

Honestly share your own feelings, thoughts, and needs. Let your opponent understand you, just as you are trying to understand your opponent: "I feel frustrated by the old paradox: you need experience to get good jobs, but only good jobs give the right kind of experience. I think I have what it takes in terms of judgment, energy, and dedication. All I need is a chance to show what I can do. How about a three-month trial assignment?"

State the Problem in Terms of Interests

Behind conflicting positions lie shared and compatible interests as well as opposing ones. The shared interests are the reasons people keep negotiating. You'll never hear a TV news announcer say, "Talks between the hospital and the nurses broke off forever today. The hospital board of directors quit and decided to go into the franchise food business, and the nurses quit and took up gardening." You'll never hear it, because shared interests will drive both sides back to the bargaining table again and again until a new agreement is forged.

When an opponent states a position or demand, uncover the interest behind it by asking: "Exactly why do you want [state what the opponent is demanding]? Why don't you want [state an option]?"

For example, ask the owner of the house you want to rent, "Exactly why do you want a $1,000 cleaning deposit?" You may find out that the last tenant stabled a horse in the back bedroom, or that $1,000 is exactly what it cost to clean the house the last time it was vacant, or that the landlord is $1,000 short of money she needs to buy a car. By uncovering the landlord's interests in the matter, you may uncover a way to compromise: a written no-pets clause in the lease, three months in which to pay the deposit, or a deposit that's partially refundable in six months upon inspection of the premises.

In looking for the interests behind positions, be sensitive to basic human needs for security, trust, intimacy, and self-esteem. They can be more important to you and your opponent than dollars and cents. For example, more and more American companies are being reorganized to show a consistent concern for their employees' emotional needs. These companies often enjoy high productivity and profits, low staff turnover, and excellent worker morale because employees feel that they are valued for more than their contribution to the bottom line.

Often your opponent will stick to a position not because he or she needs the additional $300 but because giving in on the $300 means losing self-esteem. You can help your opponent save face by reframing the compromise as generosity rather than giving in. Labeling the act of compromise as a positive virtue is often very helpful.

It takes time to explore interests. You should avoid blurting out your preconceived solution until you and your opponent have each had a chance to air your concerns. You may discover some flaws in your own solution or find ways to improve it as the discussion continues.

Stating problems in terms of interests makes you focus on the future, since that's almost always where your interests lie. Focusing on future desires is helpful because it discourages old, familiar foes from raking up past complaints. For example, suppose you want to have a room added on to your house. You have $25,000 to do the job, but the lowest bid you've received is for $27,500. You state your interests to the low-bidding contractor like this: "We want another bedroom because my sister is coming to live with us next January. We have exactly $25,000 saved up to do the work. I think the specifications I gave you are as simple and economical as possible. I don't want to settle for a smaller room or cheaper materials that won't match the rest of the house. Is there any way you can see to get this job done for $25,000?"

The contractor reveals his interests in this manner: "I've done a careful estimate on materials and labor, and there's just not that much slack. At $25,000, I'd be losing money. This is my busy season and there's plenty of work around at top rates, so it doesn't make sense for me to squeeze in a job like this now at less than a full profit."

You're quick to sense where his interests lie, so you ask, "What about your slow season? You could do the foundation, framing, exterior walls, and roof now, at full rate. Then, this fall, when you have more time and need the work, you could come back and finish up the interior at a reduced rate."

By exploring your mutual interests, you have uncovered one of the classic tradeoffs: time for money. You're on your way to getting what you want at a fair price without alienating the contractor.

List Options

Adopt the attitude that there are probably several possible solutions that will be acceptable to both sides. Get rid of the notions that there is only one best way to divide up the pie, that the pie is only so big, and that you absolutely must get the biggest piece. These are all self-defeating ideas. There are actually several good ways to cut up a pie. You may even find a way to make the pie bigger. And ending up with the biggest piece isn't always ideal, especially if you antagonize people and end up getting pie in the face.

Do your homework so that you really know what's fair. Find out what's common practice, how much others are earning, what similar items are selling for, the rent on comparable houses in town, the medical benefits supplied by other companies, other respected teachers' grading practices, other departments' sales figures or absentee rates, and so on. Precedents and benchmarks help you generate reasonable proposals.

Brainstorming

To generate different opinions, you can brainstorm with the other interested parties. Gather together five to eight people in a place somewhere other than your usual surroundings. Pick one person to keep the meeting on track, enforce the ground rules, and encourage participation. Seat the people side-by-side or in a circle; the feeling of formality that comes from being squared off across a table may inhibit creativity. Have the leader explain these ground rules: criticism is absolutely forbidden, the session is off the record, and ideas won't be attributed to the individuals who suggest them.

Come up with a long list of ideas, the more and the wilder the better. Approach the problem from all angles. Record all the ideas on a blackboard or large sheet of paper so that everyone can see them. When no new ideas are forthcoming, declare the freewheeling part of the session over.

Now you can be critical. Underline the most promising ideas. Try to combine and alter the best ones to make them better. You should end up with a list of good ideas, any of which could become an acceptable proposal in the next negotiation session.

If you're on your own and don't have any brainstorming partners handy, try looking at the problem through the eyes of many imaginary experts. How would the problem be solved by a judge, a cop, your mother, your father, an engineer, a lawyer, a psychologist, a priest or minister or rabbi, a salesperson, a politician, or any other kind of expert? Looking at the problem this way can momentarily free you from your personal set of blinders.

To increase your options, consider some of the time-tested methods of compromise. Even very young children understand the obvious fairness of

"I'll cut the pie, and you'll choose your piece first." A classic way of fairly dividing disputed property or goods is splitting it down the middle. The buying-and-selling equivalent is splitting the difference.

If you think the options you've come up with are too hardheaded for your opponent to accept, consider the many ways in which the options can be softened. Fundamental changes in policy can be made into merely procedural changes. Permanent alterations can become only temporary. Comprehensive plans can be applied partially. Final agreements can be changed to agreements in principle. Unconditional demands can be made contingent. Binding decisions can be made nonbinding.

An example of generating options is the case of Thelma's raise. Thelma worked for an advertising firm that had come on hard times. She was up for her annual salary review, and she wanted a 20 percent raise. However, her coworkers had been getting annual raises of 5 percent, so her chances didn't look good. She decided that despite the unpromising precedents, she would adopt the attitude that there were probably several ways for her to get the raise she wanted from the company.

Thelma brainstormed her options with her family, friends, and a colleague from another department. Putting several people's imaginations to work gave her many different ways to look at her problem. Some of the suggestions had to be tossed out. Threatening to quit was impractical, and embezzlement and blackmail were illegal. However, one suggestion made Thelma realize that more fringe benefits might be just as good as a raise in pay. She could ask for a company car to drive, a nicer office, better equipment, secretarial help, time off, or a flexible schedule. The company might be willing to give her some of those goodies in addition to the 5 percent raise that everybody else got.

Thelma also realized that she had been thinking in terms of getting paid more for the job she was doing. Brainstorming made it clear that a promotion or transfer could mean more money automatically, without the company having to leap the psychological hurdle of a larger-than-average raise.

Thelma then tried looking at the situation through the eyes of raise experts—her boss and the head of the personnel department. This simple exercise made it clear that the only compelling reasons for giving raises were increased cost of living, increased productivity, increased profit, or increased responsibility. Her personal financial needs would carry little weight with management.

Thelma faced the fact that she might have to compromise or soften her requests. She decided that she would be willing to split the difference between the 20 percent she wanted and the 5 percent she was likely to be offered, especially if the pot was sweetened in some other way. She was also prepared to spread her raise over time or to make it contingent on increased productivity.

She found that her original option—demanding a big raise because she needed it—had now expanded to a long list of strategies and options. She decided to do the following:

> Point out increased cost of living and increased productivity in her present position.

> Show that her productivity could be increased by secretarial help and the use of a company car.

> Ask for more responsibility, such as taking over the quality control reports when Rachel retires.

> Volunteer to head up the market research project that everybody says should be done. Offer to work some free overtime to get it started.

> Ask for 20 percent, secretarial help, company car, and flexible hours.

> Compromise on 15 percent now and the remaining 5 percent in six months if productivity increases as predicted.

Thelma was now ready to go into her boss's office and negotiate effectively.

Turning Options into Proposals

You've established a good working relationship with your opponents. You've stated and discussed the problem in terms of your mutual and conflicting interests. You've privately prepared your list of acceptable options, and now you're ready to make a proposal.

Approach the proposal slowly. Describe the option you like best in detail. Then move on to the next best one. Ask your opponents which option they prefer. By offering choice and inviting discussion, you avoid confronting them with an ultimatum that will lock them into a defensive position. Sometimes the opposition will even start brainstorming with you in a genuine attempt at joint problem solving.

If at any point in describing your options you find your opponents in an agreeable frame of mind, hit them with an approvable proposal. An *approvable proposal* is one of your acceptable options stated as a direct question to which yes is an easy answer. For example, if you want a 20 percent raise, you should ask, "If I can straighten out the production bottleneck and increase productivity, would you be willing to give me a 20 percent raise?" This proposal is much better than "I really need a 20 percent raise. Why can't I have it?" The first proposal is conditional on something the boss wants and can't be denied without implying that increased productivity is undesirable or that excellence shouldn't be rewarded. The second proposal is poor because it's based only on your needs and invites the boss to make a list of reasons why not. The following is a list of deniable proposals restated as approvable proposals:

Deniable	Approvable
"I want this apartment painted, and I want it painted by the time I get back from vacation."	"Would you rather paint our apartment right now or next month when we'll be out of town?"
"Give me the preliminary report on the fifteenth and the final figures no later than the thirtieth."	"If I give you until the end of the month to get the final figures, can you provide a preliminary report by the fifteenth?"
"No matter what you say, I'm not paying more than $250,000 for this house. How about it?"	"Assuming we can agree on all the other terms and contingencies, I'm prepared to offer up to $250,000 for this house. Does that seem like a reasonable offer?"

Note: If you are having trouble getting a yes from an otherwise agreeable opponent, make sure that the person you're dealing with is actually empowered to make the decision. If not, you'll need to approach the person who does have the power to say yes.

When the Going Gets Tough

Sometimes negotiations can get difficult. Perhaps you're dealing with an opponent who has all or most of the power, your opponent won't cooperate, or your opponent plays dirty tricks to try to get you off track.

When Your Opponent Has All the Power

When you are faced with an opponent who has all the power, you have to be realistic. The odds are that you'll lose. Before going into the negotiation, you should figure out your best alternative to a negotiated decision. What are you going to do if you get turned down flat? Knowing this before you go in gives you some certainty.

If your best alternative is a strong one, you can let your opponent know about it in the form of a threat: "If you don't give me this promotion, I plan to quit and go into the dry cleaning business with my brother-in-law." Be sure that your threat is believable and that you're really prepared to go through with it. When your best alternative to a negotiated agreement is a weak one, you should conceal it. For example, you should keep quiet if you have no brother-in-law in the dry cleaning business to fall back on. If your alternative to getting the promotion is to continue meekly in the same dead-end job, you're in no position to make threats.

Whatever your alternative, make sure you've done your homework. Have all your facts and figures complete and accurate. Come down very hard on objective criteria. Appeal to your opponent's sense of fairness and hope for the best.

If many other people share your one-down position in relation to a powerful opponent, you can adopt the tactics of minority power politics. This means pulling power out of thin air. You go around drumming up support among like-minded people. You form a committee or a party. You hold meetings and rallies and press conferences. You become an expert on the problem. You focus the harsh light of publicity on your opponent's unfairness.

When Your Opponent Won't Cooperate

Sometimes an opponent will dig in to a position and refuse to budge. When this happens, resist the impulse to launch an all-out attack on the position. Instead, look behind the position for the underlying interests. If management absolutely refuses to even consider a dental plan, make a list of all the reasons they might have: funding a plan will be too expensive; new employees will run up huge bills for long-standing dental problems; people will get expensive cosmetic work done; it's too hard to administer; available plans conflict with the existing medical plan; and so on.

When you think you understand your opponent's interests, ask a question: "Why do you refuse to consider a dental plan?" Then sit back and wait for an answer. Let the silence drag on and on. If you get a nonanswer like "It's against company policy," counter with the question "Why is it against company policy?" Then try asking a more specific question like one of the following: "How expensive is it?" "What would it cost to administer?" "Are you afraid employees will take advantage of your generosity?" Don't forget the long silence after each polite question. Your goal is to get the hard-liner talking about the problem.

Other times an opponent talks too much, and the entire response is an attack on your position. When this happens, resist the impulse to dig in and defend your position. Rather, adopt the judo tactic of diverting your enemy's force. You divert attacks on your position by welcoming criticism: "That's very interesting. What other ideas do you have about my plan? How could we improve it?" You involve your opponent in helping you create additional options.

Sometimes a hard-liner will attack you personally. The way to divert personal attacks is to redefine them as attacks on the problem. For example, when the management spokesperson accuses you of "irresponsibly stirring people up with this ridiculous dental plan fantasy," you must stifle your impulse to call the spokesperson a hypocritical stooge of reactionary management. Instead, you should reframe the attack like this: "You're right, people are very stirred up about the dental plan, and

I appreciate the fact that you feel strongly about it too. It's a serious problem that deserves the attention of all the responsible leaders in the company." Reframing personal attacks is a highly subtle use of flattery and flimflam. It defuses hostility and gives hard-liners a graceful way to start cooperating.

Then there are the times when both sides of a dispute have so much at stake that neither is willing to relax from a hard-line position. In these situations, the best solution is to use the *one-text procedure*. That's how the Camp David agreement between Egypt and Israel was reached. The United States prepared the text of a possible agreement and presented it to both sides. Each turned it down, giving specific reasons. Then the United States came up with a second draft and submitted it. Thirteen days and twenty-one drafts later, the agreement was signed. The success of this method depends on each side simply saying yes or no to successive texts, without direct confrontation or argument.

When Your Opponent Plays Dirty

There are many kinds of dirty negotiating tactics: lies, deceptions, psychological warfare, bribery, blackmail, and so on. Some books are full of tips on what to do if your opponents seat you with the sun in your eyes or how to deal with a bribe. These books make entertaining reading, but actually you need only one tactic to handle dirty tricks: call process and negotiate for fair play.

Calling process means that you stop talking about the subject of the session and talk about the process that's going on: "Before we get into the discussion of rate hikes, I'd like to point out that this chair is too low and the sun is in my eyes. Surely we're not going to play one-upmanship games in a serious negotiation like this?"

Expose the dirty trick for what it is. Then negotiate for an agreement to proceed according to the rules of principled negotiation. Explain that you understand the temptation to take every possible advantage, and that you don't take it personally. But point out that everyone's interests will be better served if you approach the problem as honest people who are amenable to reason. Explain that you're here to find some options that will serve your shared interests and reconcile your opposed interests. Invite your opponents to help you look for options that will benefit everyone.

Suggest some objective criteria by which these options can be judged. Conclude with the following: "If we're agreed that we should proceed in a civilized manner, then let's find me another chair and get on with it." Most of the time, this approach will work. If it doesn't, it may be time to call in a neutral mediator.

You may encounter a conflict that can't be negotiated. This happens when your opponents want the conflict more than they want a resolution. For example, the union may want to keep tempers and uncertainty high until the contract deadline is closer. Management may want to prolong negotiations until the union's strike fund is exhausted. Student demonstrators may want publicity more than they want grading reform or job placement programs. Until you uncover and deal with such hidden agendas, negotiation is impossible.

PART IV

. . . .

Social Skills

12 | Forming Accurate First Impressions

When you meet someone new, you form a first impression by a process called *prejudgment*. You take in and interpret information about new people based on your past experience, your needs and wishes, and the context in which you meet. The prejudgment process happens almost automatically and unconsciously.

Prejudgment is an immensely useful skill for categorizing the many strangers you meet—when it is accurate. But sometimes you infer a great deal about a person from too little information, forming a hasty and distorted first impression that taints all further communication with that person.

For example, a young man at a party sees a tall, slender woman standing awkwardly by herself and frowning. He infers that she is a boring wallflower and heads in the other direction. Later he almost spills his drink when the boring wallflower introduces herself. Somehow she has learned his profession and asks about his job. The young man feels trapped and avoids eye contact. He answers her "boring" questions with curt replies. Eventually he mumbles an excuse and retires to the bar. There he sees his best friend, who tells him that the very woman he is trying to avoid is a beautiful, fascinating creature. The first young man thinks his friend has taken leave of his senses and says, "She's a total dud. She reminds me of my old Aunt Sally."

Inaccurate first impressions often go uncorrected. Research indicates that your first impression of another person will remain unchanged, even after weeks of regular interaction (Sunnafrank and Ramirez 2004). You are likely to freeze your first impression of a person with only minor modifications. The young man in the example above ends up working in the same department with the woman he labeled a dud. He concedes to his friend months later that she is indeed very attractive, but he cannot fathom how she can be so popular with the other people in the office. He continues to find her as boring as Aunt Sally.

Prejudgment Traps

Since first impressions are so important, it's equally important to become aware of some of the most typical traps of prejudgment.

The Limits of Perception

You never get complete information from a first impression because the perception process itself simplifies and eliminates some of the data. Your eyes, ears, and skin are constantly bombarded with stimuli that are not intense enough to excite the nervous system receptors. Once messages enter the nervous system, the process of inhibition further simplifies them by eliminating messages inconsistent with the dominant messages received. For example, if your friend nods his head, smiles, and says "yes," you are unlikely to notice that the knuckles on his fingers are white from clutching his arms. The latter nonverbal cue is inconsistent with the dominant message and is therefore inhibited.

Generalization of Expectations

In a new or unfamiliar situation, your brain jumps to conclusions to fill in any missing pieces, basing its conclusions largely on past experience. You tend to perceive what you are in the habit of perceiving.

Exercise 12.1

Connect the nine dots with only four straight lines without lifting your pencil from the paper or retracing a line. Spend at least ten minutes on this puzzle. A solution appears at the end of the chapter.

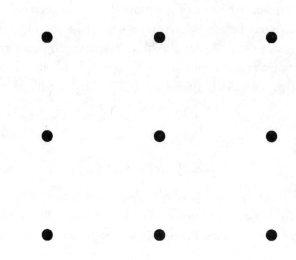

If you solved the problem within ten minutes on your own, you are indeed the rare person. Most people add an extra assumption that isn't part of this puzzle. They assume that they can't draw the four straight lines beyond the square formed by the eight outside dots. This assumption makes the problem unsolvable. If you made this erroneous assumption, try to solve the puzzle again, allowing the lines to extend beyond the square.

This exercise points out the importance of checking out the assumptions underlying your perceptions. When you make unverified assumptions about new people and new situations, you run the risk of communication breakdown. For example, you assume that a party means inviting everyone you know, and your new live-in boyfriend assumes that a party means inviting close friends only. If you don't check out each other's assumptions, you are likely to be in for a bitter awakening at the first party in your new home.

Perceptual Accentuation

When you need something, even a poor version of it will do. If you are lonely, even a boring date is better than no date at all. Suddenly your job seems more valuable when six of your coworkers have been laid off due to an economic slump. Perceptual accentuation causes you to see what you expect and want to see. You are also likely to assess people whom you like as more attractive and more intelligent than people whom you don't like.

Visit http://www.newharbinger.com/41719 to download the next exercise.

Exercise 12.2

Ask yourself which of the following activities you would most like to do right now. Which would you like to do the least? Rate the activities on a scale of 1 to 8, with 8 being the activity you most want to do. Repeat this exercise at a later date at a different time of day. Compare your ratings.

_____   Smell a freshly cooked steak

_____   Smell a rose

_____   Smell peppermint

_____   Smell the air after a rain

_____   Smell a fire in a fireplace

_____   Smell freshly baked bread

_____   Smell your favorite perfume or aftershave lotion

_____   Smell a pie baking

Depending on your current needs, different items will seem more attractive to you at different times.

Stereotypes

Without much difficulty, you are able to generalize from almost no information to form expectations about people based simply on their membership group. Stereotyping is a shortcut to forming impressions of others.

Exercise 12.3

Read the following sentences and fill in the blanks as fast as you can. Do not ponder your responses.

Italian men make excellent _____.

Politicians are often _____.

Most basketball players are _____.

Women with big _____ are very _____.

Fat people are _____.

Hardworking, energetic people usually _____.

Sunday school teachers are usually _____.

People born to wealth are _____.

Based on as little as one trait or behavior, you may classify an individual as belonging to a group of people to whom you attribute common qualities. For example, if you classify a person as being attractive, you may think that he or she is friendlier, has a better character, is more exciting on a date, has a higher occupational status, and would be a better marital partner than a person you classify as unattractive.

On the positive side, stereotyping helps you avoid cognitive overload by allowing you to package stimuli into manageable numbers of categories. Although many stereotypes are inaccurate, many others have at least some truth to them. For instance, women are disproportionately represented in clerical positions, blacks in athletics, and Jews in academia.

Stereotyping becomes dangerous when negative or inferior traits are ascribed to a group on a biological or ethnocentric basis. Racism, sexism, and ageism are all negative products of stereotyping. Stereotyping is most dangerous when there is no accommodation for new information. The person doing the stereotyping dogmatically holds on to an opinion, no matter how much contradictory data are presented otherwise.

Another danger of stereotyping is the self-fulfilling prophecy. The best-known example of the self-fulfilling prophecy is the *Pygmalion effect*. As part of a study, teachers were told that certain students would be expected to do exceptionally well because they were "late bloomers." The names of these students were selected at random by the researchers. The results were spectacular: the students whose names were given to the teachers actually did perform at a higher level than the other students. The selected students even made greater improvements on IQ tests than the others did (Rosenthal and Jacobson 1992).

Self-fulfilling prophecies are an important part of first impressions and ongoing relationships. If you expect others to act in a certain way, you are likely to communicate your expectations to them with subtle cues, increasing the likelihood that they will act as you anticipate. If you expect people to reject you, you are likely to avoid eye contact, frown, speak in curt sentences, and have a rigid, closed body posture. Seeing your behavior, others in turn fulfill your expectations, which makes you more confident of the accuracy of your predictions. In the future, your expectations are apt to be still more definite and rigid when you encounter a similar situation.

Self-fulfilling prophecies can be used in positive ways. For example, you may expect that your mate is going to be very loving and generous with you. If you behave in a manner that conveys your expectation, your mate is likely to act accordingly. For example, by what he says and does, a successful salesman conveys to his customers his confidence that he is going to make the sale. A positive self-fulfilling prophecy can be created in just a few words. For example, a speaker introduced to her audience as an expert in her field will be perceived as much more persuasive than a person who is given no introduction.

Exercise 12.4

In a social setting where at least several strangers are present, comment to yourself about each of the people. Say to yourself, "I notice ..." Add something you perceive about the person. Then add, "I imagine ..." Add something you infer about the person but cannot perceive with your five senses.

Here are some examples: "I notice that man is very fat. I imagine that he does not exercise, has no willpower, and is lazy." "I notice that woman is very neatly dressed. I imagine that she is very organized, perfectionistic, and demanding." "I notice that black man is very tall. I imagine that he is a basketball player."

As this exercise illustrates, many of your impressions about people are based on inferences drawn from minimal perceptual cues. It is from such minimal cues that you stereotype others.

Approval and Disapproval in Prejudgment

On first meeting people, you tend to make judgments about them in such terms as "intelligent" or "stupid," "strong" or "weak," "warm" or "cold," and "active" or "passive." These critical pairs of opposite traits form a core from which you infer many other traits. They help you arrive at an overall evaluation of the "goodness" or "badness" of people you meet. The next exercise explores this idea. Visit http://www.newharbinger.com/41719 to download this exercise.

Exercise 12.5

Rate a person you like and a person you don't like in terms of the following pairs of opposite traits. Put a checkmark on one of the blanks between each pair indicating your evaluation of the person. The blanks at either end represent extreme evaluations. The middle blank indicates no feelings or opinion at all, and the blanks in between represent moderate evaluations.

hardworking	____ ____ ____ ____ ____	lazy
warm	____ ____ ____ ____ ____	cold
active	____ ____ ____ ____ ____	passive
trustworthy	____ ____ ____ ____ ____	untrustworthy
knowledgeable	____ ____ ____ ____ ____	uninformed

strong   ____ ____ ____ ____ ____   weak

intelligent   ____ ____ ____ ____ ____   stupid

friendly   ____ ____ ____ ____ ____   aloof

attractive   ____ ____ ____ ____ ____   ugly

To make these scales complete, add any other trait pairs that you frequently use in making judgments. When you finish the scales for each person, make an overall evaluation of the person:

good   ____ ____ ____ ____ ____   bad

Repeat this scale for four additional pairs of people.

These scales reflect the kind of judgments you make daily. Although they are highly intuitive, such evaluations largely determine how you interpret the messages that come from others.

In the above exercise, did you find that certain traits went together? For instance, did you rate a person as good, warm, and friendly? Or bad, passive, and weak? In our culture, warmth and friendliness are traits that are perceived as being closely allied with goodness, as are physical vigor and strength. Do you think that your clustering of certain traits in the exercise is truly reflective of the people you evaluated? Or is this clustering more a function of your expectation that these traits occur together?

To further explore this question, make a new list of five people whom you like and five people whom you don't like. You can include public or fictional characters as well as acquaintances and family. For each individual, list his or her traits. Examine the traits of the five people you like. Do they have certain traits in common? Examine the traits of the five people you don't like. Do they have certain traits in common? Do you find yourself using the same scales of opposite-trait pairs for people you like and don't like? For example, do you often rate people on the warm versus cold or knowledgeable versus uninformed scales?

You may discover that you use certain trait scales repeatedly in evaluating people. If you were to compare your lists of traits with lists filled out by other people, you would likely find some evaluative traits that would not normally occur to you. Remember that how you evaluate others will be largely determined by the specific trait scales you habitually use.

The famous personality theorist Harry Stack Sullivan provided a possible explanation for why certain traits reoccur in your evaluation of others while other traits are never used. Sullivan (1968) suggested that from a very young age, we become attuned to those things we do that either result in approval and satisfaction or result in disapproval and dissatisfaction. The child focuses only on those behaviors that are cause for approval or disapproval. Much like looking through a microscope, this narrow focus interferes with noticing the rest of the world. What the child is aware of through this very narrow field, the child identifies with and calls "self" or "I."

The self doesn't notice parts of the personality except those that are approved or disapproved of by significant others. And one can find in others only what is in the self. A favorite saying of Sullivan's was "As you judge yourself, so shall you judge others." Many times when you respond strongly to something in another person, it has more to do with you than with that person. Your microscope is focused on traits that you habitually find significant. To explore this point, do the following exercise.

Exercise 12.6

On a separate sheet of paper, fill in the blanks for ten people: "When I think of [give the person's name], I become aware of the part of me that notices [describe a behavior or trait]."

Here's an example: "When I think of Madeline, I become aware of the part of me that notices physical fitness."

Note for each person that the behavior or trait you notice is only one of many ways that this person could be described. Your awareness of each particular trait is based on how strongly significant it is to you. Madeline may be in great physical condition, but it is something in you that causes you to pick this particular trait of hers to focus on.

Correcting Parataxic Distortions

Have you ever had the experience of walking into a roomful of strangers and almost immediately being drawn to a particular person? You instantly like the person and may have a sense that you've known him or her a long time. Perhaps the person reminds you of someone out of your past. You may be able to recall who that someone is, or you may just have a vague sense of something familiar that you can't quite put your finger on. Usually the association between the person in front of you and the person out of your past is small and superficial: he or she has the same hairstyle, the same name, the same profession, or a similar accent.

When you do have a strong positive or negative reaction to someone you are meeting for the first time, consider the possibility of *parataxic distortion*—that the person in front of you is reminding you of someone else. Proceed with caution, because you may superimpose on the new person a set of inferences and assumptions that really belong with the person out of your past. The result can be confusion and misunderstanding.

Parataxic distortion is sometimes easier to spot when someone is relating to you as though you were someone else. You notice that this person has either a strongly positive or a strongly negative attitude about you from the beginning of your contact. The way he or she treats you is inconsistent with objective reality. You may find yourself thinking that this person has little idea of what you are really like. A good example of parataxic distortion is presented in the introduction of this chapter: the young man who associated a woman he met at a party with his Aunt Sally.

You might think that once you have uncovered your association between the person in front of you and the person out of your past, the influence from the past association would be done with. However, if you feel that the person in your history is similar to the person with you in the present, no amount of reality testing with current contradictory information is likely to change your feelings and attitudes about the present person. For instance, you might meet a young woman at the party with a "special smile." You realize as you talk with her that she reminds you of your old girlfriend, whom you still care for. Later your best friend tells you that this new woman is really the two-timing, deceitful person who's broken the heart of two other mutual friends. You shake your head in disbelief and say that may be so ... but that smile is so sweet that deep down you know she is good, and you decide to ask her for a date.

Parataxic distortion doesn't always function as an instant like or dislike. Sometimes it only influences specific interactions. One man kept interpreting his new lover's depressed feelings as a complaint and a demand that he change. Every time she talked about feeling sad and lost, he inferred that she was really trying to badger him into marriage. He responded with anger instead of support. And his lover, hurt and bewildered, became more depressed. Unconsciously, the man had confused his mother with his girlfriend. It was the mother who used her unhappiness like a club, whose sadness was always a veiled complaint. Because of parataxic distortion, the two women became one.

Unless the association between the person in your past and the person in your present can be separated in your mind, you will continue to react to the traits of the person from your past and relate to the new person accordingly. However, you can correct parataxic distortions. For example, you see new person at a meeting at work and instantly distrust him. You think that it must be something about his eyes and mouth, and then you realize that he bears a slight resemblance to a politician you hate. You decide to talk to him after the meeting. He has an easy, direct manner, which causes you to set aside the negative association with the odious politician. You feel comfortable with him as sales manager of the company.

Whenever you have a strong, immediate attraction to or revulsion for someone, whenever you find yourself making assumptions, ask yourself if you associate the person in front of you with anyone out of your past. Compare the person in front of you with the person out of your past by contrasting how each would respond to a similar situation and checking out what the current person actually wants or feels rather than assuming you know what these wants and feelings are.

If you suspect that someone is superimposing a parataxic distortion on you, try the following. Ask him or her, "Do I remind you of anyone else in your life? Perhaps someone in your past?" If the other person says yes, then explore the similarities and differences between you and the remembered person. If the other person denies that you remind him or her of someone else, but you have an idea of who it might be, cautiously suggest the specific person: "Perhaps I remind you of some young girl out of your past, maybe your little sister. You sometimes treat me as though I were an eight-year-old playmate." Sometimes the origin of a parataxic distortion escapes conscious awareness, and no amount of exploration will cause it to surface. That can spell trouble for any ongoing relationship.

Perpetuating Illusions

First impressions are interactional. More often than not, when you first meet someone, you are both on good behavior. However, if you try to maintain an unrealistically good image to win the approval or affection of the other person, you create an uncomfortable relationship that is likely to break down eventually. You can't delude other people forever. Sooner or later, they are likely to notice that you are not living up to your idealized image, and they will probably feel disappointed if not cheated. Consider the following dialogue:

Alice: You don't want to go to the party tonight? In the six months since we've been married, you've gone to only two parties with me. When we were single, we went to a party almost every weekend.

Jacob: I'm not really all that much of a partygoer. I can't stand all the noise.

Alice: I met you at a party and you were the life of it! You said you loved to be center stage.

Jacob: Oh yeah. I guess what I meant was that I like to be center stage with you.

Alice: That's nice to hear, but I miss our friends and parties.

Jacob: Why don't we have our own little party?

Alice: It's just not the same. You're not the same. You seem different now. I want your old self back.

In this example, Jacob clearly led Alice to believe that he was a much more extroverted person than he really was. He was only able to maintain the facade for a little while before it became too unnatural to continue. As a result, Alice's initial expectation that they would be a party-going couple is being disappointed. She holds on to her first impression and feels cheated by Jacob for denying her his more sociable side. An acknowledgment that she was mistaken in her initial assessment of Jacob would be a threat to her self-confidence. She would have to admit that her ability to evaluate people—in particular, potential mates—is not foolproof.

Clarifying First Impressions

Misleading first impressions can lead to later disillusionment. It is much easier to replace illusions with reality by checking out and sharing first impressions as soon as possible. You don't have to be potential best friends or lovers to make clear where you stand with a person. If you want to or have to continue relating to a person after your initial meeting, the following steps should clear up most illusions you have about each other. Take these steps before the initial meeting is over.

1. Let the other person know that you are interested in getting to know him or her better, or at least let the other person know how you feel about him or her.

2. State what happened during the meeting from your point of view.

3. State what you expect and hope in regard to the other person.

4. Give the other person an opportunity to object to or correct any false perceptions.

Returning to our conflicted couple, note that Jacob might have avoided misleading Alice had he taken those steps when they first met.

Jacob: I really had a great time with you tonight, and I want to see you again soon so that we can get better acquainted.

Alice: I really enjoyed you. You had us all in stitches until my ribs ached. How about going to a party next week?

Jacob: I guess I was a little rowdy tonight. I get that way when I've had too much to drink and I'm trying to impress a pretty woman. That's not my usual style. Basically, I'm a homebody.

Alice: Boy, you could have fooled me. You looked as though you were really in your element tonight.

Jacob: Not really. I wouldn't want you to get the wrong impression about me. Actually, I'd like to spend some quiet time with just you.

Alice: That's fine with me.

These four steps should reduce considerably the illusions of first impressions. As a relationship develops, it is essential to continue to check out each other's assumptions to keep communication lines clear. Never assume that you know what the other person is thinking or feeling until you have checked it out with him or her in plain language. Once you treat an assumption as a fact, it's very hard to change your opinion and acknowledge that you have misread someone. To avoid this trap, maintain a healthy skepticism about your assumptions and continue to test their reality by considering information contradicting as well as supporting your perspective.

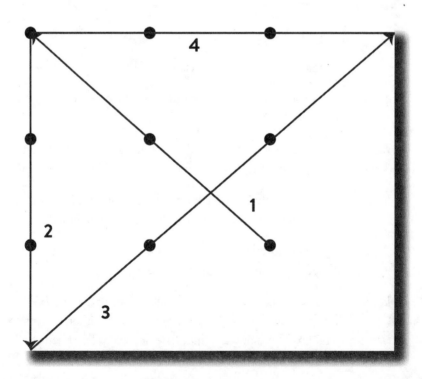

13 | Making Contact

The world is full of interesting strangers. Every day potential friends and lovers pass you in the hallway and the parking lot. They eat next to you. They wait on you in the store. Your glances meet and shyly slide away. It's frightening to step out of your anonymous role and make contact. What would they think? What would you do if you were rejected?

This chapter is about breaking the ice and making conversation with the people who attract you. It's the art of beginnings. By following a few simple rules and suggestions, you can vastly reduce your shyness with strangers. You can learn to talk with virtually anyone, anywhere.

Fear of Strangers

Fear of strangers can come from several sources. You may believe in outmoded social restrictions that say it's impolite to impose yourself on someone you don't know. Or you may fear that strangers will reject you if you make an overture. But by far the most common source of fear of strangers is your own self-deprecating internal monologue.

You may say things like this to yourself: "They don't want to talk to me." "They probably wouldn't like me." "It's hopeless." "I'm too awkward, too ugly, too short, too stupid." You view yourself as someone inferior, unworthy, and unattractive. You imagine that other people are always heroes while you are always the goat. The belief that you are unworthy inevitably leads to awkward self-consciousness and the painful conclusion that people you could enjoy won't enjoy you. The following sections will show you how to cope with your fear of strangers.

Analyze What You Say to Yourself

Imagine that you are in a doctor's waiting room and have just started a conversation with an attractive person. The person listens for a moment, makes a few perfunctory responses, and returns to reading a magazine. Now notice your internal monologue. Are you blaming yourself for the rejection? What fault have you found with yourself for the other person's disinterest? Are you using global labels to describe yourself, such as "stupid," "lame," "ridiculous," and so on?

Exercise 13.1

Negative judgments and labels should be changed. Make a list of your negative labels and devaluing statements. Next to each of the statements, write the same thing in a purely descriptive manner. For "stupid," you might write, "My mind periodically goes blank when trying to think of conversation." Instead of "dumpy," you might put your actual height and weight. Make a commitment to yourself to use descriptive rather than negative labels in your internal monologues.

The hard part, of course, is sticking with your nonjudgmental descriptions when trying to approach someone for the first time or after you've been rejected. These are the times when all your old habitual put-downs come on strong. You're so used to hearing them from yourself that you hardly notice. The solution is to make a list of your significant positive and negative qualities, five or six of each. The negative qualities are nonjudgmental descriptions. The positive qualities are things you realistically like or take pride in. Every time you find yourself tempted to approach someone, go over the memorized list. Give yourself a shot of reality rather than the old distorted labels and judgments.

Reframe Your Approach Behavior

Your fear of rejection is largely a product of how you conceptualize, or frame, your meeting with an interesting stranger. Here are some negative frames that will inhibit you when meeting people:

"They'll think I want something from them."

"He probably wouldn't be attracted to me."

"They're nice but wouldn't want to be friends with me."

"She's gorgeous. What would she see in me?"

Notice that all these statements leave you hoping for something undeserved. It's time to reframe the meeting experience so that the stakes aren't so high. Meetings with interesting strangers shouldn't be a test to see if they want to sleep with you, want to be your friend or mate, or even particularly like you. It's merely an opportunity to begin getting to know someone who interests you. You're curious about what will happen but not worried about it. You don't want anything from the other person; you are merely offering your time and interest. A refusal of your interest is a lost opportunity, nothing more or less.

Reframe Rejection

When you approach a stranger, you are offering a gift—the gift of interaction. If he or she declines the offer, you may frame the rejection in a variety of ways. You may see yourself as inadequate and unworthy, you may focus on your physical and character flaws, or you may beat yourself up as socially incompetent. The trouble with these frames is that they assume facts not in evidence. You are mind reading.

There could be literally hundreds of reasons for any particular refusal or rejection. Let's suppose you invited someone at the office to lunch. The person smiles and says, "Not today, but please ask me again." You will be crushed if you conclude that your big nose has again turned someone off. But that's just one of many explanations. The person might be on a diet, might have just eaten, might be meeting someone else, might be too busy to eat, might be in some emotional turmoil, and so on.

Right now, as an exercise, list at least twenty-five reasons why you might turn down a relative stranger for a lunch date. Now examine the list. How many items would you consider rejections of the core person, of some basic emotional or physical characteristic? The fact is that you don't know strangers well enough to reject them. If you don't want to go on a lunch date, it probably has more to do with you—your schedule, your willingness to meet someone new, your mood.

Mind reading will almost always get you in trouble by leading you to the most negative possible interpretation for any refusal. The best thing to do if you are rejected is to assume there are personal reasons for the refusal that have little to do with you. If you want more information, ask for clarification. For example, if someone declines a lunch date, you could check to see whether it would be okay for you to ask him or her again another time.

Plan to Get Rejected

Even a minor rejection can take your breath away. To deal with the emotional blow of rejection, take a few deep breaths and tune in to how your body is doing. Feel your feet against the floor, the chair against your buttocks, the sensations in your stomach. Concentrating on your body can turn off for a few minutes the negative internal monologue that may follow rejection. Your deep breathing and body awareness can act as a sort of thought-stopper and keep you from psychologically kicking yourself.

You should expect to get soundly rejected at least three times a week. This means that you've found yourself interested in someone who, for one of hundreds of possible reasons, wasn't receptive to your interest at the moment. Try initiating conversations for the express purpose of experiencing and learning to deal with rejection. As an exercise, pick someone out whom you like but who might not like you. Before initiating anything, think through the answers to these questions:

"What wouldn't he or she like about me?"

"How would he or she probably act?"

"What would I do to salvage the situation if I were rebuffed?"

After you've answered the questions, approach the person. As you interact, observe what's going on between you. Also keep track of what you're thinking and feeling. Later, when you're in a quiet place, think back and notice how many of your assumptions were right or wrong. Did you enjoy yourself at all? Did you experience any sense of accomplishment in meeting a challenge?

Guidelines for Making Contact

There are only two basic rules for successfully making contact: First, you have to give what you would like to receive, which means that the attention, interest, respect, and liking that you want must also be something you offer to others. Second, you have to have an outward rather than an inward focus. You listen to the other person instead of rehearsing your next remark or worrying about your hair or your awkwardness.

Giving what you would like to receive and staying focused on the other person are easier said than done. Fear of strangers may have the effect of making you awkward and self-conscious. No matter how much you want to reach out, your attention is riveted on your own appearance and behavior. The following sections will show you how to make contact so that others will feel your genuine interest.

Use Body Language

One of the biggest ways you can turn people off is through body language. Shy people characteristically avoid eye contact, keep a blank and expressionless face, and physically retreat from others. The message sent is "Don't bother me." Here's the body language you need for making contact:

Move toward the other person. This means getting into the circle or group rather than watching from the outside. It also means that you don't converse from ten feet away. You must find a distance at which you can talk and interact comfortably.

Lean forward. Leaning back against the seat communicates fatigue or disinterest, while leaning forward indicates that you are engaged and ready for contact.

Uncross your arms and legs. Crossed arms and legs indicate a defensive, protective position, while an open posture indicates a willingness to listen.

Make eye contact. Most people have trouble looking someone in the eye and trying to think of what to say at the same time. Eye contact can be anxiety provoking and make you lose your train of thought. The solution is to focus your eyes somewhere else on the other person's face. For example, you can keep your eyes glued to the person's nose, mouth, or left ear. As long as your focus is within eight inches of the nose, the other person won't be able to tell that you aren't looking him or her in the eye.

Smile. A smile is the most universally understood statement that you are open and interested in making contact.

Let your responses show. Nod, frown, raise your eyebrows in surprise, and so on.

Here's how to practice your body language skills. Sit in front of a TV talk show and imagine that the guest is speaking directly to you. Keep a checklist of the skills nearby and refer to it while you practice your responses to the talk-show guest. Make a point of using body language to help you express feelings and opinions in everyday conversations.

Use Icebreakers

The only way to begin a conversation is to start talking. It's safe to assume that other people want and enjoy contact just as you do. They need that excitement that can only come when two people express genuine interest in each other. And just as you want the same things, you are probably afraid of the same things too: embarrassment, rejection, or being forced to do something you don't want to do.

It doesn't matter a great deal what you say to get a conversation started. What's important is that you say enough to invite some response. When you need an icebreaker, stop for a moment and focus on your immediate experience. Relax, open yourself to what you see and feel, and wait for an awareness you can share. What's unusual? What can you deduce from the other person's appearance or behavior? Notice the environment you're sharing. How would you describe it to a friend? Check your feelings. What's it like to be you right now? How does it feel to be poised on the edge of making contact?

At the end of your moment of reflection, choose which awareness you will share. One woman who was seated next to an attractive man on a train was racking her brain for a conversational opener. Finally she paused to meditate on her experience. The train was taking her to a new job and a new town. She thought how hard it had always been to meet people. And that gave her the icebreaker: "You know, I'm moving to a place where I don't know a soul. I've been thinking that I better get in practice for meeting people. Hi, my name is Jill." A university student, observing a young woman in his class, smiled and said, "You haven't taken a note either. Are you as bored as I am?"

If a few moments of reflection fail to suggest an icebreaker, try one of the following standard openers:

Ask for information: "Can you tell me where Filbert Street is?" "Is there a gift shop in the lobby?" "How do I get to the nearest bar?"

Give a compliment: "Your purse has some of the most intricate tooled leatherwork I've ever seen."

Employ a little humor: "Do you mind talking to a man who's lost?" "You could get old waiting for a table in this restaurant." "I was looking for the manager, but I'd rather talk to you."

Use current events: "This city's full of muggers. Look at that guy. Right now he's doing an appraisal on my watch." "I'm starting to like the idea of a moratorium on high-rises. This street is a wind tunnel."

Certain ritual questions are tried-and-true icebreakers: "Hi, what's your name?" "How are you?" "How's it going?" "Do you live around here?" "Do you work in this building?" "Is this your son?" "How did you like the play?" Ritual questions don't require a lot of work to think up, and they don't require a lot of work to answer. Therein lies their strength and their shortcomings. It's easy to elicit a brief remark. But then, almost immediately, the ball is back in your court and you have to follow up with specific questions and comments to generate a real conversation.

One of the most challenging and rewarding of conversational icebreakers is the direct approach of telling the other person exactly what you feel and what you want: "I feel attracted to you, and I want to spend a few minutes talking and getting to know you." "It's a little scary walking up to a stranger, but you seem like an interesting person to me." "I see you're reading Gaiman's latest book. What do you think of his style?"

When searching for an icebreaker, two things to watch for are similarities and differences. Anything you have in common is a good way to start a conversation. Noticing that you both like the same book, admire the same view, are slumped in your chairs, or are wearing Band-Aids is a good way to initiate a conversation. Noticing contrasts is a provocative way of encouraging self-disclosure: "I'd never have the courage to come here alone." "I was always more drawn to the Impressionists, but I see that you like the Hopper prints."

The Art of Conversation

Once you break the ice, the question is how to make satisfying contact with another person. You only have to know how to do three things to make good conversation: ask questions, listen actively, and disclose a little about yourself.

Questions

There are basically two kinds of questions. *Ritual questions* focus on learning a person's name, where he or she is from, and what he or she does. Ritual questions are most often used as the opening gambits of a conversation, but these soon give way to *informational questions*. These are more specific and are designed to elicit important facts about the other person's experience, beliefs, and feelings. While a ritual "How are you doing?" might reap a "Fine, how are you?" an informational question, such as "What's it like to work with children?" will promote more intimate contact.

Whenever you pose an informational question, you will probably find out a little more than you asked for. This is called *free information*. If you ask the woman sitting next to you on the bus whether she lives in town and her answer is "Yes," you receive no free information. But in most cases, you will get a more specific response, such as "I just moved up to Twin Peaks because I really love the view." You've gotten two free pieces of information: that she is new to the neighborhood and that she prefers an expansive view. Through a series of questions, you might get such free information as her marital status, number of children, taste in art, and the story of a past vacation.

Informational questions allow you to begin sketching a picture of who this other person is. The secret to exciting conversation is to follow your curiosity and ask questions that you really want the answer to. You may want to know how she could survive on a windswept hill like Twin Peaks. Go ahead and ask. You may want to know how much she pays in rent. You may want to know if she lives alone. The most basic rule of conversation is to pry. People are their own favorite topics of conversation. They're flattered by your attention and interest. Be outrageous, because each question continues the excitement and pleasure of a growing intimacy.

In modern society there remain some well-established social rules about minding your own business. You can get around those rules by tempering really direct questions with the techniques of active listening and self-disclosure.

Active Listening

The second hallmark of a good conversationalist is the ability to listen in such a way that others feel heard. To be an active listener you need to feed back in your own words what's been said. You do this for three reasons: to make sure that you understood and got it right, to give the speaker the reassurance that he or she was listened to, and to promote more disclosure on the part of the speaker.

For example, if a mountain-climbing woman was explaining the details of a difficult ascent, you might listen actively by putting a little amazement in your voice: "And you were able to sleep in a hammock suspended by only two pitons!" She might say, "No, I had three, but that was only for safety." Then, encouraged by your attention, she might go on to describe how it feels sleeping with nothing but a piece of nylon keeping her from a two-thousand-foot drop.

It should be clear that listening is more than merely keeping your mouth shut. You need to carefully attend to what is said, remember it, and feed it back. Lack of active listening is the most common cause of conversational disaster. Some people can't listen, because they are preoccupied with their fears of embarrassment, others are constantly preparing their next remark, and still others fail to listen because they are too busy advising or arguing. If you are unable to listen, you are unable to give the interest, attention, and respect that you would want to receive from others. People grow bored with you and slide away. For more information on the blocks to listening and how to overcome them, read chapter 1.

Self-Disclosure

Disclosure makes intimacy possible. Trying to achieve closeness without revealing something about yourself is like trying to hit home runs with a toothpick. You haven't got what it takes.

If you have difficulty talking about yourself, try this exercise: Write a four- or five-page autobiography. Think back to important incidents in your life that helped make you who you are. Focus on information that will enable others to understand you better. Include the following:

- Important or formative events in your childhood

- What school was like for you

- Your favorite teacher

- A few of your more interesting jobs

- The people you've loved and cared for

- Your biggest loss

- Your most wonderful moment

- Your greatest achievement

- Your hobbies

- Your best vacation

- The funniest thing that ever happened to you

Add anything else that you think is important or appropriate. You can reread your autobiography whenever you anticipate being in a social situation. It will give you a wealth of information for stories and anecdotes.

Self-disclosure doesn't mean that you have to reveal your deepest needs and secrets. There are three levels of self-disclosure. The first level is purely informational: describing your job, your last vacation, a funny experience. This level persists during the first few minutes of a conversation, when you aren't yet ready to reveal your feelings to someone you would like to know better.

To deepen the contact, you can move to the second level of self-disclosure. This level of intimacy involves thoughts, feelings, and needs—

but only about the past or the future. Typical statements at this level might include the following:

- A belief or an opinion that you've felt committed to

- A story that makes you seem foolish

- An emotional event from your childhood

- A fear you once had or a concern for the future

- Some of your hopes for the future

- General preferences and tastes

- Problems in old relationships

Each thing that you reveal about yourself adds spice to your relationships. The other person feels flattered to be let into your world, and you both enjoy the excitement of deepening contact. When you talk about your hopes and fears, preferences and beliefs, you become a unique individual rather than a cardboard character. You are making an impact.

Some people are afraid to express their tastes and feelings because they feel that disclosure might destroy an illusion of similarity with the other person. They worry that revealing differences will undermine potential closeness. On the contrary, contrasts are exciting, and differences in taste and viewpoint can enliven a relationship. Withholding your feelings may spare you some anxiety, but you will eventually suffocate your relationship.

Many conversations never get past the second level of self-disclosure, in which the feelings and events under discussion tend to be safely in the past or the future. To get to a deeper level of intimacy with someone, you need to go to a third level of self-disclosure, in which you reveal your current feelings about the person you're speaking to. This means doing some of the following:

- Saying what attracts you to the person

- Saying how you are affected by the other person's behavior at that moment

- Telling about your reservations and some of the things you don't like about the other person

- Saying what you hope for from the encounter

- Saying what you feel about how the other person responds to what you say

The key to this deepest level of intimacy is to say what you feel right now. It's risky, and you may get a little anxious. But you will also feel undeniable excitement. As you take risks, particularly by revealing your negative feelings, you are creating strong bonds. Just as soldiers in combat feel a special intimacy, people who risk sharing their hidden feelings can quickly become close.

To get practice at this level of intimacy, try an exercise for sharing your reservations. Seek out a friend you feel close to. Tell him or her this: "I'd like you to share your reservations about me. I won't defend myself, but I'd also like to share mine with you at the end." Explain that you're trying to get practice hearing and saying negative things.

Putting It All Together

Conversation is the art of combining questions, active listening, and self-disclosure in such a way that people keep talking with you and enjoy it. Remember that the basic rule of conversation is to pry. But your probing questions must be tempered with self-disclosure so people feel they're getting a fair deal, getting to know you while you're getting to know them. Two examples: "I have a hard time saying no to my daughter. How do you manage to keep good discipline?" "I've always wanted to ski. Do you go up to Squaw Valley often?"

Another way to avoid being obnoxious is to combine informational questions with active listening: "So you've had a series of relationships that seem to end when you finally stand up for yourself. Did you tend to wait until you just couldn't bear it anymore to stand up for your rights?" "You toured Europe for five months all alone at the age of seventeen. Incredible. Was it your father's death that brought you home?"

Prying is fun. It helps you satisfy your curiosity and also get more information so you can keep the conversation going. When you are no longer curious enough to pry, it's probably a good sign that the conversation has run its course and you should look for a graceful close.

Here's how a conversation might go if you used questions, active listening, and self-disclosure to the best advantage.

Warren: That was a tremendous analysis of the populist movement. I think Professor Sims loved it. [*icebreaker*]

Beth: Thanks. You're Warren, aren't you? [*ritual question*]

Warren: Right. You can always tell when Sims likes something. He gets all excited and starts wiping his glasses. Are you enjoying the seminar? [*ritual question*]

Beth: Not much. In fact, I haven't a single class I really like this quarter. I'm a little depressed about it. Are you worried about finding the primary sources Sims wants, the old newspapers and all that? [*self-disclosure/informational question*]

Warren: No, they should all be online, and, frankly, I sometimes just make it up. [*self-disclosure*]

Beth: (Laughs) Are you going home this Christmas? [*informational question*]

Warren: I'm going to stick around here. I had a horrible time last year when my stepmother got drunk and fell into the tree. She's a lot younger than my father, unfulfilled and bitter. I'd just as soon stay clear of it. [*self-disclosure*]

Beth: There's no family feeling, a lot of hassling? [*active listening*]

Warren: Yeah. I think they're ready to split. Is Christmas any better at your house? [*self-disclosure/informational question*]

Beth: We don't stay home. We all go to the mountains for cross-country skiing. Every year there's this cabin we rent for the holidays. I have three sisters. There's a real close-knit feeling. [*self-disclosure*]

Warren: I'd give a lot to have a family like that. Especially this time of year. Sometimes I wonder if there's any hope for a decent marriage. I mean, it's scary. I think even if I find someone who's wonderful now, five years later it might be a night-mare, just like my parents had. [*self-disclosure*]

Beth: It's like you can't make a commitment for fear the whole thing will turn into some terrible trap. I worry about that; time changes people incredibly. My sister was really in love with this guy, and she hates his guts now. I worry about my own affection changing suddenly as much as I do about the other person's. [*active listening/self-disclosure*]

Warren: Yeah, you worry about something breaking the spell, so suddenly you're not in love anymore. [*active listening*]

Beth: That's it. It's fun talking. By the way, how did you get Sims to let you do a paper on Dashiell Hammett? Now there's something that would be fun doing. [*self-disclosure/informational question*]

Warren: I love detective novels—as long as they have lots of cigar-smoking cops and Sam Spade–type gumshoes. I'm addicted to them. I've even been to that place in San Francisco where Miles Archer was supposedly killed in *The Maltese Falcon*. Do you like Hammett too? [*self-disclosure/informational question*]

Beth: Not as much as Raymond Chandler. I've read every word Chandler ever wrote. In fact, I've written some short stories imitating his style. [*self-disclosure*]

Warren: You write? How do you find time? [*informational question*]

Beth: Well, I guess between writing and studying, there isn't time for much else. [*self-disclosure*]

Warren: I hope you won't be offended, but I have always thought you were kind of asocial, just preoccupied with books and not very interested in people. I was kind of attracted to you and always wanted to talk to you, but you seemed so ... reserved. [*self-disclosure*]

Beth: I think that's true to some extent. But I'm enjoying talking right now. The only trouble is that I'm five minutes late for class.

Warren: I'm a little scared to ask you, but I'd love to take you to a movie tonight. *The Thin Man* is playing. [*self-disclosure*]

Fortunately for Warren, Beth suspends her prejudice toward Dashiell Hammett and accompanies him to *The Thin Man*. Their initial conversation moved easily from point to point. It got off the ground with icebreakers and ritual questions. Informational questions were the lubricant that kept it going, while active listening and self-disclosure deepened the contact. Neither person was afraid to abruptly change the subject to follow a new line of interest. Beth learned a lot about Warren in a few minutes. She reassured him that she was listening by feeding back what he said in her own words. She offered him information about herself, so her questions came in the context of her own disclosures. Warren allowed Beth to see into his painful family situation. He exposed some of his fears and even offered a reservation about her. Each of these disclosures increased the opportunity for bonding and made it more likely that Beth would say yes to a date to see *The Thin Man*.

14 Digital Communication

Many messages are delivered via digital channels—email, texts, voice mail, social media, and video. Each channel has its pros and cons, its advantages and disadvantages. An effective communicator knows how to maximize each medium's strengths and avoid its pitfalls.

In this chapter you will learn how to choose the most appropriate medium for your message and how to be efficient, effective, clear, direct, and appropriate in your digital communication.

Email

Email has turned every computer or smart phone user into a potential Saint Paul, Eleanor Roosevelt, Ernest Hemingway, or Abraham Lincoln. None of those famous letter writers enjoyed the scope, power, and ease of written communication that modern email provides us. And yet we use it too often to confuse, confront, and control and too seldom to inspire, influence, and inform.

Pros and Cons

There are many advantages to email that have lead to its supplanting almost all physically delivered snail mail. It is fast, allowing you to get a message to someone almost instantly. At the same time, it preserves a written record of what was said, the date, the sender, the recipient, and any other people who were copied. With email you can send to just one intimate or you can simultaneously address thousands of recipients all over the world. Your message can include color graphics and all sorts of additional material in the form of links or attachments. With threading software, you can organize and keep track of a complex series of communications among several parties. All that, and it's cheap too.

Email does have some real drawbacks. Perhaps the most serious is that email has become so familiar that it almost feels like full, face-to-face communication. But it's not. In an email you can't see body language and you can't hear tone of voice, those nonverbal components that make up a huge portion of human communication. Because of this limitation, an email message has only about 7 percent of the effectiveness and impact of a face-to-face message (Mehrabian 1980).

In addition, email is sometimes too fast and too easy. Typos abound, with sometimes comic, sometime tragic consequences. It is all too easy to fire off an angry, inaccurate, or incomplete email that you will later regret sending. For example, Caroline was emailing back and forth with her sister and her best friend about whom she should pick for her bridesmaids in her wedding, the dresses, logistics, and so on. They made some pretty sarcastic remarks about how her chubby cousin Janie would look in her bridesmaid outfit. Then late at night, after a couple of glasses of wine, Caroline emailed cousin Janie the details about the wedding party. Right after she hit "send," Caroline realized that she had included, way at the bottom of the information, some of the catty remarks she had made about Janie in the earlier interchanges. Janie was offended, boycotted the wedding, and didn't speak to Caroline for two years.

Guidelines for Effective Email

The next time you are catching up on your email, slow down a little and try some of these ways to be more effective:

Proofread. Cramped keypads and keyboards, fat thumbs, distractions, and quirky autocorrect functions create a lot of typos. Before hitting "send," scan your message for spelling, factual accuracy, proper tone, and completeness. Almost every time, you will find something you'd like to change or add. Proofing slows you down just a little, but it pays off.

Maximize your subject line. The subject line is the most important part of an email. After the sender's name, it's the first thing a recipient sees. It identifies this message from you, motivates others to open your email, and remains visible in recipients' mailboxes so they can find your message again later. Use your subject line to summarize your content clearly and briefly, including key details like dates and times and requests for action. For example, "Bring driver's license to 3PM escrow closing" is a much better subject line than "See you tomorrow."

Use appropriate style. Is your message formal or informal? Are you asking for a favor from an authority figure, or are you reassuring a subordinate? Are you dutifully answering your sister's endless questions or asking an urgent question of your own that needs an immediate response? Being aware of these kinds of considerations will help you strike the right tone, use appropriate language, and achieve your desired results. You won't be too slangy or too stiff, overly laudatory or excessively critical.

Cool off. You can compose a message when you're angry or excited, but don't immediately send what you've written in the heat of the moment. Go get a cup of tea, walk the dog, or otherwise cool off before committing yourself. Remember, this email is going to be floating out there in cyberspace forever.

Be brief. Get to the point quickly and don't ramble.

Be kind. Be as respectful and careful of peoples' feelings as you would be in person, in a face-to-face conversation. In fact, you should be even more careful in email than in person because you cannot immediately see the reactions of your recipient and adjust your tone.

Be empathetic. Try to anticipate how your words will affect the recipient of your email. Choose words and tone based on how the reader is most likely to receive them. In other words, put yourself in the other person's shoes.

Be clear. Complex or subtle emails are often misinterpreted and lead to hurt feelings. If your message isn't understood, or if it is understood incorrectly, stop emailing and talk directly.

Include your feelings. When appropriate, include how you are feeling about the person or the situation. If it is your style and it is appropriate, use emoticons and emoji, the keyboard symbol combinations or the small smiley face images that have evolved for conveying emotion digitally.

Be discreet. When you're all alone with your computer, email can feel like a very private form of communication. But it's not. Emails can be forwarded all over the place and even hacked by the malicious. So assume that your emails are at least potentially public, and don't blab all of your secrets or use language that you would not employ in public.

Listen. In the email universe, the equivalent of being a good listener is to be a good responder. Check your email frequently and respond to queries promptly.

Minimize attachments. Many people don't have the bandwidth, current software, or experience to handle a ton of attachments in various file formats. Whenever possible, paste extra content into the body of your email, so it displays automatically with the text of your message. That way your recipient doesn't have to struggle opening an attachment.

Respect privacy. When sending an email to a lot of people at once, don't assume that everyone in the group wants everyone else to know their email address. Put your own name in the "to" space and use the bcc (blind carbon copy) space for the recipients' addresses. That way you are not violating anyone's privacy. The only time it's all right to expose everyone's name and address is when you know they already know each other's addresses and would welcome further contact.

Texting

Text messaging, or texting, became popular in the early 2000s as a way for private mobile phone users to exchange messages when voice communication was impossible or undesirable. At first you could only use a phone to send straight text to one other person, but now you can use many different devices, send images and links, and send to more than one other person at a time. The popularity of texting has spawned several blogging sites, most notably Twitter. Texting is also used commercially for reminders, notifications, and promotions.

Pros and Cons

Texting is a fast, convenient, cheap way to send a short, simple message to someone who is busy or not available to take a phone call. It is a very informal medium in which brevity, abbreviations, slang, emoji, and a casual tone have become socially acceptable. Instead of disappearing into the ether like a phone call, a text message is saved on our devices for later reference. Popular all over the world, texting is used in many countries as part of emergency services systems and has become a potent tool during times of social unrest.

Texting is remarkably effective in binding together small groups of intimates. Most people send over half their texts to three to five intimate friends and relatives. Texting allows you to stay in touch, send photos of your lunch plate, and carry on conversations with loved ones in the many small moments of the day that might otherwise be lost to boredom or daydreaming.

On the other hand, texting can be a colossal waste of time. Sometimes it takes much longer to make a plan using texting than it would take with just a phone call. Some people think that texting is destroying school kids' ability to write standard English essays, and bullying texts are a problem in some schools. Others blame texting for the global anglicization of languages—English abbreviations such as lol (laughing out loud), brb (be right back), and gr8 (great) have become common in eleven different languages. Finally, we all know the dangers of texting while walking or driving, but many do it anyway.

Guidelines for Effective Texting

Before you push "send," consider whether you have followed these guidelines.

Be clear. Don't use too many abbreviations and acronyms, especially when texting someone whose texting literacy you are not sure of.

Proof before sending. Make sure your text has not been garbled by your elephant-thumb typos or your phone's autocorrect function. Save yourself having to send three more texts by checking that all pertinent information is included.

Consider a phone call. After two or three texts back and forth, it would probably be faster to just make a phone call and talk in real time.

Be considerate. Although people expect texts to be short and to the point, you can still offend or hurt someone's feelings by being too abrupt. Take a few extra seconds to consider your recipient's feelings.

Add feeling. As with email, texting lacks all body language and voice tone, the important channels by which we interpret the emotional content of communication. Add some feeling words or use emoticons and emoji to add emotional clarity to your texts.

Remain casual. Stick to casual topics, nothing too heavy. It is not appropriate to use texting to deliver serious messages such as breaking up a relationship, turning down a job applicant, or announcing a pregnancy.

No all caps. It's the boorish equivalent of shouting.

Voice Mail

Voice mail has been around longer than any other electronic medium, and yet we still haven't mastered it. How many times have you received two consecutive voice mails from someone who twice rambled on past your recording device's time limit and still forgot to tell you the crucial information?

Pros and Cons

Voice mail is a convenient way to leave a short message when the recipient isn't there to answer the phone in person. It creates a more or less permanent record of your message, and some of your feeling comes across because your tone of voice can be heard.

On the other hand, some people hate "talking to a machine." They freeze when they know their voice will be recorded and that their time is limited. This tends to make them sound nervous and rushed, and they forget to include important information.

Guidelines for Effective Voice Mail

As you dial a number, be prepared to have the call answered by a machine, and follow these simple guidelines.

Pretend you're really talking to the person. Forget that you are being recorded by a machine, and talk as if there were a live person on the other end. Your personality and feelings will come through and make the message more conversational.

Who, what, where, and when. While you're waiting for the beep, run over the crucial information in your mind so that you can lead with what you most want to communicate, when and where the appointment is, or whom you are calling about.

Include name, time, and number. Even if the person you're calling knows your voice and your phone number, identify yourself, when you called, and the best number to call back.

Wait for the final beep. There's always a chance that the person you want to talk to is actually there, screening calls or perhaps frantically rushing in from the yard, trying to pick up before you hang up. Even if your message is short, wait until the final beep, just in case.

Social Media

In 2004 on the Harvard campus, sophomore Mark Zuckerberg launched an early version of Facebook, the first widespread social media computer network. A year later, Google launched YouTube, an innovative way for people to make and share short video clips online. In the next decade there was an explosion of social media sites such as Pinterest and Instagram for sharing photos, Twitter and Tumblr for blogging, and Google+ and LinkedIn for interest-based and career networking. By 2015 it was estimated that 84 percent of adolescents in the United States had Facebook accounts. The proliferation of social media continues today, with new sites coming online and older sites morphing and merging.

Pros and Cons

With nearly two billion worldwide users of Facebook alone, there is no denying the popularity of social media. It has become an important tool for connecting people, a way for you to stay in touch and feel close to family, friends, and various online communities. Businesses, nonprofits, and political interest groups also use social media widely to market goods, raise funds, and get their message out.

However, there are some downsides to social media. Several studies have linked heavy Facebook and other social media use to depression in adolescents (Selfhout et al. 2009). Many young people are victims of cyberbullying, harassment, and trolling behavior perpetrated through social media. A less serious but more common problem is the amount of time that social media can consume. Trying to achieve more "likes" and positive responses can be addicting. You can easily spend a couple of hours a day just keeping up with your friends, family, and acquaintances on Facebook, as well as seeking attention and approval.

Also, it's possible to overexpose yourself by revealing personal information on social media that on second thought you would have preferred to withhold from authority figures, employers, or strangers. For example, Gerard was a gay man who publicly posted several photos of himself and his boyfriend dancing and hugging at a party. Months later his application to rent an apartment was denied by a prospective landlord whom he had friended on Facebook years before. Gerard couldn't prove anything, but he suspected that the prospective landlord had checked him out on Facebook and rejected his application because of homophobia.

Guidelines for Effective Social Media

Here are ways to fine-tune your use of social media so that you maximize the benefits and avoid the pitfalls. These guidelines refer mainly to Facebook features and practices, but they also apply to other social media platforms.

Don't friend people you don't really know. Anyone in the world can Google your name and send you a friend request. Don't compete for the greatest number of Facebook friends in your crowd. It can backfire like it did for Gerard. A stranger may be a mutual friend with someone else you know, but that does not guarantee that the stranger will be a good friend to you.

Pay attention to what's public and what's private. Unless you've specifically blocked them, anyone to whom you've ever sent a friend request can access your Facebook page and see what you have posted for public consumption. Whenever you post anything on Facebook, consider whether it is public information or private for confirmed friends only, and make sure the appropriate button is selected for that post.

Group your friends and followers. If you are very active on social media, consider grouping people as immediate family, intimates, casual friends, acquaintances, business contacts, and so on. You can use the default categories on Facebook or make up your own. To help figure out what you want to disclose to whom, reread chapter 2 on self-disclosure.

Manage access. Under your settings, you can turn off someone's ability to follow your public account at any time. Likewise, you can unfriend or block anyone you no longer want to have access to your personal information. You can hide some posts from specific people on a case-by-case basis: select sharing options from the drop-down menu at the top right of a Facebook post, or by editing your privacy setting on a mobile device. You can hide your list of friends from everyone but yourself. You can also hide a relationship-status change from some or all of your friends.

Look at your own profile. You can see your profile through the eyes of your friends and followers by using the "view as" function. This is a good way to check on what you have made visible to whom and how it's working.

Edit your old posts or comments. If you have old stuff on Facebook that's now a little embarrassing or no longer relevant, you can delete or edit it at any time.

Video Communication

The idea of the TV phone is almost as old as television itself, but it was not until the 1990s that peer-to-peer video conferencing became practical, affordable, and widespread. Now there are Skype, FaceTime, and other applications that let you see and hear the person on the other end of the line. Also various devices let you easily record videos, send them to others, and upload them so that the whole world can see as well as hear your message.

Pros and Cons

The big advantage of video communication is that it delivers the 93 percent of impact that words alone fail to convey (Mehrabian 2007). Using video communication, you and the other person can hear tone of voice and see facial expressions and other body language cues that humans depend on to amplify and clarify meaning.

On the downside, video communication sometimes involves technical difficulties that hinder communication. People are so busy fussing with the camera angle and maintaining digital contact that they neglect the human contact. For example, when Charlene Skyped her mother, she was often frustrated because her mother spent so much time marveling over the video experience, wandering out of frame, or talking so loudly her voice was distorted.

Guidelines for Effective Video Communication

Prepare. Be considerate about calling other time zones at a moment when people may be sleeping, bathing, busy, and so on. Test your equipment ahead of time and make sure you know how to operate the hardware and software. Prearrange a time when you won't be interrupted. Turn off phones and alarms and anything that might make unwanted background noise. Make sure you are dressed and groomed appropriately. If there is something you want to show the other person, make sure it is close at hand.

Know your purpose. A lot of video communication is casual, a chance to see a loved one's face and make contact. But if your video communication has a business or an important personal purpose, set an agenda. Know why you are communicating and what you want to say. Make notes beforehand of key information or ideas. Figure out exactly what you want the person or people on the other end to hear, think, feel, and do.

Compose your scene. Consider the background that your camera will pick up behind you. Avoid clutter and very bright contrasts. Clear the space of distractions and possibly embarrassing personal possessions. Position yourself so that there is enough light on your face and you are not too close to or too far from the camera.

Act naturally and focus. To get the full benefit of video communication, use body language and facial expressions naturally, as you would if the other person were actually in the room with you. Pay attention to the other person all the time as if really in the same room. You are not just watching a video of the other person—it's live.

Listen. Because this is a live, ongoing interaction, you need to practice good listening skills: again, pay attention, acknowledge what is said, and paraphrase it back if necessary.

Follow up. If important points have been made or agreements reached, it's a good idea to follow up with a text or an email so that there is a written record documenting the conversation.

The guidelines from this chapter will help you choose the most appropriate digital medium for your messages and make you more efficient, effective, clear, direct, and appropriate in your digital communication.

PART V

. . . .

Family Skills

15 Couples Skills

Successful relationships don't just happen. They are nurtured by the people in them. A strong relationship is based on the couple paying attention to the way the relationship is going, and making changes in how they interact together based on what the relationship needs to keep it healthy. A relationship is like any living thing: if it doesn't get enough nourishment, it will die; but if you give it what it needs to grow and blossom, it will thrive.

What makes a good relationship? Researcher John Gottman and his team have studied thousands of couples and have discovered that couples typically need a five-to-one ratio of positive to negative interactions in the relationship. That means five positive interactions, such as physical touch, smiles, spontaneous kisses, compliments, and other signs of positive regard, for every one negative interaction, to overcome the effects of negative interaction (Gottman and Levenson 1992). Gottman's research has also found that healthy couples tend to interpret neutral events in a positive way, which he calls "positive sentiment override." At-risk couples, on the other hand, are more likely to interpret neutral events as negative, because they are victims of "negative sentiment override" (Gottman 1999).

What this means for couples is that the best way to build a healthy, strong, lasting relationship is to genuinely like and respect each other, act in a positive and caring way most of the time, and develop good couples communication skills.

This chapter will teach you skills to identify and change negative patterns that may be interfering with your relationship with your partner, and it will offer effective alternatives to some common unhealthy communication styles.

Schemas

A *schema* is a label that you put on someone else based on his or her behavior. It's how you might sum up a person in just a few words. Schemas are based on all the experiences and interactions you've had with someone else. They help your brain organize your experiences into categories. Although your brain's tendency to make quick judgments can be helpful in some situations, it can be a problem in the context of close relationships. Negative schemas, like concluding that your partner is lazy, stubborn, selfish, or uncaring, can be extremely powerful and damaging.

Schemas can include labeling another person's personality, such as thinking of someone as crazy, boring, vain, or selfish, and assigning motivations or intention, such as assuming that your partner is trying to make you jealous or only cares about sex. Schemas can also include assumptions you make about your partner's feelings about you, such as "She thinks I'm incompetent" or "He thinks I'm ditzy." Negative schemas are strengthened by what you see as evidence that the schema is true, while evidence to the contrary is often ignored or downplayed.

For example, Susanna tends to need a lot of time to herself and isn't a big partier. Her husband, Marlon, is more of an extrovert, so he sometimes gets frustrated with Susanna's tendency to withdraw into herself. He's developed some negative schemas about her, thinking of her as "unfriendly" and a "loner." Conversely, Susanna doesn't understand why Marlon has a problem with her need to have time alone, and she has a negative schema of him as "selfish" and "immature" because he loves loud parties and frequently tries to drag her along to them when she'd rather be at home reading a book.

Marlon conveniently forgets the times that Susanna has agreed to party with him and even seemed to enjoy herself, and Susanna similarly doesn't take into account the time that Marlon surprised her for her birthday with a candlelit dinner at home and the times he has wanted to go out but agreed to stay in with her instead and watch a movie. Their schemas about each other are often at the core of the fights they have, especially during the weekends, when their different personality styles tend to clash.

Identifying Negative Schemas

The first step in identifying negative schemas is to keep a thought log. In just two weeks of logging your interactions with your partner, you'll discover the assumptions and conclusions you regularly make about your partner, often without even knowing that you're doing it.

Your thought log should have three columns, labeled "Situation," "Thoughts," and "Consequences." In the situation column, write down the circumstances surrounding any conflict you've had with your partner, especially a situation where you've felt strong negative emotions in relation to your partner, even if there was no overt argument or fight. In the thoughts column, write down what you were thinking about yourself or your partner in that moment, or how you explained your partner's behavior. Did you say bitterly to yourself, "My feelings don't matter in this relationship" or "She's so selfish!" or "There he goes again. All he cares about is hanging out with the guys"? You might have also been making assumptions about how your partner feels about you, such as "She obviously thinks I'm dumb" or "He's not attracted to me anymore." In the consequence column, write down what happened as a result of those thoughts or assumptions, such as how you or your partner reacted. Here's a sample log from Marie about her relationship with Tina:

Situation	Thoughts	Consequences
It's Saturday. I want to go do something different today, but Tina doesn't want to do anything I suggest.	She never wants to do anything fun. God forbid we go out and do something I like! She's a stick-in-the-mud, never wants to take any risks!	I'm very cool as I put away the breakfast things. Unresponsive to her comments.
Tina and I planned to go to dinner. She called at five saying she was getting ready to leave the house, but she didn't get to my house until seven.	She's always late; it never fails. Just tack on two hours to the time she says she'll be ready.	Frustrated but try to put a good face on it during dinner. Give her a quick kiss afterward, and when she starts to pull me closer, I pull away and say I'm tired, just want to go to sleep.

Tina says something judgmental about my father and pretends to be joking.	I just want to smack her. How dare she judge my family! She's always making fun of me. It's like it's her way to feel better about herself.	I snap at her, bring up her own crazy family members. She gets hurt and pissy.

Schema-Driven Responses

As Marie continues to keep her log, she realizes that she's quick to assume that Tina's behavior translates to Tina not valuing her very much. Marie tends to feel judged by Tina, even by such things as Tina being late or not feeling like going out on a Saturday. Marie assumes Tina thinks she's uninteresting and not worth a great deal of effort. Marie also sees that she tends to withdraw and punish Tina for any infraction. Even when Marie tries to forget an incident, it's hard for her to do so, and she often acts passive-aggressively, pretending that things are fine but then withdrawing, saying she's "too tired" to spend time with Tina when, in reality, she's upset at Tina. Although some of Tina's behavior is genuinely a problem, Marie's reactions don't help matters. More often than not, both women just end up tense and angry, and nothing ever gets resolved.

As you analyze your own thought log, look for patterns of reactions on your part and how they contributed to the conflict. What are the core assumptions you tend to make about your partner's behavior? How do you react when these schemas come into play? How might your reaction reinforce your partner's behavior? Do your schemas help or hinder your closeness with your partner during conflict? List five of the core schemas you've noticed from your log. You can use one word or a sentence or two to describe your schema. Here's what Marie wrote:

1. "Tina is irresponsible."

2. "She thinks I'm boring."

3. "She's dull and boring."

4. "She doesn't care about me."

5. "She's selfish."

The Cost of Your Schemas

Now look at your record of consequences. How do you tend to react when your schema surfaces in your partner's behavior? What do you say? How do you feel? Marie gets cold and distant and withdraws from Tina, or she snaps at Tina, because she feels rejected whenever Tina doesn't respond to her the way she wants her to. Marie's reactions create more distance, when what she really wants is to be closer to Tina and to feel more accepted by her.

Imagine how you might respond to conflict if you weren't interpreting your partner's behavior through the lens of your schema. For example, if Marlon didn't have the schema that Susanna is unfriendly, because she often doesn't want to party with him, he might not get so irritated at her for declining his invitations to parties, and they might not fight so much on the weekends. If Susanna didn't operate from the schema that Marlon was immature for partying so much, she might be more open to suggesting alternative ways for them to be together that they both might enjoy.

Take this opportunity to list five ways you commonly react when your schemas are triggered and the effects of these reactions on your relationship. Here's an example of what Marlon wrote:

Reaction	Effects
"I get irritated at Susanna and say something sarcastic or mean, like 'Oh, I guess you just want to sit at home with a book again. Wow, sounds like fun!'"	"She gets pissed off and goes into her room or outside, shutting me out."
"When I'm getting ready to go, I sing or whistle really loudly, which I know annoys her. It takes us at least a day to get over it. That's the whole weekend, gone!"	"By the time I leave, we're both so mad that we don't even say good-bye."

Now write how you might react if you felt totally neutral about the situation and what the result might be if you reacted from this neutral place. Here's what Marlon wrote.

Reaction	Effects
"If Susanna says she doesn't want to go out, I could kiss her and say, 'Okay, honey. I'd love to spend time with you, but I'll see you when I get back.'"	"We wouldn't get in a fight that weekend, and we could spend some time the next day doing something we both enjoy. No fighting. Imagine that!"

Checking Out Your Schemas

The best way to put your schemas to rest is to examine them objectively. Schemas gain strength through your brain's tendency to see only supporting evidence that your assumptions are true and to ignore or trivialize evidence to the contrary. Schemas seldom withstand close scrutiny, because simplistic assumptions cannot account for the complexities of human behavior.

To disprove a schema, you can look for evidence that your assumptions are untrue. For each of your schemas about your partner, write down three things your partner has said or done that disprove the schema. For example, Marie's schema about Tina not caring for her was disproved by the time Tina rushed her to the emergency room, leaving an important work meeting and staying with her at the hospital for two days.

Another way to take power from your schemas is to check them out with your partner. This may be scary, but it can open up a dialogue, clear the air, and vastly improve the quality of your interactions. With your list of core schemas in front of you, pick one that is the least threatening and seems the easiest to face. Write a script for how you might check with your partner about that schema's validity. The script should open with a neutral phrase, such as "I've been wondering if …" or "Sometimes I feel as though …" and conclude with a nonattacking, nonblaming description of your schema.

For example, Paul had a schema that his wife, Doris, thought he was not very smart. She corrected him frequently in conversation, and he often felt lectured by her. He sometimes heard her making jokes at his expense with friends and family about how "he was pretty to look at" but that she really "wore the pants in the family." His script to check out this schema with Doris went like this: "Doris, I've been wondering about something lately. I sometimes feel like you might think I'm not very smart. I've heard those jokes you make with your family about me being window dressing, and I've noticed that you correct me a lot when we talk. Is it true that you think I'm not smart?"

When Paul got up the nerve to check out his schema about Doris thinking he was stupid, he discovered that Doris felt a lot of anxiety about her own intelligence because she often felt dull and stupid around others. She overcompensated by correcting Paul and playing up her competence in running the household. After they spoke, she realized that what she was doing was hurting Paul, and they were both able to reassure one another that neither thought the other was stupid. The conversation permanently altered how they related, and it led to several other intense, honest, and ultimately eye-opening conversations between them about their other schemas.

Couples Systems

Another way to understand couples' interactions is from a system perspective. A *system* is a negative behavior pattern that couples repeat over and over. Even though you can sometimes see that the pattern is destructive, you can't seem to stop fighting the same old battles.

Negative couples systems are circular patterns of action and reaction. One person will react to something the other has done, then that person will react, and so on. Reactions can include anything from physical actions to comments to emotional outbursts. The origins of the fight are lost in the mist of history, and there is no end in sight.

For example, Sheila and Octavio's system looks like this: For the last few months, Octavio often has worked on weekdays until nine or ten o'clock at night, and many weeks has gone into the office for four or five hours on Saturdays. He's worried about money and wants to pay down his credit card debt. His longtime partner, Sheila, who works nine to five Monday through Friday, has started getting anxious when she returns home at six o'clock and Octavio isn't there. She often waits for him until he comes home, telling him, as soon as he comes through the door, that they need to talk about their relationship. After being home for hours worrying, she seems anxious and needy to Octavio, who usually feels tired and hungry after working long hours. Faced with what he sees as Sheila's neediness, he feels overwhelmed and will often disappear into the bedroom for an hour or so, telling her that he's too tired to talk and that they can talk later. Sheila, overwrought from thinking all evening about the trouble with their relationship, sees this as a sign that he doesn't care about her. She gets more and more emotional and frantic, demanding that Octavio come out and talk to her. Octavio eventually comes out to get something to eat, complaining that he never gets any peace and quiet when he's home. As the evening wears on, the couple will often alternately snipe at and avoid each other, leaving them both unhappy and exhausted. The next day, Octavio, wanting to placate Sheila, will try to be extra sweet to her, sometimes leaving her a loving note before he leaves for work or calling her on his lunch break to say hello. She will often withdraw, speaking in monosyllables on the phone, her voice sad and quiet. Octavio sometimes feels as if he must seduce her all over again, but he always wins her over. Usually, though, his attention only lasts for a day or two before he focuses back on his work and continues the old pattern of staying at work late and working on the weekend. After several days of this, Sheila once again begins to get anxious about the relationship, and the cycle continues.

In this system, you can see that Sheila and Octavio are reacting to each other. Sheila feels lonely when Octavio works so much, so she pushes him for more contact. He feels overwhelmed and blamed in her attempts to get closer to him, so he withdraws, leaving her feeling anxious about his love for her. His habit of spending long hours at work may even be, at least partly, an attempt to distance himself from an uncomfortable situation. To both of them, the other person is at fault. Octavio thinks to himself, "If only Sheila would just let me have some time to unwind and relax, I'd enjoy being with her more." And Sheila thinks, "If Octavio spent more time with me, I wouldn't have to always be pushing him to talk to me." But in reality, the two of them are enmeshed in an unhealthy system that leaves them both unsatisfied with the relationship.

Three Common Couples Systems

Although every relationship is unique, researchers and couples therapists frequently see three couples systems: pursuer-distancer, blamer-placater, and overfunctioner-underfunctioner.

Pursuer-Distancer

Sheila and Octavio are a good example of a pursuer-distancer couple. Sheila demands Octavio open up about their relationship, and Octavio, in turn, distances himself from her demands by withdrawing. The more she pursues, the more he distances. They both fail to get their needs met, and both are dissatisfied with each other's role in the system.

Blamer-Placater

In this system, one of the partners takes on a blaming role, often criticizing the other's appearance, behavior, or opinions, or blaming him or her for being "the problem" in the relationship. The other partner, eager to avoid conflict at all costs, agrees with the blaming partner and tries to "do better" next time. Because the placating partner concedes to the blamer, the criticizing partner gets positive reinforcement for the blaming behavior, and the placating partner gets what he or she wants, which is a temporary end to the criticism.

Overfunctioner-Underfunctioner

An overfunctioner-underfunctioner system may operate in one of several ways, but in all of them, one partner acts as the adult or caretaker and the other acts as the child or the sick or irresponsible one.

There are three types of this system. The first is *child-parent*, in which one partner acts as the parent—paying bills, staying in touch with friends, making medical and dental appointments, buying clothes, and so on. The other partner acts as the child, being taken care of most of the time.

The second over/under functioner system is *alcoholic-enabler*. One partner abuses alcohol or drugs, while the other partner enables the use by partaking in it, taking care of the other partner when he or she has overindulged, or lying to friends and family about the extent of the partner's use.

The third type of over/under functioner system is *sick person-caretaker*. In this system, the relationship is organized around one person's psychiatric or physical illness with the well person taking care of the sick person, in effect becoming the sick person's nurse. While taking care of your partner is not in itself unhealthy, this dynamic can get in the way of the relationship.

Diagramming Your System

Do any of the systems above seem familiar to you? Most people find that they play different roles at different times, but one role is particularly problematic. You know your particular couples system is in play when you have that *here we go again* feeling. You may see it coming from miles away and may even have resolved, this time, to change your reactions. Then you find yourself and your partner having the same old fight all over again. This pull to keep the system stable and unchanging is called *homeostasis* and is one reason why changing an enmeshed system can be so difficult.

Try this exercise: Think about the last time you thought, "I am so sick of having this fight all the time!" On a blank sheet of paper, describe the situation that caused you to have that feeling of familiarity. Be as detailed as possible. Then begin to trace the fight backward, writing down what was happening before that moment, when things were just starting to become tense or conflicted. Next, write what was happening even before then, when you were still feeling good about things, before the tension arose.

Read your description and see if you can place blame for starting the fight. If it seems obvious to you who started it, keep tracing back the conflict until you can no longer assign blame to one or the other of you. For example, if you think, "He started it. All I did was ask where he put the dish towels Aunt Maude gave us for our anniversary. Then he snapped at me and we had a big fight!" go back to that question about the dish towels. What was your tone? What were you thinking when you asked the question? Were any of your negative schemas in play, such as "He never puts anything where it should go. I always have to do everything around here!"? What was happening between you at the time? Had anything happened earlier, such as a fight or difficult interaction? Were either of you angry, anxious, irritated, tired, busy, or sad, and how did that affect your interaction? If you're willing to honestly look at the elements of your conflict, you'll see that there are often very old issues underlying the fight.

You should eventually be able to complete a circle, drawing an arrow from the beginning of the conflict to the end, from the place where both people are at peace, but there are seeds of conflict, to the place where the fight has occurred and both people are at peace again. Here is how Sheila and Octavio's system can be traced:

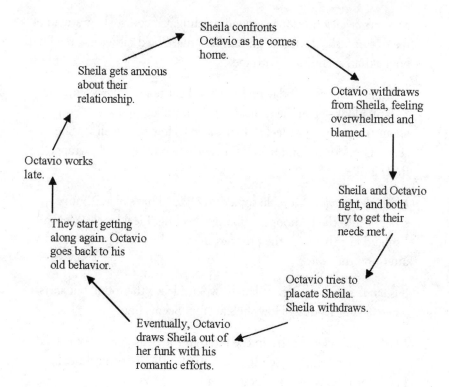

Now, rediagram your description in this circular format. Include how you and your partner were feeling emotionally at each step. Get your partner to help you diagram your system. The purpose of this is to trace the pattern of interaction from one person's feelings to his or her actions to the partner's reactions, feelings, and actions, and so on around the circle, showing how each step in a conflict is a reaction to a previous one. Here's how Marlon traced his conflict with Susanna:

Marlon's behavior: Tuesday I get an email from a friend about a party on Friday, so I forward it to Susanna. Feeling: Excited, he throws great parties!

Susanna's behavior: She emails straight back, saying, "I was really looking forward to staying in tomorrow, reading my book by the fire. It's been a stressful week. Sorry, hon." How she's feeling: Seems fine.

Marlon's behavior: I don't respond. Feeling: Of course, how stupid of me to think she'd want to go out with me! She'd rather just read her books than spend time with me.

Susanna's behavior: Friday night, when I get home from work, Susanna looks up at me from the couch, smiles, and says, "Sorry about the party, I just feel so exhausted." How she's feeling: She seems comfortable and happy sitting there on the couch, wrapped in a blanket.

Marlon's behavior: Mumble something like "That's okay," but go straight into the bedroom to change. Feeling: I feel lonely. Maybe I should just flirt with the other women at the party, get some attention that way.

Susanna's behavior: Sort of laughs when I leave the room, but stays where she is, reading. How she's feeling: Seems fine.

Marlon's behavior: I turn up the radio in the bedroom to some loud dance music, to get myself in the mood for the party. Feeling: I feel like I don't care anymore. Screw her.

Susanna's behavior: Shouts over the music, "Thanks, Marlon, that's really relaxing. I'm so glad you understand." How she's feeling: Seems pissed.

Marlon's behavior: I don't do anything. Just keep dressing, dancing in the room. Feeling: Glad she's pissed.

After getting dressed, Marlon shuts off the music, tells Susanna he'll grab something to eat on the way, even though it's too early to leave, and slams the door. He comes home after Susanna has gone to bed. Marlon's log continues:

Susanna's behavior: The next morning, she gets out of bed early and takes the car. Doesn't leave a note or anything. How she's feeling: Probably pissed from last night.

Marlon's behavior: I lie in bed. Feeling: Lonely and stupid, like I messed up again.

Intervening in Your System

Unhealthy systems change faster when both partners are actively involved. If that is not possible, one partner acting unilaterally can make real changes. But it will take longer to overcome the homeostasis of the system. Either way, change takes time, so be patient.

To intervene is your system, look over your diagram and find the weak links, the times when it's easier to interrupt the pattern:

- Early in the interaction, before anyone is highly upset.

- When you are calm enough to stop your impulse to attack your partner.

- When your behavior is reinforcing problematic responses in your partner, often the very behavior in your partner that causes you the most grief.

In the example of Marlon and Susanna, Marlon might identify one weak link as the moment when he interprets Susanna declining a party invitation as proof that she doesn't want to spend time with him, the moment when he experiences a familiar sinking feeling in his heart. At this point, he can choose whether to lash out at her, get defensive and hurt, or act in another, healthier way.

Once you identify the weak link, follow these five steps to intervene in the system:

1. *Stop doing what you always do.* This may be easier said than done, but it's the crucial first step in interrupting an entrenched pattern. Even if you choose to say nothing in a situation where you usually criticize your partner or defend yourself, the pattern will be interrupted.

2. *Describe your feelings using whole messages.* (See chapter 3 for more on this.) In this step, you'll need to talk to your partner directly about your feelings and needs in this situation rather than resort to indirect behavior or speech that typically reinforces the system. You've already identified your normal reactions and behaviors in your pattern, so now take the time to write out a script that states your needs in the familiar situation and without criticizing or blaming your partner.

3. *Reinforce new behavior.* The reason why your system has become so entrenched is that your behavior reinforces your partner's behavior and vice versa. The only way to create a new, healthier system is to reinforce new, healthier behavior. Think of what you would like to happen *instead* of what normally happens in your current system and then consider how you can reinforce this desired behavior.

4. *Describe your system.* If you are working with your partner to change your system, take the time to describe what you see happening in the system. This step is optional if your partner is not involved in this process with you or if you feel like describing your system would create more problems than it would solve. Be careful to describe your system in neutral language, without blaming either your partner or yourself for what's happening. Make it clear that you're both trapped in old patterns of behavior that don't serve either of you, and you're trying to change the cycle for the better of the relationship.

5. *Negotiate new solutions.* This step is not necessary if your partner is uninvolved in the process or if he or she is not open to negotiation. If negotiation is an option, though, it can be a powerful tool for changing your pattern. Remember that you and your partner

both have valid needs, and your negotiations should be focused on getting both your needs met, not on forcing your partner to change to meet your needs. (Refer to chapter 11 for help on negotiating.)

Sheila realized, finally, that if she and Octavio didn't change their pattern of relating, their relationship would be perennially frustrating and unfulfilling for both of them. She realized she wasn't getting what she needed by hounding Octavio for reassurances that he loved her, so she decided to work to change their system. Sheila's guidelines looked like this:

1. She pledged to herself to stop her pattern of jumping on Octavio as soon as he came home from work, wanting him to talk about their relationship. She realized this behavior caused Octavio to withdraw to escape what he saw as unreasonable demands on his energy. She decided she'd concentrate more on living the life she wanted to live rather than worrying excessively about her relationship with Octavio.

2. After thinking about it for a while, she wrote a script that expressed her needs without blaming Octavio. Her script read, "Octavio, when you spend so much time at work, even on the weekends, I feel as if I'm losing you. I feel sad, like your work is more important than I am. I love you and I want to spend time with you, just being together. I also know your work is important to you, and I don't want to take you away from it. But I'd like it if we could work out a plan where you can spend some weekends and evenings with me instead of at the office."

3. Sheila decided that she would reinforce Octavio's behavior of coming home at a reasonable hour by greeting him with a hug and kiss, or a sincere inquiry about his day, when she was at home. If she went out, she'd leave him a friendly note letting him know where she was and when she'd be back. If she was at home feeling unhappy or anxious when Octavio returned from work, she would tell him what was happening for her in a calm tone with non-blaming language, taking responsibility for her own feelings. She

also decided to ask Octavio to save one weekend day a month where they could spend quality time together, letting him choose the weekend based on his work schedule.

4. Sheila picked a time when she and Octavio had a Sunday together and they were feeling close to one another. She didn't want Octavio to feel defensive or blindsided, so she brought up the topic of their relationship by first kissing him and ruffling his hair affectionately, which she knew he liked, and asking if she could be serious for a moment. She told him she'd been anxious about their relationship for a while and wanted his help in changing their pattern, so they wouldn't fight so much. She then described what she thought their system was, asking for his input along the way, using validation and whole messages as she described what happened for her in their pattern.

5. Since Octavio wasn't on board at first, Sheila didn't negotiate any solutions.

Octavio had a hard time admitting that he might have any role in the situation. In his eyes, all he wanted was some peace and quiet after working long hours. He figured Sheila should do all the changing; after all, she was the problem, wasn't she? He listened to her frustrations but thought the idea of intervening in the system was silly. "Just don't nag me when I come home from work, okay?" he said, effectively ending the discussion.

Sheila was frustrated that he couldn't see her side of things but decided she didn't have any choice but to change her own actions anyway. If she didn't change, they would both stay stuck in their unhealthy system. Instead of sitting at home thinking about why Octavio was once again working late, and worrying about their relationship, she started to make plans with friends once or twice a week to go out to a meal or a movie, and often came home after Octavio did. She recommitted herself to learning Spanish, which she'd always wanted to do, and made a list of books she had always wanted to read. After two weeks of her new behavior, she felt more relaxed, less anxious, and better about her place in the relationship.

Now, when Octavio came home late, Sheila was sometimes home studying or reading, and sometimes he would find a note she had left him saying she was out with friends or at a museum or a gallery exhibit. At first

Octavio felt relieved and enjoyed being able to decompress after work without needing to defend his right to work late. But then a funny thing happened: he started to miss her. When she wasn't at home in the evening, even though he was glad she was out living her own life, he missed being able to tell her about his day and to ask her about hers. When she was home reading or studying, even though she usually greeted him with a smile, it seemed clear that she was content whether or not he was there. So after about two months, he asked her if they could spend more quality time together. Sheila told him she'd love nothing more than to spend more time with him, and she showed him the list she'd made that had helped her change how she behaved in the relationship. Then she asked him if he'd come up with a similar list so that they could make a plan to strengthen their relationship together. Octavio's guidelines looked like this:

1.   He not only resolved to commit to spending two nights a week and one weekend day with Sheila, but he also decided to call Sheila each night that he decided to work late, to let her know when he thought he'd be home. He also decided that if Sheila was upset or anxious when he came home, rather than disappear into his room he would take some time to ask her what was wrong and to respond in a caring way. He decided that if he needed some time alone after his workday, he would tell Sheila of his need, using nonjudgmental language.

2.   Octavio's script read like this: "Sheila, when I come home from working hard and find you immediately wanting to talk about the relationship, I feel overwhelmed and resentful. I'd like some room in this relationship to do what I need to do—which is to work overtime, so I can pay off my debt—and spend some time alone and with other friends without feeling like I'm abandoning you. But I also love you and I want to spend time with you when we can be relaxed around each other, not always talking about 'the relationship.' I'd like us to decide on some time that's 'our time,' but then also be free to do other things on other days, like work late, play basketball with the guys, or just read my book in the living room."

3. Octavio decided to reinforce Sheila's new behavior by sincerely asking her about her day and her feelings, once he had some time to relax after his day, and to use more active listening and validation techniques to show his care for her. He also resolved to be more affectionate in general and to try to be more present on the days that were designated as their time together.

4. Sheila and Octavio had some differences in how they saw their system, so they spent some time comparing their versions of things. Although they never fully agreed on what was happening between them, in the end they came to a mutual agreement on the basic structure of their system and understood each other's feelings better, because they took the time to honestly listen to one another.

5. Sheila and Octavio negotiated the days that he would be fully available to spend time with her and also agreed to revisit their new pattern after a month to see how it was working for each of them.

Exploring Needs and Solutions

Marlon and Susanna went through this process also, and they found it helpful to write down their needs and solutions. Each kept the final list of solutions with them, to remind themselves of what they'd agreed to. Here's what was on it:

1. Marlon agreed that he tended to overreact to Susanna choosing not to go out with him, so he agreed to explore alternate ways of reacting to his feelings of being rejected by her. He decided he'd try to take some deep breaths when he felt that familiar sense of being rejected and to remember that it wasn't necessarily that Susanna didn't want to be with him. If this didn't work, he agreed to explore different techniques for slowing down his impulse to lash out when he felt rejected.

2. Susanna discovered that she tended to instantly reject Marlon's invitations because she felt they were a test of her love for him.

She agreed that she would consider each invitation closely, instead of just rejecting it out of hand, and that if she really didn't want to go, she would tell Marlon in an honest, nonblaming way.

3. Susanna also knew he was sensitive about being rejected, so she agreed to be sensitive to that and to show him affection and love more consistently throughout the week.

4. Susanna also agreed to curb her impulses to withdraw from Marlon when he was upset and to be sarcastic and mean in response to his feelings of hurt. She agreed to explore other ways of reacting and to communicate her feelings in an honest, nonblaming way.

5. Marlon and Susanna agreed to spend at least one weekend evening and one weekday evening together, alternating between things Marlon wanted to do and things Susanna wanted to do.

Keeping Your Relationship Strong

A healthy relationship takes two partners who are willing to honestly face the inevitable problems that will crop up. If problems aren't dealt with, one or both of you will begin to harbor resentment, anger, and disappointment, which can easily smother the love and positive regard you felt for each other in the beginning. This chapter gives you a set of skills to use to look honestly at your unhealthy patterns of communication and take steps to make changes in how you interact together, which will go far in ensuring that your relationship remains strong, vibrant, and healthy.

16 Communicating with Children

To be an effective parent is to realize two things: that you are a human being with problems and that your children are human beings with problems.

As a human being, you have basic needs for food, clothing, shelter, warmth, affection, love, security, relaxation, and so on. You go about getting these needs met in ways that are more or less effective. Sometimes you succeed and sometimes you make mistakes and fail. Sometimes other people thwart your attempts to get your needs met, and then you have a problem.

As a human being, a child has the same needs, tries to get them met, makes mistakes, and has problems when needs are thwarted.

How well you and your child communicate will determine how well you solve your problems. There are three critical communication skills required for effective parenting: listening, expressing, and joint problem solving. These are applicable whether your child is a three-year-old or a teenager.

Listening

Reread chapter 1, on listening, realizing this time that it applies to communication with children as well as adults. If you're like most people, you don't listen to children the same way you listen to adults. You fall into adult chauvinism. When you're being an adult chauvinist, you tend not to listen to kids, because they are smaller, younger, weaker, uninformed, inexperienced—what of value could they possibly have to say to you? You automatically assume that you know how they feel because, after all, you were a kid yourself and you know all about it.

When you talk to your children, you are likely to engage in many of the common blocks to listening outlined in chapter 1, especially these:

Listening Block	Statement
Judging	"That's where you're wrong." "You're too emotional."
Advising	"Try asking Jack over here to play." "Why don't you do your math first, when you're fresh?"
Placating	"Right, right, you'll feel better tomorrow." "Uh-huh, these things happen."
Derailing	"Haven't I heard this story before?" "Just blow their stupid clubhouse up, then." "Can't we talk about something pleasant at dinner for a change?"
Mind reading	"He's just jealous of his sister." "You're doing this to spite me."

You are also prone to special listening blocks that you'd seldom fall into with your adult friends but that arise out of power struggles between children and adults:

Listening Block	Statement
Ordering	"Go to your room and clean it up now." "Don't you ever use that tone of voice with me."
Threatening	"You'll be sorry." "If you don't behave tonight, there'll be no allowance for you for a month."
Moralizing	"Nice girls don't talk like that." "You should always respect adults."

Lecturing	"Let's analyze this rationally." "Your college years are the best time of your life."
Ineffective praising	"Well, I think you look just fine." "But you did really well for your age."
Pitying	"Poor baby." "I'm sorry you're in such a mess."
Shaming	"You're disgusting." "What a rotten, dirty thing to do."
Interrogating	"So how do your friends spend their money? On what? How much?" "Exactly what will you do if you drop out of school now?"
Denying	"You don't miss that ugly old neighborhood." "You don't hate Grandma."

Your child needs to express important feelings and desires. These feelings and desires can't be denied, shamed, interrogated, or threatened away. Nor can they be ignored. If you fail to listen, the feelings may go underground or turn into confusion or rage. They won't simply disappear.

In actively listening to your children, the most important ability a parent needs is empathy. Children have intense feelings and little experience in effectively communicating them. Sometimes you may need to decode your child's feelings. To do this, you have to separate the feelings from the content of what's said and give the feelings a name.

Here's a father responding to a question from his three-year-old son:

Son: Are there big kids in preschool?

Father: No, they're all about the same age as you.

Son: Oh.

In this case, the father has responded to the content of the question. He thinks nothing more about this interchange, and his son throws a tantrum the first day of preschool, refusing to get out of the car. Here's the same question, with a response to the feeling:

Son: Are there big kids in preschool?

Father: You're nervous about preschool.

Son: Big kids might hit me.

Father: You're afraid of being hit.

Son: Yeah, and they don't play with you.

Father: You'd feel left out if they wouldn't play with you.

The father doesn't have to reassure his son by making up lies about the complete fairness and safety of preschool or to shame him for being afraid. Responding to the feelings by naming and feeding them back is enough. The son gets to work through some of his vague fears before they mount to panic in the car on the way to school.

Another effective strategy this father is using is that of making his responses in the form of statements rather than questions. This may seem artificial and contrived at first, but it can be very helpful. All too often, questions asked of children take on a badgering, cross-examining tone. Making simple statements instead of asking questions is a way of avoiding the temptation to cross-examine your child. Also, since questions require answers, they have a way of leading the conversation. When you make simple statements that can be confirmed, denied, or ignored, you allow your child to retain more control of the conversation.

Exercise 16.1

To get practice in recognizing feelings, read these typical messages children send. Listen carefully for feelings. In the second column, write the feelings you heard. Discard the content and write in only the feelings in two or three words. Some of the statements may contain several different feelings.

What Child Says	How Child Is Feeling
Example: "I don't know what is wrong. I can't figure it out. Maybe I should just quit trying."	Stumped. Discouraged. Tempted to give up.
1. "Oh boy, only ten more days until school's out."	
2. "Look, Daddy, I made an airplane with my new tools!"	
3. "Will you hold my hand when we go into preschool?"	
4. "Gee, I'm not having any fun. I can't think of anything to do."	
5. "I'll never be good like Jim. I practice and practice, and he's still better than me."	
6. "My new teacher gives us too much homework. I can never get it all done. What'll I do?"	
7. "All the other kids went to the beach. I don't have anyone to play with."	
8. "Jim's parents let him ride his bike to school, but I'm a better rider than Jim."	
9. "I shouldn't have been so mean to little Jimmy. I guess I was bad."	
10. "But I want to get my lip pierced—it's my body, isn't it?"	

Possible answers: 1. Glad, happy, relieved. 2. Proud, confident, pleased. 3. Afraid, fearful, nervous, apprehensive. 4. Bored, restless, stumped. 5. Inadequate, discouraged, envious. 6. Defeated, discouraged, overwhelmed. 7. Left behind, abandoned, lonely, jealous. 8. Discriminated against, competent, confident. 9. Guilty, regretful, sorry, repentant. 10. Resentful, defiant, threatened.

Active listening alone will often clear up your child's problem without any further input from you. For example, this mother's eight-year-old son has had a run-in with his teacher:

> *Son:*   Why did she make me stay after school anyway? I wasn't the only one who was talking. I hate her.

> *Mother:*   You're really angry at that teacher.

> *Son:*   Yeah. But I don't hate her for making me stay after. It's the other guys who got away with it.

> *Mother:*   You feel persecuted. She singled you out.

> *Son:*   She just picks on one kid to punish so that everybody else will shut up.

> *Mother:*   You don't like that.

> *Son:*   Aw, I can take it. I guess I was just unlucky she saw me first. Next time I'll be more careful, and she can pick on someone else.

> *Mother:*   You'll play it cool.

> *Son:*   Yeah.

When active listening alone doesn't clear up a problem, you'll have to move on to joint problem solving. But you'll be surprised how listening can solve apparently impossible problems by reducing your child's anxiety to the point where it can be endured or ignored.

Expressing

Reread chapter 3, on self-expression, noticing that you need to make yourself clear to your children just as carefully as you do with adults. As with listening, adult chauvinism can be a trap: why take care when a mere child is bugging you? The following sections cover five basic principles for effectively expressing yourself to your child.

Specificity

What you want and feel should be communicated as specifically as possible. Children want and need clear limits—boundaries within which they can operate freely and securely, and outside of which they can expect natural consequences. Here are some examples of clearly stated expectations:

"I expect that you will take your bath before doing your homework."

"I want you in tonight by five o'clock."

"Please clean the counters, the stovetop, and the sink when you're working in the kitchen today."

The following are examples of nonspecific expectations:

"Don't go to school stinky again."

"I want you in early."

"I want you to clean up the whole kitchen."

Praise should also be specific. Such superlatives as "great," "fantastic," or "beautiful" aren't always believable and don't help your child learn to praise himself or herself. Specific praise tells exactly what you like and why you like it. Here are some examples:

"You did the dishes without my asking."

"You were warm and friendly to your cousin and included her in everything right away."

"Your homework was really carefully printed and showed a lot of effort."

Hearing specific praise that describes exactly what he or she is doing right, your child can begin to tell himself or herself the same things:

"I do chores without being asked."

"I'm a warm and friendly person."

"I do much neater work now."

Feelings can also be expressed specifically. I-messages that describe what you feel and what provoked the feeling give your child important information about what goes on inside you: "I feel hurt and unappreciated when you forget to thank me for driving you to Becky's house." Your child learns much more from this I-message than if you angrily accuse her of ingratitude.

Immediacy

Say what bothers you when it bothers you. Reward good behavior right away. Studies show that children learn best when they are rewarded or punished immediately following what they do. The longer you wait to express your reactions, the less impact you'll have on your child's behavior.

When you establish a consequence for misbehavior, it should be immediate. For example, suppose your four-year-old daughter doesn't stop jumping up and down on the couch when you tell her to stop. Putting her in time-out for five minutes, right away, would be an immediate consequence that would adequately reinforce your rule about standing on the furniture. The delayed consequence of "no TV tomorrow" would be harsher but would actually be less effective because it would occur long after the misbehavior.

Some parents always try to be nice. They stockpile their negative feelings until some minor infraction triggers a massive explosion. Children get the message that they're bad and worthy of rejection. And the behavior doesn't improve, because there's no way of linking your anger to the specific things they've done.

Nonjudgment

All your communication to your children should include the implication that they are basically lovable and capable. Blaming, name-calling, and sarcasm communicate that the child, and not just the behavior, is not okay.

Let's say that your son, who's habitually messy, can't find a vital homework assignment in his room. You have a choice. You can vent your feelings by labeling him inept and stupid. Or you can take the position that this is a problem that needs attention. The room needs to be cleaner, and homework needs to be kept in a special place.

When things go really wrong, you can still express strong disapproval without attacking your child's character. "Stop that right now. There will be no playing with your food at the table" is a stern but not assaulting message. The child can still feel basically loved. "Why do you have to act like a slob? You're always making a mess" communicates contempt. The message is "You're not an okay person."

There are three good ways to avoid blaming and name-calling:

1. *Omit the word "you" when describing a situation or problem:* "I see a little boy with dirty hands and dirty face at the dinner table." "I see a bedroom with toys on the floor and dirty and clean clothes mixed up in the drawers."

2. *Give information:* "Dirty dishes belong in the sink." "Milk gets sour if it's left out of the refrigerator." "Toys get ruined when they're left outside."

3. *Say the message in one word:* "Bedtime." Not "What are you doing up past bedtime?" Or "Teeth." Not "You always forget to brush your teeth."

The development of good self-esteem in your child very much depends on the messages you communicate. Consistent "you're bad" messages eventually create an "I'm bad" self-concept. A commitment to nonjudgment is a major step toward raising a healthy child.

Consistency

Children are confused by inconsistent messages. If you tell your son that he has to be in by five but you only enforce the rule once in a while, you'll find that your son habitually ignores the five o'clock deadline. The rule ceases to affect his behavior, but it can afford a perfect opportunity for you to vent some anger when you've had a bad day. If homework is supposed to be done before your daughter gets on the phone but most days you're too tired to remind her, the rule will soon be forgotten. You can always resurrect the rule, however, when you feel annoyed about something else.

Allow children to consistently experience the consequences of misbehavior. Letting them off teaches a lesson you don't want them to learn: that irresponsibility pays. If you and your child have agreed that failure to clean the bedroom on Sunday will result in grounding on Monday after school, keep your word. You'll be a believable person, and your child will learn that misbehavior does have consequences.

It's easier to be consistent if your consequences are natural—if they follow logically from the infraction. For example, the natural consequence of forgetting your coat is to be cold until you retrieve the coat from where you left it. The natural consequence of not doing your chores is no allowance this week. The natural consequence of not sharing a toy is to have the toy taken away for a while. The natural consequence of rowdiness at a birthday party is sitting quietly in a corner or leaving the party early. The natural consequence of not making your lunch before the school bus arrives is going to school without lunch. Sometimes these consequences seem extreme, but they work much better than nagging, lecturing, or applying unrelated punishments inconsistently.

Praise should also be consistent. Children need to hear when they've done well. They need approval the first time and every time until they've mastered a particular developmental skill. Each Saturday when your son keeps his promise to vacuum, he needs to hear how nice the carpet looks.

Disclosure

In most families, disclosure is a one-way street. Parents know everything about their kids, but kids know almost nothing about their parents' inner lives. Letting your child in on some of the things you feel and want makes you a real person. You cease to be an authority figure who hands down rules and punishments. The limits you set make more sense to your child when presented in the context of your feelings and needs. "Turn down the stereo" is just another irritating command unless it goes with a little self-disclosure: "They were doing some construction in the office next to mine, and my nerves are shot—would you please turn the stereo down?"

The key to effective disclosure is the use of I-messages in place of you-messages. Notice how I-messages are more self-expressive, include more feelings, are more specific, and are less likely to provoke resistance:

You-message: "How dare you waltz in here at one in the morning? You're getting damned irresponsible."

I-message: "I was very worried when twelve-thirty came and you weren't home yet. I imagined something terrible had happened. I'm relieved that you're all right, and I feel really angry about having stayed up worrying."

The rules for composing effective I-messages are very simple.

Use appropriate force. If you feel strongly, let your child know it, but don't overshoot by erupting over a relatively minor irritation.

Include all feelings. If you feel relieved, frightened, concerned, or loving, in addition to feeling angry or disappointed, be sure to mention these other emotions too.

Avoid you-messages in disguise. "I feel that you are a stupid, lazy bum" is not a legitimate I-message. It's a name-calling you-message with "I feel" pasted on the front like a clown mask on a battering ram.

Persist if ignored. Sometimes children ignore I-messages, especially if they have been receiving a heavy barrage of you-messages. You say, "I feel very sad and upset when I see my flowers pulled up," and little George just grins as he goes by on his tricycle, plowing up more of the flowerbed. Persist. Restate with more force: "Hey, George, I really mean it! I'm real sad and mad about these flowers."

Switch to active listening if you get an I-message back. Let's say you complain about the dishes not being done and your daughter says, "Yeah, but why do I have to slave in the kitchen while Bill has it easy in the yard?" You should then switch to active listening ("You resent how chores are divided") until you hear out your daughter's problem. This may lead to a full-scale joint problem-solving session, or it may result in a brief interchange after which you can return to your original I-message.

Joint Problem Solving

The most difficult time to be an effective parent is when there is a genuine conflict of needs. You have a legitimate need that interferes with your child's legitimate need, or vice versa. Common areas for this kind of conflict are chores, neatness of shared rooms like the kitchen, TV programs, loud music, the family car, where to go on vacation, and so on. There are three possible approaches to resolving these conflicts: authoritarian, permissive, and cooperative.

Authoritarian. This is the traditional approach to problems. You are the boss. You make the rules and enforce them. This solution sounds easy in theory, but unfortunately it doesn't always work. If you are overly authoritarian, your children may resist and resent your solutions to their problems. And because their behavior is externally controlled by your strict rules, they may also fail to develop self-discipline. As adolescents, they can become rebellious, withdrawn, or both. You'll then find that you spend an inordinate amount of time nagging, yelling, and punishing. A vicious cycle starts: the more they resist, the more you punish, and the more they resist. Authoritarian orders do have their place in emergency situations when you genuinely do know best and there's no time to discuss matters. You don't let your three-year-old topple into a roaring fireplace or allow your intoxicated daughter to stay overnight at a party.

Permissive. This approach is also traditional, but less common. You give your child whatever he or she wants. The trouble is that you eventually feel resentful about giving up your own needs, and your kids will pick up on that resentment, making them feel insecure about your love.

Additionally, because you don't take the trouble to provide structure for your kids, they may get the message that you don't care about them. The final problem with being overly permissive is that the rest of the world isn't so indulgent. School, work, and most peer groups have rules and expectations. Spoiled, demanding kids have a hard time surviving in a world that doesn't bend to their wishes. The time to be permissive is when you genuinely don't have a strong opinion in the matter, when your child can be trusted to make an acceptable decision, or when a poor decision won't hurt you or your child.

Cooperative. The most consistently effective approach to resolving conflict with your children is the cooperative approach. It avoids the drawbacks inherent in being either overly authoritarian or overly permissive.

The root of the evil in authoritarian or permissive systems is power—your power over your child or your child's power over you. Power at its most effective can only compel or prevent behavior. It can't change behavior in the sense of making someone else want to do what you want him or her to do.

You automatically have considerable power over your children simply because you are physically and psychologically bigger than they are. In the cooperative approach to resolving conflicts, you have to be willing to set that power aside and act as a reasonable adult meeting younger people who are also reasonable and capable of making decisions.

The goal is to jointly solve problems and find solutions that are acceptable to everyone. You have to sincerely want this and convince your kids that you are sincere. At first they may be resistant and suspicious. Try a frank approach: "I'm learning about a way to be a better parent, and I want you to try it out with me."

Implementing the Cooperative Approach

There are seven steps to joint problem solving. Sometimes a mutually acceptable solution will pop up before you have progressed through all these steps, but generally you should go through all of them in the following order:

1. **Identify and define the conflict.** If this is your first attempt at joint problem solving, pick a problem that is a long-standing one,

but not one that will make tempers flare. Pick a time when the kids aren't busy, distracted, or about to leave. State clearly, concisely, and firmly that there is a problem that must be solved. Use I-messages to convey your feelings as strongly as you feel them. Avoid you-messages that put down or blame the kids. Use active listening to elicit your kids' view of the problem. You may find the real problem is different from the apparent problem you started with. Explain that you want to find a mutually acceptable solution.

2. **Brainstorm possible solutions.** Get the children's solutions first. Younger kids may not come up with anything at first, but keep asking them. It helps develop their thinking ability and shows that you want their contribution. Treating kids as valuable sources of solutions is a good idea for two reasons: it improves their self-esteem, and it produces a lot of good ideas. At this point, only variety and quantity count. Brainstorm freely. Keep pressing everyone for one more suggestion, no matter how far-out, until all the ideas are squeezed out. Accept all solutions without judgment. Evaluation comes later. No one should say, "That won't work" or "I can't accept that." Write all the solutions down so you can remember them.

3. **Evaluate solutions.** Now is the time for judgments. Narrow down your written list by crossing off the solutions that are unacceptable to anyone in the group, for whatever reason. Eliminate any solutions that are crazy, dangerous, or too expensive.

4. **Pick the best solution.** The best solution is the one that is most acceptable to both parents and kids. The key is the acceptability of solutions, not arriving at the "correct" solution; the same problem will have different solutions in different families. Keep testing the remaining solutions against your kids' feelings. Make sure no one is being railroaded into acceptance. Point out that the chosen solution may not be the final word. The plan is to try it for a while and see if it works.

5. **Secure commitment.** Be sure everyone understands that by accepting this solution, they are taking responsibility for carrying it out and making it work. This will motivate the kids and make any agreement easier to enforce. Be sure to identify contingencies. What happens if someone breaks the agreement? Is there a penalty? Extra work? Loss of privileges? Another problem-solving session? Discuss the penalties as matter-of-fact consequences that will happen if anyone doesn't follow the plan. This lets kids know the cost of breaking an agreement, and they can weigh it in an adult manner.

6. **Implement the decision.** Agree on who is to do what, when and where, how, and under what conditions. What are the standards to measure success? Is there a time limit to the agreement? A way to call an end to a trial period? Now, go do it.

7. **Evaluate results.** Not all solutions will work well. Check from time to time that you and your kids are happy with how the solution is working. Circumstances may change. If your solution needs to be scrapped or modified, return to the brainstorming step.

Doug and Diane want to try joint problem solving with their twelve-year-old, Mark, and their ten-year-old, Susan. Susan is supposed to sweep the kitchen floor and put the clean dishes in the cupboard after the dinner dishes are done. Mark is supposed to empty all the wastebaskets whenever they're full and wheel the trash can out to the curb on Wednesday nights for pickup Thursday mornings. Here's how the family identified and defined the conflict:

Dad: I want to talk about chores. I really think evening chores are a problem. I get angry and depressed when I come into the kitchen at ten o'clock and the dishes are still sitting in the dish drainer and the trash is overflowing onto the floor. I'd like to solve this problem together.

Mom: I'm tired of nagging two or three times before the work gets done. I feel like I have to crack the whip, and I don't want to. Does this chore stuff bother you?

Mark: But I almost always do the trash before Susan does the dishes.

Susan: I can't sweep the floor until you're through making your trash mess.

Mark: It's not in your way.

Dad: Sounds like you guys do have some problems with chores. Do you want to find a way to get chores done, so everybody's satisfied?

Mark: Sure.

Susan: Yes.

Mom: Let's make sure we know what the real problem is. We want the chores done each evening. And you want not to get in each other's way. Right?

Susan: And sometimes we just can't do it, like when there's company and you don't even wash the dishes until the middle of the night.

Mark: And I can't stand the nagging.

Mom: So you feel sometimes it's impossible to do the chores, and you don't want to be nagged.

Mark: Right.

Dad: Okay, we want chores done by a reasonable time—say eight-thirty. And you want to not interfere with each other, to get out of chores when they're unreasonable, and to not get nagged?

Susan   Yeah.
and
Mark:

Next the family went on to generate a list of possible solutions.

Susan's solutions:

1. "Use paper plates."

2. "Do trash first, then floor, then dishes."

Mark's solutions:

1. "Everybody takes turns doing all chores."

2. "Do the dishes and floor first, then trash."

3. "No blaming the other guy for not doing your job."

4. "Put up reminder signs."

Mom's solutions:

1. "No dessert until chores are done."

2. "No nagging."

3. "If chores aren't done by eight-thirty, no dessert at all."

4. "Post a calendar in the kitchen for keeping records."

Dad's solutions:

1. "Buy a dishwasher and get a maid."

2. "Susan and Mark do each other's chores for variety."

3. "Allowance is cut if chores aren't done."

4. "One day a week off."

The family evaluated their solutions. They went down the written list and crossed off what was too silly (paper plates), too expensive (dishwasher and maid), unacceptable to kids (doing each other's chores, no dessert), and unacceptable to parents (parents having to take turns doing kids' chores).

To come up with the best solution, the family combined the remaining solutions:

The kids have until eight-thirty to do chores.

No blaming the other guy for preventing you from doing your job.

Mark has Thursday nights off for baseball practice.

Susan has Friday nights off because that's when company usually comes and there are many dishes that aren't ready to put away by eight-thirty.

Mom and Dad won't remind or nag.

For every night the kids don't do their chores, they lose fifty cents of their allowance.

Try this solution for a month and see how it works.

Everyone was clear about what they had to do. Mom agreed to buy and post a calendar in the kitchen for keeping records. Mark made himself several signs reminding him that Thursday was trash day.

After a month, chores were getting done consistently and everyone was satisfied. They agreed to continue the contract indefinitely. Later, Susan was allowed to choose Friday or Saturday for her night off, depending on her parents' plans for entertaining.

When to Let Go

Sometimes chronic conflicts can be alleviated if you recognize that some decisions and problems belong completely to your child. How he does his hair, whom he picks for friends, how she dresses and keeps her room, or how she spends her allowance may best be left up to the child.

To be sure, you undoubtedly have strong feelings and opinions about these things. That's only natural. And there is an almost overwhelming impulse to cast your opinions into a set of rules that must be strictly enforced. But if you try to involve yourself in these decisions, you're likely to get caught in a protracted conflict. If no basic harm is being done, you may be better off letting your child deal with these decisions.

When You Have to Say No

When you say no, you run the risk of generating tears and resistance. A good strategy for saying no is to say it indirectly. Here are five ways to set limits without using the dreaded word.

1. *Give a choice.* Instead of saying, "No TV. You've got to finish your homework," you can say, "Do you want to finish your homework now or in fifteen minutes?" You can ask, "Do you want to brush your teeth before or after the story?"

2. *Substitute yes for no.* To the question "Can we play baseball?" you answer, "Yes, after lunch." Or to a request to go over to a friend's house, you may say, "Yes, you can go over to Tommy's as soon as you finish your room."

3. *Give information.* You might say, "We're leaving in ten minutes," instead of saying, "No, you can't go outside." Instead of saying, "No football," say, "You could get really hurt. How about touch football?"

4. *Accept feelings.* "I know you really want to stay overnight. It must be hard to come home in the middle of all the fun." "It's an awful disappointment to have gotten this cold and not be able to go skiing."

5. *Explain the problem.* "I know you wanted to go to the movies tonight, but it turns out your sister will be alone in the house—she needs to have you around."

The Point Is ...

Effective parenting is based on respect for your child. Your message must be that your child is lovable and good. You can object to specific behaviors without rejecting the essential value of this person.

The statement "Your artwork is fine, but I'm upset about the crayons on the sofa" is typical of messages that promote self-acceptance. The child is still a good person even though he or she makes mistakes. Naturally there will be times when you forget and attack your child. But a commitment to separate the child's person from his or her behavior will help your child grow toward a basic feeling of self-worth.

Some parents get discouraged when they look back and see a pattern of blame and attack: "Why do I keep calling her lazy all the time? It just seems to pop out of my mouth." The truth is that it takes a long time for a child to grow up. You have time to change old patterns and correct mistakes. Children are amazingly forgiving and will respond to your efforts. It's never too late.

17 | Family Communications

The major difference between communication within a family setting and communication with the world at large is that the stakes are a lot higher with your family. You can escape from conflicts with a neighbor down the street, the union rep, or your auto mechanic, but you can't get away from your family.

Families get into trouble when parents discourage expressing certain feelings, needs, or observations. Children grow up feeling it is wrong to ask for help or emotional support, express anger, seek praise, talk about hopes or dreams, show physical or emotional pain, talk about sex, notice mistakes, express fear or uncertainty, or show affection.

In addition to these general rules, families may have very specific regulations about what can and can't be seen and talked about: Don't notice that Daddy is drunk and dysfunctional. Don't notice hostility at the dinner table. Don't mourn or talk about Grandmother's death. Don't express your fears of a Martian invasion. Don't ask for hugs or reassurance. Don't notice Mom's affair.

The family communication rules you learn as a child become unspoken prohibitions that you pass on to your children in turn. If your father reacted angrily when you were anxious as a child, you quickly learned that anxiety should not be expressed. You were conditioned to expect to be hurt if you talked about your fears. Eventually the rule dropped out of your awareness and became a hidden influence. As an adult, you remain uncomfortable with fear and may become irritated with your children for expressing it. Your spouse may also accept your rule because it has reciprocal benefits: "I won't show my fear if I don't have to deal with yours."

For most people, the powerful rules that limit their expression are completely unconscious. In the family therapist's office, when finally asked to communicate their hurt or fear or need for support, they feel strangely paralyzed. It all seems very dangerous, but they don't know why. That sense of danger, of course, derives from conditioning long ago, when their parents rejected them for saying what they felt, needed, or observed.

Family Communication Disorders

The rules limiting expression within families result in four major communication disorders. Restricted from direct expression, you must deny, delete, substitute, or incongruently communicate aspects of your experience.

Denial

People tend to deny what they are afraid to express. Your needs and feelings can be denied overtly or covertly. Overt denial involves statements such as "I don't care," "No problem," "Whatever you want," "I'm fine," "Who's angry?" "Who's upset?" and "I don't need you to do anything." Covert denial is harder to spot but often involves shrugging, speaking in a monotone, slouching, or withdrawing contact. The message is "It doesn't matter; I don't feel anything."

Deletion

Deletion involves leaving parts of a message out, particularly the parts that directly express your needs and observations. Instead of saying, "I'd like to go to a movie," you may catch yourself saying, "It's sure a lousy TV night, isn't it?" With deletions you have to say everything roundabout. Statements don't specify who, what, where, or when. The following are some typical examples:

"It's been a little lonely." (Meaning: "I've missed you the three nights a week you've been in class, and I hope you take fewer night classes next quarter.")

"There's a new French restaurant down the street." (Meaning: "Let's eat out tonight.")

"Damn, the threads are stripped. I'll never get this running." (Meaning: "Give me a little sympathy and bring me a cup of coffee.")

"Now what do you want me to do?" (Meaning: "Leave me alone right now. This is the first time I've relaxed all day.")

"I guess you're a little tired." (Meaning: "How come you're so angry all of a sudden?")

Deletions are usually constructed in one of three ways:

1. *Statements in the form of a question*: "Are you still here?" (Meaning: "I would like to be alone for a few hours.")

2. *Requests in the form of neutral observations*: "It's a gorgeous day." (Meaning: "Let's take a drive to the country.")

3. *Deleted references*: The message is vague and doesn't say who feels what about whom. "There's been some anger lately." (Meaning: "I have been angry at you because of all the extra work since you fired the housekeeper.") "There hasn't been much contact." (Meaning: "I've felt out of contact with my husband and oldest daughter.")

Substitution

Substitution expresses feelings indirectly. Feelings have to come out sometime, and substitution allows them to be expressed in a way that seems safer or with a safer person. If you have a rule against showing hurt, you might channel the hurt feelings into anger. If it's forbidden for you to express anger toward your wife, you might attack your son about his chores. The following are some typical examples of substitution.

Your boss criticizes your work. You're angry. You attack your wife for mismanaging the food money.

You're frightened when you see your boy run into the street. You angrily attack him as "stupid and crazy."

You feel hurt and a little lonely when your daughter spends three hours a night on the phone. You attack her for leaving the milk out of the refrigerator.

You're hurt and angry when your spouse announces the desire to take a vacation without you. Your rule against expressing anger forces you to convert the feeling to depression.

You are unable to express your secret unhappiness that the children will spend the summer with your former spouse. You express the feeling as anxiety about their health and safety.

Incongruent Messages

Incongruent communications occur when the messages carried by your posture, facial expression, tone of voice, and tempo of speech don't match the content of what you are saying. A woman says to her daughter, "I'm not upset that you were out late." But her voice has a strident, harsh quality; she talks quickly; and she's pointing her finger while her other hand is on her hip. The words simply don't match what her body and voice are saying. "I'm very sad that we can't pull this family together," a man announces at the dinner table. His eyes bore into those of his son, his jaws are clenched, and one hand forms a fist around the napkin. He says he's sad, but he's also communicating something else. It may be anger, or it may be a kind of agitated despair.

When messages don't match, family members are forced to decide which message is the true one. They have to read minds and try to guess what the speaker is really saying. The following examples of incongruent communication are each presented in four parts: words, voice and body language, listener's interpretation, and the real message.

Example 1

Words: "I'm terrifically glad to see you home."

Voice and body language: Flat monotone, eyes looking at the floor, a half smile, body turned slightly sideways.

Listener's interpretation: Chooses to respond to voice and body language. Assumes that the speaker is uncomfortable and disappointed. Listener feels hurt.

Real message: "I'm glad you're home. Unfortunately I couldn't finish the work I wanted to do, and I'm afraid I won't complete it now that you're back." The speaker has a rule against expressing anything but joy at a reunion. The result is incongruent communication.

Example 2

Words: "I don't mind not going. There are lots of things to do around the house."

Voice and body language: A bright smile that fades unnaturally fast, stooped shoulders, neck bowed, a high, placating voice.

Listener's interpretation: Chooses to respond to the reassuring words, but feels anxiety and discomfort because the body language shows extreme disappointment.

Real message: "I'm extremely disappointed that we couldn't go to the movies tonight."

Example 3

Words: "I just want some more support, the feeling that you care about me."

Voice and body language: Voice high and loud, almost whining, mouth drawn out in a flat line, shoulders and arms shrugging, looking over the top of glasses.

Listener's interpretation: Chooses to respond to the voice and body language. "He sometimes shrugs like that and stares over his glasses when he's angry," the listener concludes. "He must be angry." The listener experiences the message as a demand.

Real message: A request for help and a feeling of hopelessness that any will be forthcoming. The speaker's body language for expressing hopelessness is apparently similar to that used for anger. The listener, confused by incongruent messages, assumes that the speaker is hiding irritation.

Example 4

Words: "I worry terribly about you when you're late like this."

Voice and body language: Arms crossed, weight on one leg, mouth drawn in a thin line, voice harsh and loud.

Listener's interpretation: Chooses to respond to the words. Feels vaguely uneasy that the words don't match the body language.

Real message: "I waited for you and worried about you. I'm angry that you didn't have the courtesy to call."

Example 5

Words: "Why don't you get the kid a couple more toys?"

Voice and body language: Voice slightly high and singsong, torso leaning forward, head shaking from side to side, finger pointing.

Listener's interpretation: Chooses to respond to the voice and body language. The voice and finger pointing are interpreted as critical, taunting.

Real message: "It worries me that she has nothing to play with at your house. I'm afraid she'll stop wanting to be with you because she's bored there." Because the speaker has used finger pointing and a singsong voice in the past to express annoyance, the listener mind-reads annoyance and responds by getting angry.

Incongruent messages form the basis of much family pathology. People usually assume that voice and body language communications are always consistent. But these messages are easily misinterpreted because of over-generalization. This is the tendency to believe that a particular posture or intonation always means the same thing: "When Harry shrugs, that always means he's upset with me." "When Jane frowns and points her finger, that always means she's making a demand." "When Natasha has a high, strident voice, that always means she's anxious." Overgeneralization cancels out any other meanings the gesture could have. It increases the opportunity for misinterpretation.

Family Pathology

There are several common patterns of behavior that occur in families that can increase tension between family members. These include mind reading, forming alliances against one another, and using various covert manipulation strategies to achieved desired outcomes.

Mind Reading

Because family members have rules about what can and cannot be expressed, they are forced to communicate covertly. Through deletions, substitutions, and incongruent messages, family members say what they need to say. But often no one understands them. When you try to interpret covert messages, you are forced to mind-read. You have to make a guess as to what the covert request or feeling really is. Take the example of a man who remarks that the house is infested with fleas. Since he has deleted his feelings and needs about the matter, his wife must try to divine if his hatred for the cat has surfaced again, if he wants her to have the house flea bombed, or if he wants her to acknowledge and commiserate about the problem. If he has a history of substitutions, she may be worried that he brought up the flea business because he's angry about her purchasing new drapes. The matter is further complicated if there are incongruent messages. If he stands with his hands on his hips and talks very rapidly, his wife may conclude by virtue of overgeneralization that her husband is violently angry.

All this guesswork results in just one thing: mistakes. If you are mind reading, you are going to be wrong a certain percentage of the time. You will respond to what you think is going on rather than to the real message. Your inappropriate response then creates a chain reaction like the proverbial falling dominoes. Consider the following interaction: Margaret, whose husband, Al, demands peace and quiet when he arrives home, hastily ends a fight with her son as she hears his keys in the front door. She's anxious when she greets him. Her voice is high and clipped. She avoids eye contact.

By virtue of overgeneralization, Al assumes that the clipped, high-pitched voice means that his wife is angry. He mind-reads that she is irritated with him for being late. He makes himself angry by telling himself that she doesn't care about the long, hard hours he works. Al can't express the anger and instead substitutes by complaining about the toys left on the floor. Margaret feels hurt but substitutes by complaining that he's late again. The ensuing melee is entirely a result of mind reading.

There are two ways to break out of the mind-reading trap.

As a speaker, you have to ask yourself these questions: "What feeling, request, or awareness have I left out of my message? Do my tone of voice and body language match the content of my message?" If you find that you are simultaneously communicating more than one message, break it down into two separate communications. Suppose, for example, that you have a rule against expressing anger. You're telling your child to clean up his room, but you notice a lot of anger in your voice and that you are pointing your finger. You might separate and express the messages in this way: "I want you to clean up your room by an hour from now. I asked you to do it this morning and now I find myself a little frustrated and angry that it's still not done."

As a listener, you can combat mind reading by checking out all ambiguous messages. If you notice that the content doesn't match the voice or body language, describe in a nonjudgmental way what you observe. Ask if there is more that needs to be said: "I notice your shoulders were kind of hunched and you were staring at the floor while we talked about the kitchen remodeling. Is there something more that you feel about that?" You need to catch yourself when you make assumptions about the needs and feelings of others. A red flag has to go up inside when you mind-read. As you catch yourself, you'll notice that certain assumptions typically come up over and over again. You may be prone to imagining that people are angry, disappointed, or making covert demands on you. These typical assumptions derive from overgeneralization, in which you invariably read certain gestures or tones of voice as anger, disappointment, or demands.

Alliances

Family alliances are formed to help you express forbidden feelings and needs. If Dad gets angry when his son discusses problems in school, maybe

Mom will listen. And perhaps Mom will also share some of her negative feelings about Dad. As the mother-son alliance develops, Dad becomes more and more isolated. He doesn't hear the anger and the hurt, and he is also cut off from any warmth or support. Dad, as he feels increasingly peripheral, may seek an alliance with his daughter. They may complain to each other about how cold Mom is and secretly collude to support each other in family conflicts.

Sibling alliances are a good way to deal with a punitive parent who focuses more on rules than on the particular needs of his children. Parent-child alliances are helpful when a parent has been dying on the vine emotionally and feels trapped in a dead marriage. In general, alliances are useful short-term strategies for getting support and acknowledgment. But they are death on long-term family happiness. The feuding camps continue to attack and hurt each other, often until the children leave home or the parents separate.

The antidote for alliances is a family contract for directness and an agreement that feelings and wants will be expressed to the person who needs to hear them. Secrets (an implied alliance) are not allowed. Gripes are to be expressed to the offending person. For example, a mother-son alliance that would keep Dad from knowing about the boy's poor grades is prevented by a contract for openness. A father-mother alliance, in which Dad bitterly gripes about his daughter's laziness, is likewise prevented. With a contract for directness and openness, the whole family enters an alliance. They agree to support each other in expressing and hearing important messages. They agree that the feelings and needs that two of them share should be heard by all.

Covert Manipulation Strategies

All communication has an implied request built into it. You're always trying to influence people in some way: even if you're only listening to your sister, you're hoping to strengthen your alliance with her so she'll help you the next time you want to do something behind your parents' backs. The problem is that many people have rules against asking for things. If you have such rules, you can't openly ask for support, help, or acknowledgment. Nobody knows what you want. As a consequence, you are forced to use covert manipulation strategies to get the things you need. The following sections cover some manipulative strategies that are widely used in pathological families.

Blaming and Judging

The blamer attacks other family members for not meeting his or her needs. They should be more supportive, more loving, more helpful around the house. If they really cared, they would get home earlier, do more things with the kids. A blamer's weapon is the pejorative attack. He or she aims at people's vulnerable self-esteem in the way a Doberman goes for the jugular. Certain blamers have refined their strategy to an art. Some attack with a needling sarcasm that ostensibly seems funny but cuts deeply. Others make unreasonable demands and then explode with "justifiable" rage after they are turned down. Through judicious faultfinding, blamers can push family members to give them some of what they want. Blamers can get grudging attention and help. The problem is that the strategy only works for a while. Though it is initially successful and people are quite responsive to the fear of being hurt, the blamer's knives grow dull. Family members can become thick-skinned and oblivious to assaults. The blamer's once effective strategy for getting his or her way loses power. The blamer is left with a simmering, impotent rage.

Pulling for Guilt

This strategy banks on everyone's need to feel like a good person. Good people care for others, giving time and energy. They sacrifice themselves. Pulling for guilt involves subtly, sadly letting family members know that you're in pain. If they cared, they would do something about it. If they were good people, they would stay home with you instead of going bowling. If they really loved you, they would keep the lawn mowed. The best way to pull for guilt is to sigh a lot, refer bleakly to past sins and mistakes, and tell everyone you're fine while looking miserable. Pulling for guilt is very effective. People secretly resent you, but they will often do what you want.

Pulling for Pity

This strategy is designed to arouse sympathy rather than guilt. The demeanor is helpless and pathetic. There are sad stories and hopeless shrugs, all filling in the portrait of a victim. Pulling for pity has a period of maximum effectiveness. After a while, exhaustion sets in, and family members begin to lose patience with the seemingly endless stream of problems.

Blackmail

Blackmailing involves threats to withhold something other family members need. Overtly or covertly, the suggestion gets made that there will be no more sex, dinner won't be cooked, or you better forget that birthday party. Some blackmailers play for high stakes by continually threatening to leave the family. As every parent who has threatened to take away a child's allowance knows, blackmail quickly becomes ineffective if you don't make good on the threats. This puts the blackmailer in a difficult bind. He or she is either making empty threats (which are soon ignored) or must follow through on spiteful and destructive schemes. If the blackmailer follows through and family members are damaged, he or she is courting the possibility of real hatred.

Bribery

This strategy involves insincere use of flattery, favors, or affection to induce other family members to change. Sex is turned on and off like a faucet. Attention and support are forthcoming only when the briber is in need. Like most covert manipulation strategies, bribery has short-term benefits. In the long run, however, family members cease to trust the integrity and authenticity of the briber. Resentment sets in.

Placating

Placaters are nice. They fear conflict and avoid it at all costs. They try to please, to ingratiate, to garner approval. They are always quick to apologize. Placaters get their way by making people like them and owe them things. They're so agreeable and they've done so much for everyone, how could family members deny them what they need? Surely the family will be as nice and as sacrificing as the placater has been. The problem for the placater is that people take him or her for granted. In the end, the placater becomes a secret martyr with a long list of hidden resentments. The placater thought there was a deal: "I'll be nice if you'll be nice." But other family members don't keep their end of the unspoken bargain.

Turning Cold

This strategy relies on eloquent silence, the clenched jaw, the back turned in bed. The message is "You're getting nothing from me." It's a powerful strategy because it frightens people. Children, in particular, who depend for their very survival on a parent's love, are enormously vulnerable to sudden coldness. But the withdrawal of love is more than a way of influencing behavior: it is a weapon that leaves scars. Both children and spouse become distrusting. And a secret rage develops that anyone would take away the most precious and necessary of human resources: emotional energy.

Developing Symptoms

When all else fails and people have no other way of getting what they want, they develop symptoms. They get headaches, they begin to drink, they have dark bouts of depression or impulsive spending sprees, or they become unfaithful. Children get into fights at school, try to run away, stop studying for classes, or attack their siblings. The symptoms are a covert attempt to get certain needs met. Headaches may get Dad some time off work. Vaginal spasms may help a woman get time off from a sexually aggressive mate. A child may get important attention needs met by getting into trouble at school. Symptoms are useful in the short term, but in the long term they can seriously damage the family member who suffers from them. A depressed woman finally gets her husband to take her on a vacation. But she's paid for that vacation with months of suffering.

Family Systems

Covert manipulative strategies are only necessary when people have rules against the expression of needs, feelings, or observations. If two or more family members have rules limiting what they can say, the resulting covert strategies are called a *family system*. Here are two examples of family systems at work.

The Martyr

The martyr in this case is Joyce, a woman who has rules against asking for support and acknowledgment of her hard work. She also has rules against expressing anger except under extreme provocation. Joyce works seven days a week cooking, cleaning, picking up after her family, and running a little online business out of her bedroom. The money earned pays for her sons' private school. She needs help around the house, she needs recognition for what she gives, and she needs to express her anger about being taken for granted. Joyce avoids expressing her needs. Instead, she blames. She accuses her sons of taking all her time, calls her husband lazy, and says he's turned her into the maid.

The children have also been taught not to express anger. They covertly show their feelings by keeping their rooms messy, being late, and embarrassing their mother in front of friends. Joyce's husband, Sean, uses incongruent messages to express what he feels. He says, "Yes, yes, you work very hard. Of course we all know that." He speaks loudly and quickly with his hands in his pockets as he leans against the wall. Joyce interprets Sean's body language to mean he doesn't care. She assumes that her children don't care. As a result, she continues trying to meet her needs through blaming. But the children continue to wreck their rooms. Sean turns cold and repeats his incongruent "Yes, yes, we know you're working."

The problem in this family is that no one can talk straight. The children can't express anger, and Joyce interprets their passive-aggressive behavior as not caring. Sean can't express his anger either. He talks loudly and quickly and makes an elaborate show of casualness. His message is also interpreted as not caring.

This family system would be defused if Joyce could do three things:

1. Ask for the help and acknowledgment she needs, using nonjudgmental words.

2. Express anger instead of blame. This means describing what she feels, not punishing and attacking the self-esteem of others. Anger says, "I'm in pain and I don't like it." Blame says, "I'm in pain and bad people did it to me."

3. Check out Sean's real message rather than assume she can read his mind.

The Newlyweds

Jack is thirty-two and Henrietta is thirty-five. They got married with a lot of hoopla, had a weekend honeymoon in Carmel, and returned to the apartment they have been sharing for the past year and a half. Jack works in a restaurant until ten at night. He often stays around for another hour or two, having a few drinks and hanging out with the bartender. A month after the marriage, Jack is coming home later and staying out more frequently. Henrietta becomes alarmed and discovers in herself an enormous insecurity. She's afraid of losing Jack. She fantasizes for hours about his involvement with various waitresses. Henrietta has a rule against expressing her insecurity and fear of loss, however, so she deletes her feelings and tries pulling for guilt. She tells Jack she's losing sleep and can't function on her job when he stays out past eleven. Jack continues to stay out, so Henrietta changes her strategy to blackmail. She tells Jack not to bother being amorous when he comes in late. As the problem continues, she becomes increasingly desperate and tells Jack she'll move in with a girlfriend unless he gets in by eleven.

Jack, too, has feelings he can't express. Following the wedding, he feels a strange deadness and apathy. He suddenly becomes afraid that he has signed up for a joyless commitment. He also feels guilt when he yearns for the excitement of his old single days. Jack has a rule against sharing any negative feelings. Instead, he substitutes anger for the fears and guilt he's experiencing and then attacks Henrietta for being overcontrolling. At other times Jack uses the strategy of turning cold. He talks reasonably, but his voice and body language indicate withdrawal.

Faced with these incongruent messages, Henrietta mind-reads that Jack is trying to get out of the marriage. Her threat to move in with a girlfriend was an empty one. And now, in a last effort to influence Jack, she begins to develop symptoms. Henrietta starts to drink when Jack stays out late. Jack is disgusted by the drinking, and his unexpressed fears and misgivings only increase.

This system could be resolved if Henrietta and Jack communicated directly. Both are afraid. Both have rules against expressing the feelings that torment them. Jack needs to know what happens inside of Henrietta while she waits. She needs to know the fear that keeps Jack lingering at work. These feelings won't suddenly disappear, but the covert strategies may be less necessary. With everything in the open, Henrietta can begin focusing on her need to feel safe and ask Jack to call if he'll be out past eleven. Jack can directly examine his need for autonomy and decide to schedule visiting time with friends.

How to Keep Family Communications Healthy

The best way to keep a family healthy is to allow each member the freedom to say what he or she feels, sees, and wants. Here are two exercises to help you reach those goals.

Exercise 17.1

Each time a family member says something that disturbs or confuses you, write down the following:

Words: The actual content of the message.

Voice and body language: Write down your memory of the pitch and tone of voice, the posture and facial expression. What gestures were used?

Your interpretation: Notice whether the words match the voice and body language. If they seem to be saying different things, which do you believe? What do you assume to be the true message?

Real message: Ask the family member for further clarification. Describe in a nonjudgmental way any discrepancies you see between the words and the nonverbal message. Ask if some feeling or need might have been left out. Now compare what you've learned with the previous assumptions you made.

The checking out exercise helps you combat mind reading by soliciting the information you need to accurately hear a message. Do the exercise at least once a day for two weeks. At the end of that time, you'll get an idea of how much or how little you are distorting what family members say to you.

Remember that the tendency to mind-read is a natural one. Because important feelings or needs are often deleted or show up only in body language, you may have developed a habit of guessing at the "real" message. The problem is that your guesses will not always be accurate. Just as Henrietta tortured herself by assuming that Jack was trying to escape their marriage, your mind reading may be adding fuel to the fire of a painful family system.

Exercise 17.2

This exercise is designed to help you uncover your own deletions, substitutions, and incongruent messages. Whenever you take part in a painful or troubling communication, do the following:

1. Write down the first four or five sentences you said.

2. Describe your voice and body language. As you remember, how did your voice sound, what was your posture, what were your hands doing, and so on? What were you saying with your voice, your posture, and your hands?

3. Explore what was left out. What feeling did you leave out of your communication? What implied request was hidden in your communication?

4. Review the covert manipulation strategies. Notice if there is anything in your message that indicates the use of one of those strategies.

5. Rewrite your message. Include the original content of your message (if it was accurate), plus what your body and voice were saying. Include any feelings or needs that you are now aware were deleted.

Part VI

· · · · · · · · · · · · · · ·

Public Skills

18 | Influencing Others

Communication is often about influencing others to change and behave in ways that you would prefer. If you don't know how to do this skillfully, you end up feeling frustrated and bitter, while your friends, family, and coworkers feel defensive and pushed around. For example, Sonja's attempts to influence Larry are not working:

Sonja: Why don't you want to go over to Bill and Meg's house? They're a lot of fun.

Larry: I'm tired.

Sonja: You're always tired. You're a walking dead man. I can't go out for a simple evening with friends, because you're chained to the couch and that damned detective novel. Can't you just say yes once in a while? Yes to a little fun?

Larry: What can I say, Sonja? I'm really tired.

Sonja: (Loudly) Maybe it just doesn't work. Maybe it just doesn't work between us. You know? Maybe I've got to do some thinking about that.

Larry: This is a nice life, isn't it?

Sonja starts by blaming and criticizing, which only make Larry more obstinate. Then she tries threats, and Larry responds by withdrawing into sarcasm. To influence others, Sonja needs to understand the principles of change, beginning with what *doesn't* work.

Ineffective Strategies for Influencing Change

In blaming, criticizing, or complaining, your basic message to the other person is that he or she is bad or wrong. In your mind, there are basic rules of decency, fairness, and caring that are being violated. When someone breaks these rules, it feels like you have every right to let the person have it. But by blaming, criticizing, or complaining, you won't get the other person to change.

Here are some other ineffective strategies:

Threats. Here the message is "Do what I want, or else—or else I'll hurt you back, take something away that feels good to you, or just plain scare you with my anger."

Belittling. You communicate that the other person is unworthy if he or she doesn't do what you want. The other person is flawed, stupid, or contemptible.

Pouting or withdrawing. The message here is "You won't have me if you won't do what I want." This strategy runs the continuum from a brief shutdown all the way to threatening to abandon the other person.

Strategies that don't influence change all act the same way: they are aversive and they hurt people. There are two reasons why so many people rely on them. First, these strategies for change are modeled in dysfunctional families. If you grew up in a family in which people hurt each other as a strategy of influence, you'll sometimes find yourself doing the same thing. It's what you witnessed and what you learned how to do. The second reason these strategies are so popular is that they are initially effective. In the early stages of a relationship, when someone still wants to please you, blaming, threats, belittling, and withdrawing can be powerful motivators. But over time, these strategies lose their power as people stop caring about what you think. Over months and years, using these strategies makes others defensive and resistant to you. Other people stop listening. They stop caring. They build a thick emotional armor that makes them impervious to even the most stinging rebuke.

Threats are a particularly disappointing strategy. A person's initial response to your threat may be quite reinforcing. He or she may try noticeably harder to please you, but the changes you observe are created and maintained by fear; they will last only as long as the fear lasts. As soon as the threat diminishes or is forgotten, the old behavior patterns are likely to reassert themselves.

Many people use ineffective strategies for influencing others because they're angry. And they justify their anger with this kind of thought: "She sees how much pain and unhappiness she's causing me. She ought to ..." There's a strong feeling that the other person should change to mitigate your unhappiness and help you feel better. But people will only change in response to your unhappiness if two conditions are simultaneously met: First, the person whom you want to change must have a strong empathic bond with you. Your unhappiness makes them unhappy. Second, that other person's own needs, fears, and limitations must not strongly reinforce the status quo. In other words, the other person's needs can't be stacked up on the side of staying the same. Because these two conditions are very rarely met at any given time or with any given issue, your pain typically has little impact on the behavior of others.

Effective Strategies for Influencing Others

The most important principle to remember is that people change only when they want to, not when you want them to. People behave the way they do because of powerful reinforcers—mostly fears and needs—that drive them to cope and respond in predictable patterns. Because these reinforcers are so strong, change is difficult. It's often not enough to ask someone to change. The other person's fears and needs may overwhelmingly shout you down.

Consider the case of John and his girlfriend, Simone. He's asked her to be more open, to tell him more about her past and how she feels at various times when they're together. But Simone grew up in a family in which teasing and ridicule were common occurrences and information was often used to hurt people. Her sisters read her diaries and repeated passages at embarrassing moments. Simone has enormous fears of being laughed at, along with a parallel need to feel safe, even invulnerable. John's request, no matter how appropriate or well meaning, simply can't compete with the reinforcers created by Simone's traumatic past.

If people behave the way they do because of strong and complex patterns of reinforcement, it follows that changing their behavior must often involve changing those reinforcers. In other words, if John wants Simone to be more open, he'll have to find a way to make her feel more safe and less fearful of ridicule.

Effective strategies for influencing others fall into two categories: positive reinforcement and negative consequences.

Positive Reinforcement

There are four types of positive reinforcement that you can use to influence behavior: praise, trading, building in rewards, and verbal and nonverbal appreciation.

Praise

You can praise past behavior that is similar to the changes you now want to reinforce. Praising past similar behavior is a powerful reinforcer because it sends the message "I see your goodness and worth when you act like that." Everyone is hungry for esteem and appreciation. Praise is a way of giving a valued gift while at the same time pulling for behavior that you'd prefer.

Trading

The basic message is "I'll give you X if you'll give me Y." Life is full of little deals and is often made much easier by them: "If you could get those big trees trimmed, I'd help you relax with a neck massage." "If these reports get in on time, I think we can give you some more interesting assignments next week." "If you could walk me to my car in the evenings, I'd be glad to give you a lift home." "Would you mind going with me to visit my grandmother this weekend? I could make it worth your while with a dinner down at Salerno's." While trades can often sound like low-key bribery, there's nothing wrong with this. They are effective because they acknowledge the other person's needs and promise to provide something real as compensation for the desired behavior.

Building in Rewards

Studies show that positive reinforcement is the most effective way of influencing behavior. Building in rewards is much like trading, but the reinforcement in this case is woven into the desired behavior: "Come shopping with me. There's a huge bookstore in the mall. You can browse around and see what new biographies they have." "If you help me with Jennifer's birthday party, we can at least be together and talk and hang out while we're keeping things organized." "Look, I want to see Colorado, and you love trains. Let's take the Durango and Silverton, and then later we can head up the Million Dollar Highway to Ouray and points north." When you build in rewards, each person gets something from the experience; each person's needs are assumed to be important and worth planning for.

Verbal and Nonverbal Appreciation

Verbal thank-yous are important. But a hug, a pat on the shoulder, a warm smile, or even a nod and a look of contentment can also be powerful reinforcers when someone has done what you want. Appreciation conveys the message that you are grateful, you are pleased, and you value what the person has done. It greatly increases the chance that the behavior will be repeated and you will continue to get what you want.

Negative Consequences

Negative consequences should be used as a last resort when positive reinforcement isn't working. Negative consequences tend to create a backlash of anger and resentment, thereby diminishing the other person's desire to cooperate and please you. However, when negative consequences have a positive impact on the other person, they can be strong motivators for change. The following sections cover some negative consequences that you can use as strategies for influence.

Stop the Rewards

Stop rewarding the person for behavior you don't want. If you want others to be punctual, don't wait for them while they diddle with endless last-minute preparations. Leave on time without them. If you want your friend to stop drinking alcohol when you're around her, leave when she pops open her first beer. Staying has the effect of rewarding the behavior with your presence. If you want your roommate to wash the dishes, don't wash them for him when he skips his turn. You are bound to be frustrated in your attempts to influence others when you consistently reward them for staying the same.

Design Self-Care Strategies

You can design self-care strategies to meet your needs when the other person is unable or unwilling to make desired changes. If you've asked your roommate to help with household chores and he resists doing so, your self-care strategies would focus on cutting down your workload. The consequences for your roommate's unwillingness to help might include no longer doing his laundry or no longer cooking or shopping for him. If a friend keeps borrowing things without returning them, a self-care strategy might be to insist that she only borrow one thing at a time. If you've unsuccessfully requested that your partner get home earlier in the evenings, your self-care strategies might include going out to the movies and visiting friends when your partner is not home by a certain hour. Self-care strategies should not be framed as punishment or described in an angry tone that implies wrongdoing by the other person. They are merely efforts to meet your own needs without the other person's help.

Identify Natural Consequences

If someone is always late for your lunch dates, stop getting together in restaurants. If someone has a pattern of being rude to you when you attend social events together, stop going with that person to social events. If you've given your friend a ride to a party and he refuses to leave with you when you become tired, the natural consequence would be leaving and allowing him to find his own way home. The secret of natural consequences is that they aren't contrived. They are normal, natural outcomes of certain behavior. If your children haven't gotten fully dressed when it's time to leave for school, natural consequences would dictate leaving anyway, with whatever they have on, and having them finish dressing in the car.

A Plan for Influencing Change

It's time for you to develop a plan that will help you reinforce a desired change in someone else. Your plan should have six parts: a direct request, praise, trading, building in rewards, verbal and nonverbal appreciation, and consequences.

Exercise 18.1

1. **Make a direct request.** Start by identifying the person whose behavior you'd like to influence. Select a single issue or problem. If you try to deal with more than one issue at a time, your plan will falter for lack of focus. Write out a request that is specific and behavioral. This means that you're not asking the person to change his or her feelings, attitudes, or awareness. Few people are willing or able to change on that level. You're merely asking the other person to do more or less of a particular behavior: "Could you please get home by six-thirty and call me if you're going to be late?" "Could we please schedule time on Saturday afternoons for hikes and shared time together?" "When we're walking, could we stay together instead of you getting so far ahead?" "Could you listen to me when I'm talking instead of starting to read or looking around the room?" Notice that each request asks for a specific change in behavior. Once you've written down your request, plan to bring it up at a time when neither of you is emotionally upset. Be prepared to find that your request is ignored or, if you get agreement, that your request is forgotten in a few days or weeks. When a direct request is insufficient to engineer change, you'll need to implement the rest of your plan.

2. **Give praise.** Praise focuses on times when the desired behavior actually occurred in the past:

   "I really liked it when you trimmed the hedges. Could you do it again this weekend?"

   "It made me feel really good when you took Katy to the ballgame."

"I felt really special when you introduced me to your coworkers."

"I feel really close to you when you make the bed and keep the room picked up."

"I appreciated it when you asked my advice about the bills. It helped me understand our situation."

Follow up with a·description of a specific experience. Sometimes praise can be tied to a repetition of your direct request. You describe how good something felt in the past and ask for that same specific behavior in the present.

3. **Describe a trade.** Think of a trade that you could make with the other person so that he or she will be compensated for giving you what you want. It's often helpful to write down a specific script for describing the trade you'd like to make:

"If you could do more of the shopping, I could do more of your laundry."

"I know it's hard for you to help my brother, but if you could, I'd like to clean out the hall closet for you."

"Let's make a deal. I'd really appreciate it if you could go with me to the memorial. And to show you my heart's in the right place, I'll clear out next week so you can have the beer and basketball party at our house."

4. **Build in rewards.** Building in rewards starts with an analysis of the needs and interests of the other person and then looks for ways to integrate those needs into your request. Be creative. Brainstorm ideas. A request such as taking more weekend hikes may offer opportunities to meet both people's needs. For example, if your friend is a camera buff or a bird lover, it might be easy to go to areas where photography or bird watching is possible. This part of your plan for change may not always be possible with certain requests. Something simple like "Would you please not check your phone when I'm talking to you?" doesn't contain much opportunity for building in rewards.

5. **Give verbal and nonverbal appreciation.** Getting the other person to try the new behavior even once is a big step. You'll need to reinforce the behavior if you want it to happen again. Plan out what you'll say as well as how you will convey your gratitude in a nonverbal way.

6. **Identify consequences.** As a last resort, you can use negative consequences. First, analyze if you are in some way reinforcing the behavior that you don't want. What happens after the other person does what you don't like? How do you respond? Is there something you're doing that supports the behavior? If so, write down the reinforcing behavior that you plan to stop. Now write down your self-care strategy and the natural consequences that can occur in response to the old, unwanted behavior: "If I can't get your help, I have to take care of myself in some way. I think what makes sense for me to do is ..." Fill in the blank with what you intend to do.

Lisa's Plan for Influencing Change

Lisa planned to get her friend Gail to exercise her listening skills more often when they spent time together:

1. *Direct request:* "Gail, we spend a lot of time talking about what's happening with your boyfriend. I'd like you to make a point of asking what's going on with me each time we get together. It would feel good if you could pull me into the conversation and make room for my stuff."

2. *Praise:* "Remember how you asked me all about my trip back to Texas to visit my father? That felt great because I got to tell you a lot of things I might not have said otherwise. I felt invited, like you were really interested."

3. *Trading:* "If you could ask about me each time, it would make a big difference. I'd even be willing to go to that salsa club you've been wanting to try."

4. *Building in rewards*: Lisa can't think of any rewards to build in.

5. *Verbal and nonverbal praise*: When she does ask me about myself, tell her, "Thanks for asking, Gail. It really feels like you're interested." Smile and hug her.

6. *Consequences*: "Gail, I need to feel you're interested in me. If you don't ask me things and take an interest, I'd just as soon do stuff together where we go out to movies and concerts and things where we don't talk that much. Then I won't be angry about long conversations that are kind of one-sided."

19 | Public Speaking

The United Way Committee has asked you to address your fellow workers about making donations. The committee chose you because you did so well last year getting contributions from people on a one-to-one basis. As you try to gather your thoughts and prepare your talk, you realize that public speaking is very different from a casual chat on your coffee break.

Effective public speaking requires special communication skills. It is less spontaneous than personal communication, since you have to prepare your message in advance and make sure it is logically organized. Your address is more or less continuous, with little feedback from your passive audience. You have to communicate to a relatively large number of people at once, including some who aren't necessarily interested in what you have to say. Often you don't get to choose the most advantageous time or setting for your speech.

All this means that you have to take special care to determine the exact purpose and subject of your speech, organize it accordingly, and deliver it in a style appropriate to your audience and the occasion. It's no wonder you experience some stage fright!

Planning Your Talk

Ask yourself, "What is the purpose, subject, and presentation style of this speech?"

Purpose

You'll find that most speeches are intended either to inform or to persuade. Once you have determined the basic purpose of your speech, you should refine this purpose by stating it in one complete sentence. For example, you might describe the purpose of the United Way speech as follows: "This speech is intended to persuade the audience to sign up for the automatic payroll contribution plan." An informative speech about Egyptian pyramids might have as its purpose "to tell about the Pharaoh's godlike position at the center of Egyptian religion, the purpose of the pyramids, and some facts about their construction."

It's often helpful to state the purpose of a speech in terms of behavioral goals. What do you want the audience to do at the end of your speech? This is especially important in the case of persuasive speeches, after which you want the audience to contribute money, vote for you or your candidate, or take some kind of personal action such as writing a congressperson or volunteering for community service. This way of clarifying the purpose also works well when preparing an informative speech. You can state the purpose like this: "My speech will enable the audience to remember that the Pharaoh was a god, that the pyramids contained everything he would need for eternal life, and that the pyramids were constructed with massive ramps."

Subject

The next step is to outline your subject matter. A sample outline is included later in this chapter. In general, the less said, the better. If you can't sum up your speech's content in one sentence, it's probably too long. Your audience won't remember it all. Many experiments in audience retention have shown that the average audience member can only follow one main point and three sub points. All the rest is wasted breath. You're better off with a tightly focused, short speech than a long, all-inclusive speech.

Presentation Style

The purpose and subject of your speech will suggest which style of presentation will be most effective. There are four types of presentation: *impromptu*, in which you have no time for preparation and must think on your feet; *extemporaneous*, in which you have prepared a speech but not memorized it word for word; *memorized*, in which you deliver a verbatim recitation of your speech; and *manuscript*, in which you read your written speech aloud.

The impromptu speech is the most effective in terms of rapport and spontaneity. However, it is hard to pull off unless you know the subject perfectly, can think and organize as you talk, and don't suffer much from stage fright. For most purposes, the extemporaneous speech is better. It allows you to be spontaneous in your word choice and phrasing, creates good rapport with your audience, and can be carefully organized beforehand.

The memorized speech usually sounds wooden and mechanical and should be avoided unless there is no other way to conquer your anxiety or convey difficult material. The manuscript speech is reserved for formal occasions, such as political announcements or the presentation of scientific papers, when the exact word-for-word content is more important than style of delivery or audience rapport.

If you do have occasion to deliver a memorized or manuscript speech, remember to make eye contact with your audience. This keeps you in closer contact. With a manuscript speech, looking up to establish eye contact forces you to pace your reading slowly enough for audience comprehension. Mark your place with your finger as you read, so you can look up at the end of each long phrase without getting lost.

Organizing Your Talk

The advice most commonly given to beginning speakers remains the best: "Tell them what you're going to tell them, tell them, then tell them what you've told them." This advice recognizes the two most important facts about speech organization: that all good speeches must have an introduction, a body, and a conclusion; and that all important information must be repeated at least three times to be retained.

Introduction

The introduction is one of the most important parts of a speech. It gets your audience's attention, establishes your relationship with its members, sets the tone you want to take, and orients them to the subject matter. If you have already stated the content of your speech in one sentence, you have the kernel of the introduction. Most successful introductions include a capsule summary—the "tell them what you're going to tell them" part. It's a good idea to write your introduction last, or at least revise it after you know the full content and tone of the rest of the speech.

The Body

The body of your speech contains the meat. Depending on your purpose and subject, body can be organized in different ways.

Sequential Organization

Sequential organization is best when dealing with historical material, such as the history of the AFL-CIO, child development, or how your group campaigned for a new park. You start in the past and proceed in sequence toward the present and the future. The connectives are "and then," "next," "after that," "the following year," and so on. This is one of the easiest organizations for an audience to follow and works especially well for informative speeches.

Spatial Organization

Spatial organization is similar to sequential organization. It proceeds in space rather than time and is good for informing audiences about such topics as the New England colonies, the voting precincts of the city, European geography, travel stories, and so on. Its simplicity makes it easy to understand. Add a map and a pointer, and it's almost impossible to lose an audience with spatial organization.

Structure and Function

Organizing by structure and function is good when you're describing a complex organism or organization. For example, a talk about how squash grows could be organized according to structure first and function second:

Structure	Function
Root	Absorbs water and nutrients; anchors plant to ground
Vine	Carries water and nutrients; provides physical support
Leaf	Catches sun's rays for photosynthesis; shades earth
Blossom	Attracts pollinating insects; forms fruit
Fruit	Forms seeds for next year's plants; protects and nourishes seeds

Or the same talk could be organized first according to function:

Function	Structure
Intake of nutrients	Roots and leaves and energy
Conversion of nutrients	Photosynthesis in leaves and energy
Physical support	Roots and vines
Reproduction	Blossom and fruit and seeds

By thinking about a complex subject in terms of structure and function, you can often hit upon a clear way to organize your material.

Topical Organization

Sometimes you have two or three things to talk about that are not closely related by time, place, structure, or function. In this case, you can take up each topic in turn, being careful to let your audience know each time that you are changing topics. For example, a speech to your sales group at work might be broken into three parts: inventory, new prices, and overseas markets. A talk about ecology could be broken down into water quality, landfill, and legislation. This kind of organization is casual and works only when the information is simple and short. It is not to be confused with presenting a long list of arguments or other items—that's a symptom of poor organization and it never works.

Problem and Solution

Organizing in terms of problem and solution works well for a persuasive speech. You present a problem in detail and then present the solution in such a way that it clearly solves every aspect of the problem. For example, a speech in favor of a school bond initiative could be organized like this:

The problem: Overcrowded classrooms, long school bus rides, and poor performance on standard national tests.

The solution: A new school would mean smaller average class size, shorter school bus routes, and better education and thus higher test scores.

Cause and Effect

In cause-and-effect organization, you can choose to describe a cause and its effect or, vice versa, to trace an effect back to its cause. If you were to describe the western migration of Americans in the nineteenth century, you might cover the causes first:

- Economic depression in the East

- Homestead Act

- Declining fertility of eastern farmland

- Pressure of new immigrants from Europe

- Discovery of gold in California

Then you could cover some of the effects:

- Development of wagon trains and professional guides

- Indian wars

- Disruption of sod-buffalo ecology

- Formation of new states

- Great age of railroading

As you can see, some effects are in themselves causes of further effects. This is a flexible organizing principle that can throw selected facts into highlight and thrust inconvenient facts into the shadows.

The Conclusion

In the conclusion of a good speech, you summarize what you have told your audience. In persuasive speeches, the conclusion is also a call to action: to vote, to write a letter, to contribute, to volunteer, or to support a candidate or position. The conclusion is the most important part of a persuasive speech.

The conclusion should also clearly signal that you are through talking. There's nothing worse than a speech that dwindles into embarrassed silence and tentative applause. Conclude with a clear summary, statement, resolution, catchphrase, or call to action that lets the audience know you're finished.

Audience Analysis

Before preparing your speech, consider your audience. Are they all men or all women, or is it a mixed crowd? Are they mostly old or young, or all ages? How much education have they had? Are they rich or poor? Are they conservative or liberal? What are their racial or ethnic backgrounds? What are their occupations? Their attitudes? Their interests? All these considerations are important in choosing appropriate language, examples, jokes, and overall tone.

When the day of the speech arrives, give some thought to your audience's circumstances. Have they just eaten a big lunch? Is it early in the morning or late at night? Do they have comfortable seating? Is it too hot or cold or noisy? Have they just heard another speaker who bored or angered them? These considerations may make you change the length or tone of your presentation to match or counteract the mood of your audience.

During the speech, watch your audience for smiles, applause, frowns, restless movements, looks of confusion, or people leaving or talking to their neighbors. You may need to talk louder or slower, cut things short, or change your tone.

Style

The basic rule of style is that your language must be appropriate to the audience, the subject matter, and the occasion. You shouldn't talk over your audience's heads, nor should you condescend. You should use correct grammar and standard English when presenting an oral defense of your thesis and save slang and colloquialisms for proposing toasts to your football buddies.

Public speaking creates some special stylistic problems. A speech differs from a letter or a friendly conversation in that your audience has to be able to remember what you said and follow your train of thought without being able to ask you questions or reread the previous paragraph. You can ensure a good basic speaking style by following five rules: use simple terms, use short sentences, repeat yourself, put up signposts, and choose personal terms.

Use Simple Terms

Never use a two-syllable word when one syllable will do. The shorter, more common words in the English language have more impact and are more easily understood and remembered. "Now" is better than "at this point in time," and "most voters" is better than "the vast majority of the electorate."

Use Short Sentences

If you have to draw a breath before the end of a sentence, it's too long. If a sentence has more than one subordinate clause, it's too long. Before you reach the end of a long sentence, your audience has lost track of the beginning. Break long sentences down into several short, punchy sentences.

The following sentence is grammatically correct but too long for a speech: "In order to run an effective business, you must not only have a firm grasp of the day-to-day and week-to-week operations and cash flow, but you must also project your earnings and expenses several weeks, months, yes, even years into the future and plan your new products, services, and facilities."

The same sentence can be broken down into several sentences that have greater impact: "Running an effective business is hard. You have to do several things at once. You have to have a firm grasp of the day-to-day operations. You have to watch your weekly cash flow. At the same time, you've got to project your earnings and expenses. You've got to plan new products, new services, and new facilities."

Repeat Yourself

Your audience only absorbs about a third of what you say. Therefore, anything important should be said at least three times. You can actually repeat yourself word for word in a speech and sound perfectly normal, whereas the same technique employed in an essay would sound silly. Besides verbatim repetition, you should paraphrase your key points. Say them another way. Repeat your main ideas in slightly different terms. It also helps to provide your audience with short internal summaries as you proceed with your talk. It helps them remember where you've been and gives slow listeners a chance to catch up.

Put Up Signposts

Signposts are transitional words or phrases that alert your audience to a change of direction or remind them of where you are in your presentation. They are the verbal equivalent of subheadings and paragraph indentations in a written piece. Signposts can be subtle or obvious. Generally speaking, the more obvious the better:

"Now we'll move on to ..."

"This is the third point I'd like to make ..."

"On the other hand ..."

"Pay attention; this is where it gets complicated ..."

"First ... Second ... Third ..."

"In conclusion ..."

"Let me summarize what we've covered so far ..."

"Another example of this problem is ..."

Choose Personal Terms

Refer to yourself as "I" and "me." Refer to your audience as "you." Refer to people in general as "we" and "us." Do this at every reasonable opportunity. It builds rapport by underlining the personal nature of your relationship with your audience. It also makes some positions clearer. Notice how a stilted, vague statement is enlivened and clarified by recasting it in more personal terms:

Impersonal: "It has been argued that the only way to ensure a fair flextime policy is to install time clocks for use by all personnel. However, it is possible that the honor system will work."

Personal: "I've heard that the only way to ensure a fair flextime policy is for all of us to punch time clocks. However, I feel we can be trusted to follow the honor system."

Supporting Materials

Let's say you've clarified the purpose of your talk so that you can state it in one sentence. You can also summarize the content in one sentence. You've resolved to use simple terms and short sentences. In fact, your speech now seems so simple, you're wondering how you'll ever fill up the allotted time. That's where supporting materials come in.

The most important supporting materials are usually examples, illustrations, anecdotes, and jokes. These give flesh to the dry bones of the abstract point you are trying to make. The best examples are concrete—a particular person or group does a particular thing in a particular place at a particular time. Include sensory data about sights, sounds, smells, and feelings to bring the scene to life. But keep your examples brief and to the point. As a general rule, give only two examples to support a given point, then summarize the point again.

Statistics are often used as supporting material. For speeches, the best statistics are simple ones. Overly precise figures and subtle distinctions serve no purpose in a speech. Your audience will not remember that 34.657 percent of males exhibit 10.587 percent hair loss. They will remember that one man out of three goes bald.

In debates and other types of persuasive speeches, arguments are often supported by opinions, quotations, or testimony by experts or eyewitnesses. When presenting the words or opinions of others, make sure of three things: that you are quoting accurately, that the ideas effectively support your argument, and that your audience respects the authorities you're citing.

PowerPoint slides, video clips, audio recordings, whiteboards, models, displays, flip charts, and handouts are audiovisual aids that can help get your point across. If you choose to use them, be sure to practice beforehand and make sure that you have the materials you need and are familiar with their use. Clumsy audiovisual aids are worse than none at all.

The Outline

The following is an outline of a five-minute speech on divorce mediation, showing examples of most of the suggestions made so far. Visit http://www .newharbinger.com/41719 to download this sample outline.

Divorce Mediation Speech

Purpose: To persuade divorcing couples to choose mediation over litigation

I. Introduction. Mediation is better than litigation because it

   A. Protects family assets

   B. Protects children

   C. Provides emotional support for the couple

II. Body

   A. Expense

      1. Litigation costs $20,000 to $300,000 in legal fees, eating up family assets.

      2. Mediation costs $4,000 to $12,000, preserving family assets.

   B. Children

      1. Fifteen million American kids have experienced divorce.

      2. In a mediated divorce, parents are taught to take equal responsibility for the children and develop co-parenting skills.

      3. Remember, you're divorcing one another, but not the kids.

   C. Emotional Well-Being

      Example: Joe cancels all the charge cards on the advice of his lawyer. Jill follows her lawyer's advice and cleans out the joint checking account. In one week they are reduced to screaming at each other.

III. Conclusion. Mediation is better because it's less expensive, ensures continued parenting for children, and protects the emotional well-being of the divorcing couple. "Don't hate, mediate."

Notice that the introduction, body, and conclusion of this speech follow the dictum "Tell them what you're going to tell them, tell them, then tell them what you told them." Also note that the purpose and content of the speech can each be expressed in one easy-to-understand sentence.

The speech is restricted to three points: mediation is less expensive, mediation is better for the children, and mediation is better for your emotional well-being. These points are supported by statistics, examples, and quotes. The body of the speech is organized on the problem-solution principle: the expense problem, the children problem, and the emotional problem. The same two solutions are examined for each problem: a litigated versus mediated divorce. The conclusion of the speech summarizes the arguments and ends with a call to action: "Don't hate, mediate."

Exercise 19.1

Pick a topic that you know a lot about. It can be a hobby, your job, a subject in school—whatever you are very familiar with. Imagine an audience and a situation in which you could be called upon to talk about your topic for five minutes. Based on that audience and situation, compose one sentence that describes the purpose of your speech.

Proceed to outline your five-minute speech. Make sure you have a clear introduction, body, and conclusion. Organize the body according to a clear principle. Include examples, quotes, facts, and figures where appropriate. The outline should be one or two pages long.

Compare your outline with the example given above. Imagine giving the speech, and make any changes to your outline that seem necessary. Save this outline to use in exercise 19.2 at the end of the chapter.

Delivery

The most important part of your delivery is your voice. It must have the correct volume, rate, clarity, and pitch to get your message across.

To get correct volume, deliver your speech to the last row of your audience. If they still can't hear, deliver the speech to the back wall or to an imaginary point across the street. If in doubt about your volume, ask the people in back if they can hear. Avoid using a microphone. Your unamplified voice will sound more natural. If you must use a microphone, practice with it beforehand to find the optimum distance between your lips and the mike: too far and you won't be heard, too close and you'll get distortion and "popping Ps."

Most speakers talk too fast. Make a conscious effort to speak slowly. Pause at the end of each sentence. A pace that sounds painfully slow to you will probably sound just right to your audience.

Enunciate and articulate clearly. Pronounce each consonant crisply. Dwell on your vowels. Don't slur—include every syllable in every word. In public speaking, you can't get away with the lazy-lipped habits of everyday conversation.

Vary your volume from loud to soft. If you're asking a rhetorical question, let your voice rise at the end of the sentence. Let your intonation register amusement, criticism, surprise, excitement, or concern.

Once your vocal delivery is adequate, notice what you do with your body, especially your eyes. Good eye contact with your audience is essential. It implies sincerity, interest, intimacy, honesty, and other positive qualities. If eye-to-eye contact rattles you, just look at foreheads. The effect will be the same.

Your gestures and facial expressions should be natural to you and appropriate to what you're talking about. A lot of arm waving and grinning is inappropriate when delivering a eulogy but just the ticket for a pep rally. Don't put your hands behind your back or in your pockets. Use them to support what you're saying.

Move your body. Stepping to one side, forward, or back is a good way to indicate that you are about to change the subject. Movement adds welcome variety to any speech. For this reason, it's best to avoid getting trapped behind a podium.

Dealing with Stage Fright

Stage fright is a form of anticipatory anxiety. Your thoughts about having to speak in front of other people trigger a complex of fight-or-flight arousal symptoms. You feel butterflies in your stomach, your hands are cold and clammy, your mouth is dry, and your heart is racing.

Fear of public speaking is probably the most universal type of anxiety. It has been widely studied, and several effective strategies have been developed to combat it. There are things you can do before and during your speech to keep your nervousness at a manageable level.

The Week Before

If you know in advance that you are to deliver a speech, you can use covert modeling to prepare yourself to speak without nervousness (Cautela and Kearney 1993). First, write out a brief description of yourself delivering the speech well: "I step up on stage and smile at the audience. I walk to the center and take a deep breath. I begin talking in a loud, strong voice. I speak slowly, clearly, pleasantly. As I make eye contact with individual members of my audience, I notice they are paying close attention and smiling. I feel relaxed and at ease. I'm having a good time. I know my material and enjoy sharing it with the audience. When I finish talking, they applaud for a long time."

Memorize your description. Sit down in a quiet place where you won't be disturbed. Close your eyes. Take a deep breath and let it out. Visualize the place where you will give the speech: the walls, the chairs, the tables, the colors and shapes. When you have the scene clear in your mind, imagine someone very different from you getting up and delivering your speech. Pick someone you know who is older or younger than you or of the opposite sex. Imagine that person being a little nervous at first, but then delivering your speech in a relaxed, natural manner. See the smiling, applauding audience. Run through this scene twice, seeing this dissimilar model struggling, then succeeding.

Next, imagine an acquaintance of the same age, sex, and general appearance as you giving your speech. See this person being a little nervous, but then getting into the swing of the speech and really doing a good job. Run through the scene twice with this similar model.

Then imagine the same scene with you giving the speech. You're a little hesitant at first, but then you gain confidence and start speaking out with authority. You make a few mistakes, but at the end, the audience is genuinely pleased and you feel great. Run through the scene, watching yourself deliver the speech, until you feel your confidence increase.

Finally, practice the speech in front of a mirror, as described in the exercise at the end of this chapter.

An Hour Before

Just before your speech, it helps to relax your whole body, going through this progressive relaxation procedure twice:

1. Sit in a comfortable position. Tighten your shins, raising your feet and toes off the ground, flexing your ankles, and pointing your toes back toward you. Hold for five seconds and relax. Curl your toes and tighten your calves, thighs, and buttocks. Hold for seven seconds, then relax for eleven seconds. Notice the relaxation flooding your legs.

2. Clench both fists, tightening your forearms and biceps in a Charles Atlas pose. Hold this position for seven seconds, then relax for eleven seconds. Notice the wave of relaxation that goes through your arms.

3. Arch your back as you take a deep breath into your chest. Hold for five seconds. Relax. Take a deep breath, this time into your stomach. Hold for seven seconds and relax for eleven seconds. Notice the relaxation in your chest and abdomen.

4. Wrinkle up your forehead. At the same time, press your head as far back as is comfortable, roll it clockwise in a complete circle, and reverse direction. Now wrinkle up the muscles of your face like a walnut: frowning, eyes squinted, lips pursed, tongue pressing the roof of your mouth, and shoulders hunched. Hold for seven seconds and relax for eleven seconds. Notice the relaxation in the many small muscles of your head.

During Your Speech

Before you start talking, take a slow, deep breath and let it out gradually. This is the best quick relaxer, and it reminds you to fill your lungs fully before trying to speak. At any time during your speech, you can pause and take a deep breath to relax. It will seem like a natural pause to your audience.

If nervousness threatens to overwhelm you, you can try the *paradoxical admission*. This involves telling your audience frankly, "I feel so nervous, I'm sure I am going to blow this whole speech." By admitting your nervousness, you reveal what you want to hide. It is paradoxical but true that revealing hidden nervousness makes it disappear or subside to a manageable level.

Exercise 19.2

Deliver your speech in front of a full-length mirror while you make an audio recording of yourself. While speaking, watch your gestures, eye contact, and facial expressions. When listening to the playback, check your volume, speed, clarity, and pitch. Notice where you can use shorter words and sentences, where transitions are not adequately signposted, and where you should repeat yourself or use more personal language. Pretend you know nothing about the subject and see if the speech makes sense.

Deliver your speech in front of the mirror again, with the recorder's microphone as far from you as your most distant listener will be. Correct all the errors you noted the first time. Keep practicing until the speech is as perfect as you can make it. Be careful that you don't speed up too much as you become more practiced.

20 Interviewing

You will very likely be interviewed many times in your life: when you are looking for a job or a place to rent or seeking a loan for a new home; when you are applying to certain schools, clubs, or organizations; or when someone wants to gather information from you, the expert. In these situations, it's important to have interview skills.

Imagine that you've been sending out résumés for a month, and you have finally landed an interview for a new job. You're getting more nervous by the minute. How can you prepare for what feels like the Inquisition? What questions will you be asked? How are you going to make a good impression on the interviewer? What questions should you ask to be sure it's the right job for you? How will you handle questions you think you shouldn't have to answer?

Interview skills are also important when you are the interviewer. For instance, Cindy needs to buy a used car. While there are plenty of used cars available online, she has to interview their owners to decide which to go see and ultimately which one to purchase. Nick, who has an apartment to rent over his garage, wants to interview potential tenants. Trina, a member of a breast cancer survivor support group, wants to meet with women in her community recently diagnosed with breast cancer to give them important information that could help save their lives. Mary Jo plans to talk with veterans about their military experience for her research paper. Jeff supervises an employee who is often late, and he wants to motivate her to be on time. Trish's contractor quits, leaving her kitchen only half remodeled. How is she going to find reliable help to finish the job? She intends to interview three new contractors whom her friends have recommended before she makes her decision.

Reading this chapter will help you improve your skills as an interviewee and interviewer. How well you do in an interview will largely depend on how prepared you are, and preparation begins with knowing what you want to get out of the interview.

Clarifying What You Want

Knowing what you want is important, whether you are the interviewer or the interviewee. Clarifying what you want focuses your quest, motivates you to keep searching for your goal, keeps you from settling for something else, and allows you to communicate about your objective with enthusiasm.

Cindy, who needed to buy a used car, took a few minutes to imagine what she wanted: "I see myself driving to school and work in a cherry-red economy car that is safe and won't break down. It has a reliable heater, an air conditioner, and a great radio and CD player. It's big enough so that I can carpool comfortably with my three friends. I feel confident and at ease driving it. I am pleased that it was within my budget of six grand."

Cindy then asked herself what aspects of what she wanted were essential and nonnegotiable: "It must be safe, dependable, with no major repairs in sight. A heater and radio are musts. It must be comfortable for four adults. I should feel confident and at ease driving it. It must have economical gas mileage. It can't cost more than $6,000." Finally, Cindy decided that the color, air conditioner, CD player, and great sound system were optional.

The following exercise will help you practice defining what you want to achieve through an interview. Visit http://www.newharbinger.com/41719 to download this exercise.

Exercise 20.1

Think of something that you want to have or to experience that will involve at least one interview. Set aside a few minutes to close your eyes, take a few deep breaths, and relax. Think about what you want. Imagine yourself having attained your goal. What does it look like? How do you feel? What are you doing? Where are you? Are you alone or with others? If you are with people, how are you interacting with them, and how are they responding to you? Use all of your senses to fill in as complete an image of what you want as you can.

1. Write down a description of what you want:

   _____

   _____

   _____

2. Are some aspects of what you want essential and nonnegotiable? Write down these requirements:

   _____

   _____

   _____

3. What parts do you feel would be nice to have but are not essential (and are therefore negotiable)? Write down these bonuses:

   _____

   _____

   _____

Refer back to what you wrote here when you feel discouraged, when you are tempted to get sidetracked into something else, when you are preparing for an interview, and especially after you have concluded the interview.

When You Are the Interviewer

When you are the interviewer, you need to follow a written plan. It will help you save time, avoid mistakes, feel more confident, make more appropriate decisions, and achieve the outcome you want. Visit http://www

.newharbinger.com/41719 to download the following interviewer's checklist.

Interviewer's Checklist

This checklist can be used for all types of interviews: gathering information for an article or report, deciding whom to hire, choosing a real estate agent, researching what to buy, or motivating an employee to do better. In each case, you can follow the same basic steps:

1. **Decide whom to interview.** If you don't already have an interviewee lined up, a list of prospects will naturally evolve as you research what you are interested in. Learn as much as possible about your prospects, and pick one or more to interview.

2. **Define your purpose for this interview.** Your purpose may be to gather information for yourself, to report back to others, to understand a complex subject, to influence the interviewee in some way, to make a decision of your own, and so forth.

3. **List information you want to convey.** Include the most effective way to present it. Include all the practical details, such as your name and qualifications or background, the purpose of the interview, how long it will take, and so on.

4. **List the questions that you want answered in this interview.** Make sure they are questions that can't be answered readily by another source. Don't overdo it: five or six good questions are better than twenty. Put your questions in the order that you want to ask them. Start with an easy one and save the tough questions for the middle, when the person you are interviewing has warmed up to the subject. Don't hold the most important question until the end—you might run out of time and not get to it.

5. **Anticipate the interviewee's questions.** Imagine what the person is likely to ask you and prepare a response to each of their probable questions.

6. **Schedule the interview.** Contact the interviewee and get their agreement to be interviewed. Set a time and a place to meet in

person or to talk on the phone or video chat. Tell the interviewee how long you think the interview will take.

7. **Establish rapport.** Greet the interviewee warmly. Smile, shake hands, make eye contact, and use his or her name. If the interview is taking place in your office or home, make sure that the interviewee is comfortable. Reiterate the purpose and length of the interview. Explain who you are. State the purpose of your interview and how much of the person's time you want; make sure the interviewee understands and is in agreement with the structure that you are proposing. Create a connecting link by bringing up mutual interests, attitudes, friends, or experiences. If you are at a loss as to what you might have in common, start with neutral topics such as the weather and stay away from controversial topics such as politics. Pay close attention to how the interviewee responds to you. Adjust your behavior to put him or her at ease and move on to the next phase of the interview as soon as it's clear to you that this person is comfortable with you.

8. **Ask your questions.** The interaction will flow like this: you will ask a question and the interviewee will answer. You will respond to his or her answer with a comment or a follow-up question. Your responses to the interviewee's answers are as essential to gathering the information you need as your planned questions are. You can respond in many different ways: Nod your head, say "Uh-huh," summarize the answer, agree with the point being made, or ask a follow-up question. When you feel that the interaction is not going in a useful direction, feel free to change the subject and move on to the next question on your list: "I'd like to ask you about something else now ..." or "Let's take a minute to explore ..." The interviewee expects you to ask the questions and usually will not balk.

9. **End the interview.** Plan how you want to end the interview. The flow of conversation may lead you to choose a different ending, but it is always good to be prepared with a gracious and clear closing statement. At the end, you can do one or more of the following: point out that it is time to end; ask for final comments; summarize the important points of the interview; correct any

misunderstandings; thank the interviewee; and if you like, leave the door open for further contact.

10. **Debrief and follow up.** After the interview is over, review what happened in the interview while it is fresh in your mind. Jot down a brief summary of what you and the interviewee said. This is particularly important when you are just learning to conduct interviews. Be sure to separate facts from assumptions. Ask yourself if the interviewee would agree with what you are writing. If you have some doubt about what was said, you may want to call the interviewee to confirm it or send your written summary for him or her to review. If your purpose for this interview was to make a decision, do you have enough information now to make it? If you promised to get back to the interviewee for any purpose, follow up as appropriate.

After you write down what took place in your interview, take some time to evaluate your own performance. How can you do better the next time you conduct an interview?

Mary Jo Interviews Veterans

Mary Jo decided to interview four veterans about their military experience for a research paper in her English class. She came up with a list of potential interviewees among her parents' acquaintances.

She wrote an introductory script that she planned to use when she phoned the people on her list to ask for an interview: "Hello, I'm Mary Jo Anderson. I'm the daughter of Wayne Anderson, who gave me your name as someone who has had some military experience. I understand that you were a [give rank or job title] in the [name branch of military service]. I'm doing a research paper for my English class on life in the military and was wondering if I could briefly talk with you about your experience. It wouldn't take more than forty-five minutes, and I can come to your home at your convenience."

Mary Jo wrote out five questions in the order that she planned to ask them:

1. "What was day-to-day life in the military like for you?"

2. "What did you like most about your life in the military?"

3. "What did you like least about your life in the military?"

4. "What were a couple of your most memorable experiences in the military?"

5. "What were a couple of the funniest things that you experienced in the military?"

Mary Jo wrote down a brief closing statement she could modify to end each of her interviews: "I see that we are almost out of time. Is there anything else you want to add before we stop? Thank you for taking the time to share with me some of your experiences in the military. It sounds like [give summary statement]. The information that you have given me will be most helpful in writing my research paper on life in the military. May I call you if I have any more questions?"

Exercise 20.2

Pretend that you are interviewing a Marine about life in the military, and he has just said the following: "What I enjoyed most about my experience in the Marines was spending time with my buddies. We did a lot of surfing and partying. I also liked my job as a swimming instructor. Some of the recruits didn't know how to swim and were petrified of the water. I had to get them to a point where they could survive in water over their heads, all geared up."

Imagine and write down different responses to accomplish each of the following objectives.

Encourage the interviewee to keep talking:

_____

_____

_____

Probe for more information:

_____

_____

_____

State your agreement:

_____

_____

_____

Summarize:

_____

_____

_____

Change the subject to a related area:

_____

_____

_____

Change the subject to a new area:

_____

_____

_____

Nick Interviews Renters

Nick found it helpful to follow the interviewer's checklist when he decided to rent out an apartment over his garage:

1. **Deciding whom to interview.** Nick researched the rental market in his area and arrived at a fair and attractive rent. He found that the most common way to rent an apartment was to post an ad online at a popular website.

2. **Defining purpose.** Nick wanted to find the ideal renters: a non-smoking couple with no pets, both spouses working full time and able to easily afford the rent. They would need good references and be willing to stay for at least one year. He decided that it was essential and nonnegotiable that the renters be nonsmoking, be employed, have good references, be willing to stay a year, and be able to easily pay the rent. That they have no pets and be working full time were optional and open to negotiation.

3. **Listing information to convey.** Nick wrote out a paragraph describing the rental, which he could refer to when he was on the phone. He put his requirements into his online ad and made a list of important points to cover when people contacted him. The first phone conversations or email interchanges would be screening interviews to weed out inappropriate candidates. His emphasis would be on the facts. He would invite the best applicants to meet him at his rental property and decide in person whether he liked them as people.

4. **Listing the questions.** Nick wrote out a list of questions to screen the callers and arranged these questions in the order that he would ask them: "What is your full name and a phone number where I can reach you in the evening?" "Will you be living alone or with others?" If the answer is "others," the following questions would apply to them as well: "Where are you currently living and why are you moving?" "If you decide that you want to rent my place, may I talk to your three most recent landlords?" "Do you smoke?" Next he would ask: "Any pets?" "What do you do for a living and whom do you work for?" "May I contact your employer to confirm your salary and that you are an employee in good standing?" "How long do you plan to rent the apartment?"

5. **Anticipating the interviewee's questions.** Nick anticipated the questions that the interviewees would ask him and came up with

responses. Question: "How long is the lease for?" Response: "One year minimum, and then month-to-month after that." Question: "Is there a garage?" Response: "No, but there's plenty of street parking." Question: "Are the appliances gas or electric?" Response: "The heat, stove, and dryer are gas; everything else is electric." Question: "How close are the schools?" Response: "There is a grade school and a middle school within walking distance. The high school is three miles away; the school bus for it stops at the corner."

6. **Scheduling the interview.** When he got a call inquiring about the ad in the paper describing an apartment for rent, Nick introduced himself, asked the name of the inquirer, and explained that he was screening people briefly on the phone before showing the apartment. He took time to establish rapport by looking for something he had in common with the inquirer. As he gathered information about the inquirer's current circumstances and rental needs, he shared a bit about himself to encourage more open and honest communication. He went on to give a brief description of the apartment and neighborhood, asked his planned questions, and responded to the inquirer's answers. Based on the information he gathered, he made a decision on the spot about whether the person had the essential characteristics that he was looking for in a renter. If he thought that the person seemed appropriate and he or she was still interested in the rental after being screened, he set up an appointment to meet this person at the rental to show the unit. If he thought that the person was inappropriate, he said, "I already have a number of people interested in renting my apartment, and I plan to pick one of them. Thank you for your interest, and good luck in finding a place."

7. **Establishing rapport.** Nick invited back the couple who met most of his criteria and whom he liked the best for a one-hour selection interview. During that time, he asked them additional questions to get to know them better as people as well as renters: "Can you tell me more about yourself?" "What was your living situation like before?" "What made you decide to move?" "Why do you want to live in this neighborhood?" He also answered their questions about him, the rental, and the neighborhood.

8. **Asking questions.** Nick consulted his list to make sure that he had all the answers he needed. He called the other interested potential renters and informed them of his decision.

9. **Ending the interview.** The couple agreed to his terms and signed a lease. Nick made sure he had all the contact information he needed and said he would sign the lease himself in the next two days, after he had checked their references.

10. **Debriefing and following up.** Their references checked out, and Nick called the couple back to pick up the lease and schedule a move-in date. He was proud of himself for doing a good job of interviewing renters.

The Motivational Interview

Life is so much simpler when people just do what they are supposed to do. Employees should start work on time, teachers should communicate how your children are doing in school, and neighbors shouldn't let their dogs bark day and night. Unfortunately, from time to time it is necessary to sit down with people who are not meeting your expectations and inspire them to change their behavior. As the interviewer, you can encourage the interviewee's cooperation by conducting a motivational interview.

Claire is frequently late to work in the morning. Jeff, her supervisor, has received complaints from her coworkers. He reviews the company's attendance and disciplinary policies and then sets up a meeting with Claire to discuss her tardiness. After a few minutes of small talk to put Claire at ease, Jeff states why predictable punctuality enhances the efficiency and morale of the entire department, and then he describes how Claire's pattern of tardiness has negatively affected the department. Claire is quick to defend herself, and Jeff listens sympathetically. He summarizes what he hears her saying: "So are you saying that you have an illness that causes you to sometimes feel very bad in the mornings, so rather than missing a whole day of work, you simply come in late some mornings and make up the lost time in the evenings?" Claire agrees.

Jeff states that while he sympathizes with Claire's problems, he will not accept her unpredictable attendance pattern. He offers her three alternatives that take into account her illness, all of which would require her to have consistent attendance and a doctor's note to confirm her illness. She agrees to his suggestion that she start all of her workdays two hours later. Jeff points out that her colleagues, who need to know when she will be available to help them, will appreciate her punctuality and that her attendance will be reflected in her next performance evaluation. Unpredictable attendance will result in a written warning and eventually dismissal if it continues. Jeff writes up their agreement and has Claire review and sign it.

Jeff debriefs the interview by filing the written agreement in Claire's personnel file and by making notes for the follow-up interview at her next evaluation.

If You Are the Interviewee

If you are going to be interviewed, preparing for it will be easier now that you have a better understanding of the interview process. Your point of view differs from the interviewer, but many of the steps to take in preparation are similar to those found on the interviewer's checklist.

Interviewee's Checklist

The examples in the following checklist primarily relate to job interviews, but you can easily apply these ideas any time you find yourself in the interviewee's seat.

1. **Define the purpose.** It's important to define your purpose in being interviewed and the interviewer's purpose as well.

2. **Do your homework.** If you are not already an expert on the topic of the interview, do your homework. For instance, if you are applying for a job, research the person or company with whom you are interviewing. What do your prospective employers do? How do they do it? How successful are they? Who is their competition? What factors contribute to their success? How does the job that you are applying for contribute to their success?

3. **List your questions.** Based on your research, write down several questions that you can ask the interviewer.

4. **List information you want to convey.** What important points do you want to communicate about yourself? For example, think of at least three things that you have done that demonstrate how you can contribute to your prospective employer's future success. Draw on your education, experience, outstanding accomplishments, skills, interests, personal qualities, plans, and innovative ideas to convince the interviewer of your value.

5. **Anticipate the interviewer's questions.** What questions are you likely to be asked? Prepare well-thought-out responses to each of them.

6. **Anticipate objections.** If there is a screening process, anticipate any objections that the screener is likely to have toward you and come up with a good defense. For instance, if you have a pet and are responding to an ad for an apartment rental, you will want to be ready with a response for the landlord who says, "Sorry, no pets!" You can be honest about your pet and still say something like, "My little dog is very well behaved. He has never once soiled the carpet, and I make sure he doesn't have fleas. My previous landlord can tell you that I left that apartment in great condition. I would even be willing to put down an extra cleaning deposit, if you like."

7. **Rehearse.** Practice interviewing by role-playing in front of a mirror, into a recorder, or with a friend. This will make you more comfortable for the real event and give you a chance to make needed improvements.

8. **Establish rapport.** Begin with neutral topics to make a connection, such as the art on the wall and the knickknacks in the interviewer's office: "I really like that painting. Who is the artist?" "Wow, I can see by that photo that you are a golfer too. What's your favorite course?" "Now, I can relate to the slogan on that coffee mug. I like my java strong too." It is safer to stay away from politics, religion, and other controversial topics.

9. **Ask about the outcome.** Be ready to ask for clarification regarding the outcome of the interview. If you are seeking a positive

decision and the interviewer rejects you out of hand, ask for feedback. You have nothing to lose, and you may be able to counter his or her objections. If the interviewer seems positive about you but doesn't tell you what the next step in the decision-making process is, ask what it is (When will you be contacted for a selection interview? When can you see the rental property or test-drive the used car?). If you are clear that you are interested in what the interviewer is offering, say so with enthusiasm. Summarize what you have to offer. If appropriate, make an offer or give the interviewer an opportunity to make one. Push for a decision. For instance, if the interviewer can't make the decision, ask to speak to the person who can.

10. **Debrief as soon as possible after the interview.** Write down the date of the interview and the basic facts about the interviewer, company, position, or item that you are interested in. What were the main points that you made and the interviewer's response to them? What were the interviewer's main concerns and how did you respond to them? What are the next steps? What did you say that you wish you had refrained from saying? What didn't you say that you wish you had said? How do you plan to follow up on this interview? For example, plan to send a letter thanking the interviewer for his or her time. Review your key points and how they relate to your objectives. State what you think the next steps should be. Make your letter interesting and relevant. You may want to add something new or challenging.

11. **Follow up.** If appropriate, make a list of reasons to check back with the interviewer in the following weeks. Ask a question. Send a note giving your thoughts on a question that remained open. Send an article that supports your views. Follow up by asking the interviewer if the article was received and what he or she thought of it.

Making a Good First Impression

Although this section is tailored to a job interview, it applies to any interview situation in which you are seeking a positive outcome.

First impressions are crucial. You never get a second chance to make a good first impression. An interviewer's impression of a job applicant typically forms within the first five minutes of an interview. Once a negative impression is established, it's difficult to turn around.

First, be on time. Be sure that you know when and where you are going to be interviewed, and leave enough time to get there. Dress appropriately for the position and to please the interviewer. If you are unsure about what is appropriate for the position, a good rule of thumb is to dress professionally and conservatively. This is not the moment to try out a trendy new fashion, make a political statement, or wear intense perfume or cologne. Dress in colors and a style that are flattering to you. Be perfectly groomed, from your recent haircut down to your freshly polished shoes.

Know your interviewer's name and use it. People like to hear their own name.

Remember to breathe and to relax your muscles. Overcome your self-consciousness by making a point to get to know your interviewer. Tell yourself that you are prepared and dressed for success, and remember that the interviewer expects and will forgive some nervousness. Be courteous. Show the interviewer that you are respectful and appropriately friendly.

Your nonverbal communication is as important as what you say when it comes to conveying courtesy: give a warm, firm handshake, maintain natural and direct eye contact, wait to be shown where to sit, pay attention to your posture and sit slightly forward in your chair. Also pay attention to the nonverbal feedback that you receive, so you can adjust your behavior accordingly. For instance, if the interviewer is fidgeting, looking away, or glancing at the clock as you are talking, it's a sign that you should stop or change the subject.

Be flexible and tactful. Disagree only if you feel you must. When you disagree, acknowledge the interviewer's point of view and underscore any merit that you see in it before you present your point of view. Be honest and consistent. Nothing destroys trust in a relationship faster than a lie uncovered. Even the appearance of deception is usually unsalvageable. Admitting you don't know something is far better than making up an answer that can easily be discredited.

Get the interviewer interested in you. If you simply wait to be asked questions, you won't be doing anything to make yourself stand out from all the other people being interviewed. Say or do something that will break the monotony of the interviewer's day. Share something memorable about yourself. Tell an interesting story. Look for bridges between you, such as interests you have in common. Leave the interviewer with a good feeling about you. If the interviewer can identify with you in some significant way, you will have won him or her over. When the time comes to select who will get hired, the interviewer's gut feeling about you is more important than his or her recollection of specific facts about you.

As an interviewee, you are primarily a salesperson. In a job interview, your product is yourself: your assets are your experience, skills, and personality. While your résumé can communicate your background clearly, your personality can only come across in the interview.

In a job interview, the interviewer basically has one question: "Why should I hire you?" The best answer you can give to this question is that you will produce far more value than you will cost. You can demonstrate this with your accomplishments. Whatever question you are asked, try to frame your answer to indicate that you would be an asset in the position for which you are applying.

Managing Inappropriate Questions

From time to time when you are being interviewed, you will be asked a question that is uncomfortable, inappropriate, or downright illegal. When this happens, stop for a moment to take a deep breath and gather your thoughts. You can always refuse to answer a question, but your refusal is apt to be interpreted by your interviewer as a sign of noncooperation or, even worse, that you are hiding something. This can't help your chances of fulfilling your purpose in being interviewed in the first place. So how can you respond to such questions without having to reveal something that you feel is none of the interviewer's business and still not blow the interview?

If this is an informational interview in which you are sharing your experiences or expertise, you have the option before the interview begins of listing the topics that you are willing to discuss and listing the topics that are out of bounds. Famous people who are interviewed on TV and radio often do this as a condition of their participation. Imagine that a local newspaper reporter contacted you for an article on your life as a wife, mother, artist, and founder of your town's art guild. You might say that you are willing to discuss your own art and the art guild but not your family life. Should questions come up on the subject that you have made off-limits, you can simply remind the interviewer of your agreement.

Remember that when you are the interviewee in an informational interview, you are in a one-up position. Someone has come to you for information. Typically you don't have anything to lose by limiting the areas of discussion or by saying no to a question. But if you don't want to draw attention to certain topics that an enterprising interviewer might go research on his or her own, make your boundaries known only if an awkward question comes up by saying, "That's outside the scope of what I want to talk about today." What can an interviewer do other than accept this and move on to the next question?

A less abrasive option to giving a "no comment" response when asked about your opinion on a sensitive subject is to come back with a limited statement or a cliché. When asked why your marriage broke up, you can say, "Bad things happen to good people" or "It wasn't meant to be" or "She wanted to live in New York and I didn't." When asked why you haven't had children, you can say, "I guess it's just not in the cards." Most interviewers will get the message that this is something you would prefer not to talk about and will go on to the next question.

If you feel the interviewer needs a gentle reprimand for asking an inappropriate question, you might try something like pausing, looking a little shocked, and saying, "Did you really ask me that?" If the interviewer doesn't take the hint, you can always state plainly that you think that the question is inappropriate, too personal, unrelated to the subject of the interview, or none of the person's business, and you don't feel like answering it.

It is harder, if not impossible, to so boldly set boundaries when you are in a one-down position in an interview. For example, when you want to impress a potential employer or landlord that you are the right candidate for a new job or an apartment, you don't want to alienate him or her by saying certain topics are off-limits or by refusing to answer certain questions. Fortunately, there are federal, state, and local laws designed to protect you from discrimination in preemployment, prerental, preloan, and various other business-related interviews. For example, inquiries into the following areas are limited or can be out of bounds in a preemployment interview:

Race, ethnic background, or national origin

Marital status

Family makeup

Gender and, in some states and cities, sexual orientation

Age, unless related to the job

Weight or height

Membership in social clubs or organizations

Religious affiliation

Arrest record

Disabilities

Some interviewers will appreciate your pointing out when they ask an illegal question. Others will feel threatened by you and not offer you the job. You could simply say that you think the question is discriminatory and that you prefer not to answer it. But it is in your interests to be as tactful as possible if you decline to answer. For instance, you might say, "I'm certainly willing to cooperate with you in any legitimate areas of inquiry, but it's my understanding that questions that are not job related are inappropriate. I don't think that question is relevant to the job, do you?"

If you think that answering an illegal question is not going to hurt your chances of getting hired, you may choose to answer it rather than risk offending or scaring the interviewer and blowing the interview.

Conclusion

In this chapter, you have learned that a successful interview begins with you clarifying what you want and then educating yourself about your goal.

By the time you sit down for the interview, whether you are the interviewer or the interviewee, you have a list of questions to ask as well as answers to the questions you think you are most likely to be asked. You know how to establish rapport and how to make a favorable impression on an interviewer. You have learned about illegal and inappropriate questions. As an interviewer, you do your best not to ask them when you prepare your questions ahead; and as an interviewee, you know how to handle such questions should they come up. You are ready to use the concluding portion of the interview to summarize the important points of the session, correct misunderstandings, and spell out the next step.

Recommended Reading

Alberti, R. E., and M. Emmons. 2008. *Your Perfect Right*. 9th ed. San Luis Obispo, CA: Impact Press.

Axelrod, R. 2006. *The Evolution of Cooperation*. Rev. ed. New York: Basic Books.

Bandler, R., A. Roberti, and O. Fitzpatrick. 2013. Reprint ed. *The Ultimate Introduction to NLP*. New York: HarperCollins.

Bower, S. A., and G. H. Bower. 2004. *Asserting Yourself: A Practical Guide for Positive Change*. Updated ed. Cambridge, MA: Da Capo Press/Perseus.

Crowell, A. 1995. *I'd Rather Be Married: Finding Your Future Spouse*. Oakland, CA: New Harbinger.

Faber, A., and E. Mazlish. 2012. *How to Talk So Kids Will Listen and Listen So Kids Will Talk*. 30th anniversary ed. New York: Scribner.

Fisher, R., W. Ury, and B. Patton. 2011. *Getting to Yes: Negotiating Agreement Without Giving In*. Updated and rev. ed. New York: Viking Penguin.

James, M., and D. Jongeward. 1996. 25th anniversary ed. *Born to Win: Transactional Analysis with Gestalt Experiments*. Cambridge, MA: Perseus Books.

Lankton, S., and L. Bandler. 2003. *Practical Magic: A Translation of Basic Neuro-Linguistic Programming into Clinical Psychotherapy*. 2nd ed. Carmarthen, UK: Crown House Publishing.

Markway, B. G., C. N. Carmin, C. A. Pollard, and T. Flynn. 1992. *Dying of Embarrassment: Help for Social Anxiety and Social Phobia*. Oakland, CA: New Harbinger.

McCroskey, J. C. 2005. *An Introduction to Rhetorical Communication*. 9th ed. Upper Saddle River, NJ: Allyn and Bacon.

McKay, M., M. Davis, and P. Fanning. 2011. *Thoughts and Feelings: Taking Control of Your Moods and Your Life*. 4th ed. Oakland, CA: New Harbinger.

McKay, M., and P. Fanning. 1991. *Prisoners of Belief: Exposing and Changing Beliefs That Control Your Life*. Oakland, CA: New Harbinger.

McKay, M., P. Fanning, and K. Paleg. 2006. *Couple Skills: Making Your Relationship Work*. 2nd ed. Oakland, CA: New Harbinger.

McKay, M., P. D. Rogers, and J. McKay. 2003. *When Anger Hurts: Quieting the Storm Within*. 2nd ed. Oakland, CA: New Harbinger.

Newman, M. 1994. *Stepfamily Realities*. Oakland, CA: New Harbinger.

Phelps, S., and N. Austin. 2002. *The Assertive Woman*. 4th ed. San Luis Obispo, CA: Impact Press.

Powers, P. 2009. *Winning Job Interviews*. Rev. ed. Franklin Lakes, NJ: The Career Press.

Rusk, T. 1994. *The Power of Ethical Persuasion*. New York: Viking.

Satir, V. 1983. *Conjoint Family Therapy*. 3rd ed. Palo Alto, CA: Science and Behavior Books.

Scott, G. G. 2011. *Resolving Conflict: With Others and Within Yourself at Work and in Your Personal Life*. CreateSpace Independent Publishing Platform.

Smith, M. J. 2011. *When I Say No, I Feel Guilty*. Ebook. New York: Bantam.

Stein, M. 2003. *Fearless Interviewing: How to Win the Job by Communicating with Confidence*. New York: McGraw-Hill.

Watzlawick, P., J. Beavin, and D. Jackson. 2011. *Pragmatics of Human Communication*. New York: W. W. Norton and Co.

Wolvin, A., and C. G. Coakley. 1995. *Listening*. 5th ed. New York: McGraw-Hill.

References

Bandler, R., and J. Grinder. 2005. *The Structure of Magic: A Book About Language and Therapy. Vol 1.* New ed. Palo Alto, CA: Science and Behavior Books.

Berne, E. 1996. *Games People Play.* New York: Ballantine.

Cautela, J., and A. J. Kearney. 1993. *Covert Conditioning Casebook.* Pacific Grove, CA: Brooks/Cole Publishing Co.

Davis, M., E. R. Eshelman, and M. McKay. 2008. *The Relaxation and Stress Reduction Workbook.* 6th ed. Oakland, CA: New Harbinger.

Gottman, J. M. 1999. *The Marriage Clinic: A Scientifically Based Marital Therapy.* New York: W. W. Norton and Co.

Gottman, J. M., and R. W. Levenson. 1992. "Marital Processes Predictive of Later Dissolution Behavior, Physiology, and Health." *Journal of Personality and Social Psychology* 63 (2): 221–33.

Hall, E. T. 1990. *The Hidden Dimension.* New York: Doubleday.

Handy, C. 2000. *Twenty-One Ideas for Managers: Practical Wisdom for Managing Your Company and Yourself.* San Francisco: Jossey-Bass.

Harris, T. A. 2004. *I'm OK, You're OK.* Reprint ed. New York: Harper-Perennial.

Linehan, M. M. 1993. *Cognitive-Behavioral Treatment of Borderline Personality Disorder.* New York: Guilford Press.

Mehrabian, A. 1980. *Silent Messages: Implicit Communication of Emotions and Attitudes.* 2nd ed. Belmont, CA: Wadsworth Publishing Company.

———. 2007. *Nonverbal Communication.* London and New York: Routledge.

Rosenthal, R., and L. Jacobson. 1992. *Pygmalion in the Classroom.* Expanded ed. New York: Irvington.

Ross, L., D. Greene, and P. House. 1977. "The 'False Consensus Effect': An Egocentric Bias in Social Perception and Attribution Processes." *Journal of Experimental Social Psychology* 13 (3): 279–301.

Selfhout, M. H., S. J. Branje, M. Delsing, T. ter Bogt, and W. H. Meeus. 2009. "Different Types of Internet Use, Depression, and Social Anxiety: The Role of Perceived Friendship Quality." *Journal of Adolescence* 32 (4): 819–33.

Sullivan, H. S. 1968. *The Interpersonal Theory of Psychiatry.* New York: W. W. Norton and Co.

Sunnafrank, M., and A. Ramirez Jr. 2004. "At First Sight: Persistent Relational Effects of Get-Acquainted Conversations." *Journal of Social and Personal Relationships* 21 (3): 361–79.

Matthew McKay, PhD, is a professor at the Wright Institute in Berkeley, CA. He has authored and coauthored numerous books, including *The Relaxation and Stress Reduction Workbook*, *Self-Esteem*, *Thoughts and Feelings*, *When Anger Hurts*, and *ACT on Life Not on Anger*. McKay received his PhD in clinical psychology from the California School of Professional Psychology and specializes in the cognitive behavioral treatment of anxiety and depression.

Martha Davis, PhD, was a psychologist in the department of psychiatry at Kaiser Permanente Medical Center in Santa Clara, CA, where she practiced individual, couples, and group psychotherapy for more than thirty years prior to her retirement. She is coauthor of *Thoughts and Feelings* and *The Relaxation and Stress Reduction Workbook*.

Patrick Fanning is a professional writer in the mental health field, and founder of a men's support group in Northern California. He has authored and coauthored eight self-help books, including *Self-Esteem*, *Thoughts and Feelings*, *Couple Skills*, and *Mind and Emotions*.

MORE BOOKS *from*
NEW HARBINGER PUBLICATIONS

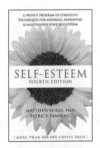

Register your **new harbinger** titles for additional benefits!

When you register your **new harbinger** title—purchased in any format, from any source—you get access to benefits like the following:

- Downloadable accessories like printable worksheets and extra content

- Instructional videos and audio files

- Information about updates, corrections, and new editions

Not every title has accessories, but we're adding new material all the time.

Access free accessories in 3 easy steps:

1. Sign in at NewHarbinger.com (or **register** to create an account).

2. Click on **register a book**. Search for your title and click the **register** button when it appears.

3. Click on the **book cover or title** to go to its details page. Click on **accessories** to view and access files.

That's all there is to it!

If you need help, visit:

NewHarbinger.com/accessories

new harbinger
CELEBRATING
40 YEARS